"Practical, but underpinned by an excellent understanding of the theory and scientific research! I can't think of a better duo to capture the essence of the ongoing debate on the relationship between governance and sustainability. Mike and George, given their experience and exposure to a wide range of issues in different parts of the world, as pioneers of good corporate governance in the early 2000s, are uniquely positioned to explain what matters and why in different contexts, and to offer stewardship guidance to investors. I also recommend this book to serving directors, investor relations professionals and corporate communications teams."

Prof. Dr. Melsa Ararat, *Director, Sabancı University Corporate Governance Forum; Member, ICGN Board*

"Investors have long known how to trade. But they are only now embracing how to own company shares to make sure boards steer responsible value creation over the long term. That's where investor stewardship comes in. Dallas and Lubrano have written the world's first comprehensive guidebook on the toolkit investors can use to safeguard the financial and social interests of citizen savers. With kudos to the International Corporate Governance Network for publishing, this is a vital, must-read manual for professionals in the rising field of stewardship."

Stephen Davis, Ph.D., *Associate Director and Senior Fellow, Harvard Law School Programs on Corporate Governance and Institutional Investors*

"Dallas and Lubrano's guide to stewardship is concise, evidence-based and implementable. Responsible investors should read it from cover to cover. I recommend it strongly."

Professor Elroy Dimson, *Centre for Endowment Asset Management, Cambridge Judge Business School*

"This book gives not only ICGN members but all governance practitioners around the globe an excellent way of understanding in depth the necessities and practical requirements for being a sustainable and successful pursuer of good governance and stewardship."

Christian Strenger, *Academic Director of the Corporate Governance Institute at the Frankfurt School of Finance*

"This is a must read for any ESG investor and a should read for any corporate governance, environmental and/or social specialist. George and Mike have effectively weaved current trends of ESG integration and stewardship into the complex corporate governance ecosystem. This modern look at corporate governance is refreshing and quite palatable even to the general public or layperson seeking to find out what is ESG."

Charles T. Canfield, *Principal Corporate Governance Officer, International Finance Corporation (World Bank Group)*

GOVERNANCE, STEWARDSHIP AND SUSTAINABILITY

The first introductory practical guide of its kind, this book brings together principles of corporate governance, investor stewardship and enterprise sustainability in the context of institutional investment.

Stewardship codes are developing in diverse markets to provide a framework for responsible institutional investment practices and fiduciary duties for beneficiaries. While codes provide a starting point, the application of stewardship in practical terms can be challenging for many institutional investors. Written by two well-known corporate governance experts, George Dallas and Mike Lubrano, and based on the ICGN training course on stewardship that they developed, this book gives needed clarity, rigour and guidance to practitioners about what we know—and don't know—about stewardship, governance and sustainability. It explores the theoretical foundations of stewardship, linking these to day-to-day decision-making and providing real-life examples and practical tools to evaluate issues that arise for companies from an environmental, social and governance perspective and generate ideas about how to make investor stewardship a practical reality in similar cases.

Investor stewardship and ESG professionals, portfolio managers, senior managers, regulators and finance students will appreciate this unique guide to developing, refining and operationalising investor stewardship capabilities in line with the respected and internationally recognised ICGN policy framework.

George Dallas has served as Policy Director at the International Corporate Governance Network since 2014, where he co-ordinates ICGN's governance polices and committees and leads ICGN's policy development and regulatory outreach. He is a visiting lecturer at Bayes Business School, University of London, and has held senior roles at F&C Investments (now Columbia Threadneedle Investments) and Standard & Poor's (now S&P Global). He has published widely and holds a BA degree, with distinction, from Stanford University and an MBA from the Haas School of the University of California at Berkeley.

Mike Lubrano is Managing Director at Valoris Stewardship Catalysts, where he advises investors and companies on the challenges of stewardship and sustainability. Mike has played a leading role in developing and delivering ICGN's ESG Integration and

Governance, Stewardship and Sustainability courses since 2011 and has trained investment analysts in the US, Europe and emerging markets for two decades. He currently teaches sustainable finance and impact investing at Johns Hopkins University. Mike earned his AB magna cum laude from Harvard College, his JD cum laude from New York University School of Law and his MPA from Princeton University.

Governance, Stewardship and Sustainability

Theory, Practice and Evidence

SECOND EDITION

George Dallas and Mike Lubrano

Routledge
Taylor & Francis Group
NEW YORK AND LONDON

Cover image: Philadelphia Museum of Art: The Louise and Walter Arensberg Collection, 1950, 1950-134-104

Second edition published 2023
by Routledge
605 Third Avenue, New York, NY 10158

and by Routledge
4 Park Square, Milton Park, Abingdon, Oxon, OX14 4RN

Routledge is an imprint of the Taylor & Francis Group, an informa business

and by the International Corporate Governance Network (ICGN)
RH.205 The Record Hall, 16-16A Baldwins Gardens, London, EC1N 7RJ

First edition published by ICGN 2021

Library of Congress Cataloging-in-Publication Data
Names: Dallas, George S., author. | Lubrano, Mike, author.
Title: Governance, stewardship and sustainability : theory, practice and evidence / George Dallas and Mike Lubrano.
Description: Second edition. | New York, NY : Routledge, 2023. | Includes bibliographical references and index.
Identifiers: LCCN 2022019542 | ISBN 9781032308791 (hardback) | ISBN 9781032308784 (paperback) | ISBN 9781003307082 (ebook)
Subjects: LCSH: Corporate governance. | Corporations--Investor relations. | Sustainable development. | Institutional investors. | Social responsibility of business.
Classification: LCC HD2741 .D349 2023 | DDC 658.4--dc23/eng/20220421
LC record available at https://lccn.loc.gov/2022019542

ISBN: 9781032308791 (hbk)
ISBN: 9781032308784 (pbk)
ISBN: 9781003307082 (ebk)

DOI: 10.4324/9781003307082

Typeset in Sabon LT Std
by KnowledgeWorks Global Ltd.

Dedications

From George: To Kathy, Will and Zach

From Mike: To Deb, Sarah, Ben and Khadijah

Cover image

The cover art is Wassily Kandinsky's *Circles in a Circle* (1923). Kandinsky wrote that 'the circle is the synthesis of the greatest oppositions.' Applied to the complex ecosystem of corporate governance and investor stewardship, where there are many actors with differing agendas and needs, this image suggests the creation of a whole and sustainable balance out of potentially conflicting tensions. This is one of the messages this book seeks to convey.

Contents

Foreword

Since 1995, the International Corporate Governance Network (ICGN) has served to promote high standards of governance and stewardship, ultimately to preserve and enhance long-term corporate value contributing to sustainable economies and wider social prosperity. Our members, led by investors responsible for assets of US$59 trillion, have developed flagship ICGN Global Governance Principles and ICGN *Global Stewardship Principles* on which our work programme is based.

The publication of this book, *Governance, Stewardship and Sustainability*, further enriches ICGN's work around the world. Co-written by ICGN Policy Director George Dallas and former ICGN Education Programme Advisor Mike Lubrano, this book takes the reader through a journey of what truly effective and impactful investor stewardship means in practice. This is artfully brought to life through George and Mike's collective wealth of professional experience as thought-leaders in corporate governance and as seasoned stewardship practitioners in investment institutions.

The important role investors play in holding companies to account for sustainable value creation is the bedrock of ICGN's work and underpins the rationale for our own *Global Stewardship Principles*. Drawn from our seminal statement on investor responsibilities in 2003, most recently updated in 2016, our own Principles remind us that '*stewardship is about preserving and enhancing long- term value as part of a responsible investment approach. This includes the consideration of wider ethical environmental and social factors as core components of fiduciary duty. In a broader context stewardship enhances overall financial market stability and economic growth.*'

And this sentiment is shared in the *G20/OECD Principles* (2015), which highlighted the important role investors play in holding boards to account, noting that '*the effectiveness and credibility of corporate governance frameworks—and therefore the oversight of companies—depend on investors that can make informed use of their shareholder rights and effectively exercise their ownership functions.*'

Now more than ever, society is questioning the role of corporations in society and their licence to operate—this extends to the effectiveness of investors in holding them to account. This book provides an excellent roadmap of how this accountability is exercised and achieved and is particularly insightful, not only for investors, but also for companies and their advisors as they build understanding of investor expectations through stewardship.

Kerrie Waring
Chief Executive, ICGN
London, June 2021

Preface to the second edition

When we signed off on the final text of the first edition of *Governance, Stewardship and Sustainability* in June 2020, 2021 was already shaping up to be a watershed year in the history of all three of the interconnected fields that are the subjects of the book. We fully expected that it would not be too long before we would feel compelled to produce an updated edition. As it turned out, developments only accelerated after the first edition went to press. Before the year came to an end, we found ourselves working on revisions.

This second edition of the book is organised along the same lines as the original and includes much of the original text. But it brings the earlier discussion up to date to give the reader an understanding of the content and impact of important recent events, initiatives and innovations, including, but certainly not limited to:

- Final ratification of the 2021 revisions to ICGN's Global Governance Principles.
- The announcement of the formation of the International Sustainability Standards Board at COP26 and its endorsement by key participants.
- Consolidation among environmental, social and governance (ESG) standard setters.
- Continued fallout from the Covid-19 pandemic and, in particular, its impact on how investors and companies think about systemic risk.
- Acceleration of mergers and acquisitions among ESG data and ratings providers.
- Intensification of the priority accorded to greenhouse gas emissions and climate risk across the ESG performance and reporting agenda.
- Introduction of the Sustainable Finance Disclosure Regulation, the proposal for a Corporate Sustainability Reporting Directive, and other major developments in the EU.
- Re-entry of the US administration into the global ESG dialogue and concomitant efforts by US regulatory bodies to reflect this in its capital markets and corporate regulatory frameworks.

The purpose of the book remains the same as it was for the first edition—to provide a primer that links the key issues and current thinking around corporate governance, investor stewardship and sustainability for practitioners and academic and professional education programmes.

We remain indebted to Kerrie Waring, the ICGN Board and the team of the ICGN Secretariat for their support of both the initial and current editions of the book. We would also be remiss if we did not thank our friends and respected colleagues Rients Abma, David Pitt-Watson and Peter Taylor for their invaluable input to the revisions.

We are also immensely grateful to Routledge for bringing this edition to press in collaboration with ICGN. Meredith Norwich, Chloe Herbert and Lauren Ellis provided immeasurably valuable advice and assistance throughout the process of revision and preparation of the final contents for publication.

One thing that has not changed since the publication of the first edition is our conviction that investor stewardship is an essential foundation for a responsible and resilient international capitalist economy. We can think of no better way of ending this preface to the second edition than how we ended the first—the voice of capital can be strong, but it must use this influence responsibly. In this broader context, stewardship is fundamental to responsible investment practices and has a role to play systematically to enhance sustainable financial markets, contribute to economic growth and build stronger societies.

George Dallas	*Mike Lubrano*
London	*Washington DC*
November 2022	*November 2022*

Preface to the first edition

Governance, Stewardship and Sustainability: Theory, Practice and Evidence is a primer that brings together principles of corporate governance, stewardship and sustainability in the context of institutional investment. The book accompanies the ICGN's signature training programme, Governance, Stewardship and Sustainability, but can be read or taught on a stand-alone basis.

Stewardship codes are developing in diverse markets to provide standards and a framework for responsible institutional investment practices and to meet investor fiduciary duties to beneficiaries. At the same time, stewardship is establishing itself as a profession within the institutional investment community, involving asset owners, asset managers, advisors and service providers. While codes provide a starting point, the application of stewardship in practical terms can be challenging for many institutional investors.

In our view, there are few, if any, books that address investor stewardship both on a theoretical and practical level. This book seeks to plug that gap, focusing on practitioners and their need to apply these concepts in their professional lives.

We believe the distinguishing features of our book are as follows:

- The linkage of the book and authors to ICGN and its own policy framework is a distinctive strength, as ICGN is well known and respected globally for articulating the perspectives and expectations of institutional investors.
- The book focuses specifically on stewardship as a growing profession in many institutional investment firms and links responsible investing to stewardship and fiduciary duty.
- It provides a theoretical framework for corporate governance and stewardship from an investor perspective and examines research and evidence relating to the effectiveness of governance and stewardship.

- It addresses the governance of stewardship within investment institutions, including managing conflicts of interest, oversight of integration of ESG factors into the investment decision-making process, and reporting to beneficiaries.
- It provides examples of practical tools to aid in the integration of stewardship into investment decision-making, including how to evaluate a company from an ESG perspective, as well as monitoring, engaging, voting and reporting to beneficiaries.
- The case study on Volkswagen provides an excellent example for applying the tools of ESG analysis in an inductive process. Readers might even want to consider reading the Volkswagen case first before the main text to sensitise themselves to some of the key ESG factors that will be discussed throughout the book.
- The authors are experienced investment practitioners with practical subject matter expertise in both corporate governance and investor stewardship. They also write and teach widely on these topics. They are both well known and recognised for thought-leadership in the professional corporate governance and stewardship community.

As a primer, we believe this book's relative brevity across a wide range of topics is a strength. But this means that some key issues of governance, stewardship and sustainability are not analysed exhaustively. Where possible, we provide readers with links to ICGN's own policy materials as well as other professional and academic references that provide greater detail on the topics in question.

There are two main audiences for this book. First, there is the professional audience: the growing number of stewardship and sustainability practitioners charged with incorporating consideration of ESG factors in investment analysis and decision-making, engagement and voting at company shareholder meetings. This audience is comprised not only of ESG specialists, but also portfolio managers and analysts who need to understand ESG and incorporate it into their analysis, thinking and decisions. But its professional relevance is not limited to investors. Given the growth of investor stewardship and activism, companies, and their boards and advisors, also need to appreciate the investor's perspective—as does the regulatory and standard-setting community.

The second audience is the educational market. The book can also be used as a lead or accompanying text in business school, academic or executive education programmes relating to finance, corporate governance or sustainable investment.

We would like to thank ICGN, specifically Chief Executive Kerrie Waring, the ICGN Board and the wonderful ICGN Secretariat, who all have been encouraging and supportive of this project. Milly Sheehan and Elle Thomas at ICGN warrant a specific call-out, and we would like to single out our friend and colleague Stephen Davis of Harvard Law School. Stephen created ICGN's first course in ESG analysis in 2011 and led this course numerous times at ICGN conferences around the world. This course is the predecessor of ICGN's current Governance, Stewardship and Sustainability (GSS) course, and so it is important and appropriate to recognise Stephen's contribution.

We have both been part of the international corporate governance 'scene' for over 20 years, including getting our hands dirty with governance and stewardship while working for asset managers and other financial services firms. We each bring distinctive, and complementary, practical investment and stewardship experience in both developed and emerging markets. This includes our collaboration in developing ICGN's eponymous GSS course.

Since we were enjoying the process of working together, we thought to take this a step further in the form of this book. It was a product of the 2020–21 Covid-19 lockdown, and we adapted, like many, to make use of Zoom technology. We were able to screen share our way through each page together, as if we were sitting in the same room and not separately in London and Washington.

Our partnership seeks to give greater clarity, rigour and guidance to practitioners about what we know—and don't know—about stewardship, governance and sustainability. It explores the theoretical foundations of stewardship, linking these to day-to-day decision-making.

The book's content draws in many places from ICGN guidance, viewpoints and comment letters. However, the opinions expressed in this book are those of the authors; likewise, the authors accept full responsibility for any errors and omissions.

We believe that stewardship and its link to corporate governance and sustainability is not only intellectually fascinating—it is today an essential foundation of a responsible and resilient capitalist system. The voice of capital can be strong, but it must use this influence responsibly. In this broader context, stewardship is fundamental to responsible investment practices and has a role to play systemically to enhance sustainable financial markets, contribute to economic growth and build stronger societies.

George Dallas
London
June 2021

Mike Lubrano
Washington DC
June 2021

Background of the authors

GEORGE DALLAS

George Dallas has served as Policy Director at the International Corporate Governance Network since 2014, where he co-ordinates ICGN's governance polices and policy committees, and leads ICGN's policy development and regulatory outreach on behalf of members, whose assets under management total US$70 trillion. He is responsible for oversight of ICGN guidance statements, viewpoint reports, public comment letters and broader thought-leadership to promote ongoing governance reform and best practice by both companies and investors. He also serves as a faculty member for ICGN's Governance, Stewardship and Sustainability training programme.

George is a visiting lecturer at Bayes (formerly Cass) Business School, University of London, where he teaches MSc and executive education courses in corporate governance. He is also a member of the Advisory Council of the Corporate Governance Institute of the Frankfurt School of Finance. In addition, George works as an independent advisor; past projects include an assignment as a staff consultant for the World Bank to develop a stewardship code in Kenya, a study of European Union corporate governance policy on behalf of the CFA Institute and teaching executive education courses in governance at the London Stock Exchange Academy. He is former chairman of Orlando Chamber Choir, a London-based registered charity.

Previously, George served as Director of Corporate Governance at F&C Investments (now Columbia Threadneedle Investments) in London, where he led F&C's global policies relating to corporate governance, including proxy voting and engagement matters. He represented F&C in several external professional bodies, including the Investment Committee of the Association of British Insurers and the Corporate Governance Committee of the Institute of Chartered Accountants of England and Wales.

Prior to joining F&C, George was a managing director at Standard & Poor's (now S&P Global), where he held a range of managerial and analytical roles in New York and London over a 24-year period, including as region head of S&P's European credit rating operations, head of its London office, global head of emerging markets and global practice leader of S&P's governance services unit. He also served on the boards of S&P affiliates in France and Spain. George began his career in corporate banking at Wells Fargo Bank.

George has published widely in the fields of finance, corporate governance and responsible investment, including the book *Governance and Risk* (McGraw-Hill, 2004) and several book chapters. He has spoken or lectured at several universities, including the London School of Economics, London Business School, the Said Business School of Oxford University, Cambridge University, ESMT Business School (Berlin), the Frankfurt School of Finance, HHL Graduate School of Management (Leipzig) and the University of Pennsylvania.

George holds a BA degree, with distinction, from Stanford University and an MBA from the Haas School of the University of California at Berkeley.

MIKE LUBRANO

Mike Lubrano is Managing Director of Valoris Stewardship Catalysts (www.valoriscatalysts.com), a firm that supports institutional investors in integrating evaluation of corporate governance and sustainability factors in their investment process. Mike has played a leading role in developing and delivering ICGN's ESG Integration and Governance, Stewardship and Sustainability courses since 2011. He served as Education Programme Advisor of ICGN in 2020.

Mike has trained investment analysts in the US, Europe and emerging markets on how to incorporate sustainability factors in investment decision-making for two decades. He has lectured on corporate governance at Erasmus University, Georgetown University's McDonough School of Business, Harvard University's Kennedy School of Government and New York University Law School. He currently teaches a course on sustainable finance and impact investing at the School of Advanced International Studies of Johns Hopkins University. Mike advises investors and companies on the challenges of governance and sustainability and is a frequent contributor to the work of OECD's Corporate Governance Committee.

From 2007 until August 2019, Mike was co-founder and Managing Director, Corporate Governance and Sustainability, at Cartica Management, LLC (www.cartica.com), an emerging markets fund manager with a concentrated, long-only portfolio of equity securities of publicly traded companies. Mike led Cartica's engagements with portfolio company management and boards to improve corporate governance and environmental and social practices to foster better performance and higher market valuations.

At International Finance Corporation (IFC) from 1997 to 2007, Mike pioneered IFC's corporate governance practice, establishing corporate governance as a central element of IFC's sustainable development strategy, and served as the first manager of IFC's Corporate Governance Unit. He developed the IFC Corporate Governance Methodology, a framework still used by IFC and other development finance institutions to assess the quality of governance of potential clients and to identify opportunities to add value by improving their boards, control environment, transparency and disclosure, and treatment of financial stakeholders. He was advisor to Chile's Ministry of Finance in drafting that country's corporate governance reforms and assisted the São Paulo Stock Exchange in designing the Novo Mercado. He was the co-organizer of the Latin America Corporate Governance Roundtable from 2000 to 2007.

Mike was a member of the Corporate Governance Advisory Council of the US Council of Institutional Investors from 2012 to 2017 and served on the Advisory Board of the Mexico Institute of the Woodrow Wilson International Center for Scholars from 2016 to 2019.

Mike earned his AB magna cum laude from Harvard College, his JD cum laude from New York University School of Law and his MPA from Princeton University.

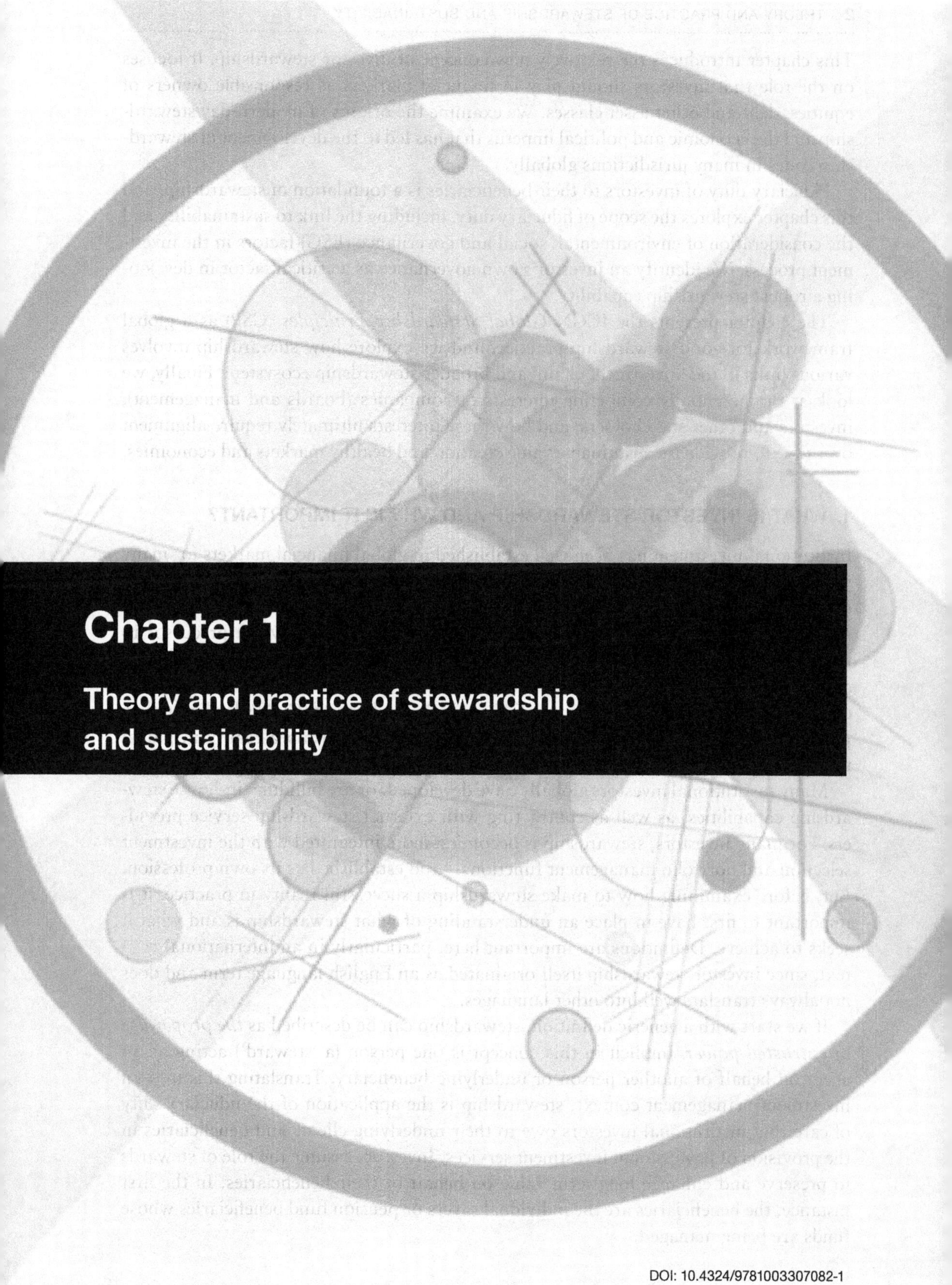

Chapter 1

Theory and practice of stewardship and sustainability

DOI: 10.4324/9781003307082-1

This chapter introduces the relatively new concept of investor stewardship. It focuses on the role that investors should play in financial markets as responsible owners of equities, debt and other asset classes. We examine the origins of modern-day stewardship and the economic and political impetus that has led to the development of stewardship codes in many jurisdictions globally.

Fiduciary duty of investors to their beneficiaries is a foundation of stewardship, and this chapter explores the scope of fiduciary duty, including the link to sustainability and the consideration of environmental, social and governance (ESG) factors in the investment process. We identify an investor's own governance as a critical factor in developing a robust stewardship capability.

The chapter presents the ICGN *Global Stewardship Principles* (GSP) as a global framework for good stewardship practice, and we explore how stewardship involves various links in the 'investment chain' and broader stewardship ecosystem. Finally, we look at the potentially competing interests of companies (boards and management), investors and other stakeholders, and how these interests ultimately require alignment over time to provide for sustainable value creation and healthy markets and economies.

1. WHAT IS INVESTOR STEWARDSHIP AND WHY IS IT IMPORTANT?

Institutional investment has been well established in global financial markets for many years; however, the concept of investor stewardship is relatively new. ICGN first came out with its *Statement on Institutional Shareholder Responsibilities* in 2003,[1] recognising that investors have responsibilities as well as rights. This was a precursor to the subsequent, and widespread, development of stewardship codes in many markets around the world, starting with the *UK Stewardship Code* in 2010. Stewardship has continued to be a prominent part of ICGN's agenda, and one of ICGN's leading policy priorities in recent years has been to make effective stewardship a reality in global financial markets.

Many institutional investors globally have developed, or are building, in-house stewardship capabilities, as well as contracting with external stewardship service providers. For many investors, stewardship is becoming more integrated with the investment selection and portfolio management functions—and established as its own profession. But, before examining how to make stewardship a successful reality in practice, it is important to first have in place an understanding of what stewardship is and what it seeks to achieve. Definitions are important here, particularly in an international context, since investor stewardship itself originated as an English language term and does not always translate well into other languages.

If we start with a generic definition, stewardship can be described as *the proper use of entrusted power.* Implicit in this concept is one person (a 'steward') acting as an agent on behalf of another person or underlying beneficiary. Translating this into an investment management context, stewardship is the application of the fiduciary duty of care that institutional investors owe to their underlying clients and beneficiaries in the provision of professional investment services. Investors assume the role of stewards to preserve and enhance long-term value on behalf of their beneficiaries. In the first instance, the beneficiaries are the individual savers or pension fund beneficiaries whose funds are being managed.

At a micro or company-specific level, the importance of stewardship lies in its protection of investor beneficiary interests and exercising basic ownership rights responsibly to oversee portfolio companies. This links into the corporate governance process and goes beyond the traditional stock picking and portfolio construction functions of investors to include more active monitoring, voting and engagement. This involves consideration of sustainability and ESG factors as part of the investment process—a topic this book will explore in detail.

In addition to a micro company view on stewardship, there is also a macro or systemic perspective. This brings on to the stewardship agenda systemic risks such as financial system stability, climate change, human rights and corruption—along with other systemic concerns that have been identified in the UN *Sustainable Development Goals* (SDGs).[2] After 2020, we can also add the social and economic challenges of a pandemic and growing geopolitical risks to this list. These systemic issues are often ESG-related and are highly relevant to investors and their beneficiaries, particularly those with long-term horizons. They address questions of economics, sustainability and ethics—all of which should feature in the practice of stewardship.

2. THE ECONOMIC AND POLITICAL BACKGROUND: STEWARDSHIP CODES AND THEIR DRIVERS

The rapid growth of stewardship activity in recent years reflects the growing awareness of regulators, investors and companies that investors have a role to play in encouraging and supporting sustainable value creation in companies and economies. This reflects a confluence of factors, including:

- *The rising levels of institutional investor ownership*: as of 2020, the global capital markets accounted for roughly US$230 trillion in value: US$123.5 trillion in publicly traded debt and US$105.8 trillion in listed equities.[3] Institutional investors hold a significant share of the investment universe—particularly in markets where ownership is widely dispersed. For example, institutional investment represents over 80% of the US stock market capitalisation. Institutional investors are a large and heterogeneous group, so the power this represents is widely distributed and decentralised. However, if this institutional investor base can mobilise, either in whole or in part, investors will have the potential to play an influential role as stewards of capital in many markets.
- *Global ownership*: linked with rising levels of institutional investment is the growth of cross-border investment—investors domiciled in many jurisdictions who are invested in the major global capital markets. In the UK and Germany, for example, over half the public equity market is owned by overseas investors. In the US and Japan, the figure is somewhat lower, but still significant—around 35%. This geographic shift in ownership brings differing cultures, perspectives and expectations to local capital markets and can create pressures for companies to adapt to new governance standards.
- *Shareholder activists and short-termism*: some corporates and regulators regard 'activist investors'[4] with suspicion. Hedge funds and other shareholder activists face public criticism over the impact of activism on companies, particularly

when key stakeholder groups may be affected. The criticisms are often linked with accusations of investor short-termism, when the long-term development of a company's business is felt to be inhibited by investor demands for short-term performance.

Short-termism is not simply a concern about hedge funds or activist investors. Even large institutional investors funding long-term retirement savings can feel pressures to encourage companies to seek near-term gain at the expense of long-term performance. Market and competitive pressures have the potential to drive ostensibly long-term investors to effectively shorten their time horizons. In Germany, overseas activist investors have been labelled 'locusts.' In Japan, a similarly negative perception of investors was reflected in 2008 by a Ministry of Economy, Trade and Industry statement: 'To be blunt, shareholders in general do not have the ability to run a company. They are fickle and irresponsible. They only take on a limited responsibility, but they greedily demand high dividend payments.'

- *2008 global financial crisis*: the financial crisis of 2008 was a devastating event that put the international financial system at risk. But it also helped to catalyse the development of stewardship. Many actors in the financial arena shared differing degrees of responsibility for this crisis, including investors. In its assessment of governance in the UK banking system in the wake of the financial crisis, the *Walker Review* identified both short-termism and a lack of an ownership culture by investors as contributing to the crisis: 'widespread acquiescence of institutional investors and the market in the gearing up of the balance sheets of banks ... with hindsight it seems clear that the board and director shortcomings discussed in the previous chapter would have been tackled more effectively had there been more vigorous scrutiny and engagement by major investors acting as owners.'[5] Investors were regarded by regulators and other observers as either too passive or too focused on short-term results—and proved to be ineffective stewards of client funds by facilitating the banking crisis that destroyed considerable value. These conclusions in the UK have relevance in other jurisdictions globally.

These diverse, but interlinked, factors have put institutional investors under scrutiny as part of the problem—but also as part of the solution. Regulators and politicians recognise the limitations of government in the oversight of companies and financial markets. They seek to both limit the negative short-term pressures of investors but also, more positively, to harness investor support—through use of ownership rights—to help achieve objectives that are consistent with public policy aims. This includes voting at shareholder meetings on a range of issues and engaging on topics including strategy, capital allocation, remuneration, board effectiveness, risk oversight and ESG matters—all to support sustainable long-term performance and value creation.

The UK took the lead in articulating this concept under the rubric of stewardship. Even before the peak of the financial crisis, the Institutional Shareholders Committee in the UK published its *Statement of Principles* in 2007. The *Walker Review* in 2009 provided further momentum to the development of what became the world's first stewardship code in the UK in 2010. Since that time, at least 20 jurisdictions globally have followed the UK's lead and have established stewardship codes with the policy aim of supporting healthy financial markets, long-term investment perspectives and sustainable

FIGURE 1.1 Stewardship codes proliferate

value creation. (See Figure 1.1.) These efforts cover six continents and a large range of markets—developed, emerging and frontier markets. Stewardship codes for investors have the potential to be as prolific as corporate governance codes for corporates.

In most cases, these different codes are 'soft law' requirements, based on a 'comply or explain' reporting system. But stewardship requirements are not always voluntary. Of specific note, the *European Union Shareholder Rights Directive*, revised in 2019, obliges European investors to disclose stewardship arrangements between asset owners and asset managers. Moreover, the EU's Sustainable Finance Initiative emphasises the exercise of stewardship responsibilities by investors, including the integration of material sustainability factors into their investment processes.

3. LINK TO SUSTAINABILITY AND ESG

Sustainability is an important concept used in many different ways, and its application in business and finance is a fundamental dimension of this book. In a general context, sustainability was defined in the 1987 World Commission on Environment and Development's (WCED) Brundtland Report as 'meeting the needs of the present without compromising the ability of future generations to meet their own needs.' From an economic and financial perspective, sustainability has been defined by the European Union's High Level Expert Group as 'making economic prosperity long-lasting, more socially inclusive and less dependent on exploitation of finite resources and the natural environment.'[6]

Taken this way, sustainability is a natural ally to the stewardship agenda, particularly with its intrinsic focus on long-term performance. Many institutional investors are either long-term asset owners, such as pension funds, or asset managers serving long-term asset owners and their beneficiaries. This implies, or at least should imply, for many investors a long-term investment horizon and an emphasis on sustainable value creation. This long-term perspective has relevance not only for individual companies, but also for markets and economies.

Investor interest in sustainability as part of stewardship is motivated by two key factors, which are not mutually exclusive:

- *Economics (value)*: increasingly, sustainability factors, often expressed as ESG factors, are recognised as reflecting material risks, and sometimes opportunities, in individual companies, markets and economies. Since evaluation of risk is a central element of investment decision-making, it is in the 'enlightened self-interest' of investors to take these broader social factors into consideration in the investment process.[7] For investors who are primarily focused on generating investment returns, the consideration of ESG factors is effectively instrumental in nature—ESG is a means towards a better understanding of risk and opportunity, not an end unto itself.
- *Ethics (values)*: in addition to seeking returns, an increasing proportion of investors also want investments in alignment with their own values. This adds ethics to the equation as a core investment criterion and is particularly the case with millennial investors (the generation born between 1981 and 1996); a 2016 Morgan Stanley study indicated that 84% of millennials cite ESG investing as a central goal.[8] A 2015 TIAA survey further indicated that 90% of affluent millennials said they were interested in realising competitive returns from their investments, while also promoting positive social and environmental outcomes. This values-based approach can translate into different applications that will be explored in this book, including ruling out investing in companies or sectors that do not meet an investor's ethical criteria (ethical investing/negative screening)[9] or seeking to achieve positive social impact in individual investments (impact investing). We will discuss the differences between ethical investing, impact investing and investing guided by ESG factors later in the book.

In turn, ESG has become the effective language for companies and investors to express and understand the specific range of sustainability issues that may have material financial, operational or reputational impact for an individual company.[10] Importantly, ESG factors often reflect how a company interacts with key 'stakeholders'—including employees, customers, communities and society at large. Companies that abuse or disrespect the interests of key stakeholders—even if it may be legal to do so—face potentially huge risks that can not only affect investor returns, but in extremis could threaten a company's social licence to operate.[11]

4. FIDUCIARY DUTY

Fiduciary duty is the obligation owed by any skilled person who takes on responsibility for looking after an asset on behalf of another. Another word for fiduciary is 'trustee.' The owner of an asset entrusts it to the fiduciary on the understanding that the latter will safeguard and manage it for the owner's sole benefit. In the context of professional asset management, the asset manager owes fiduciary duties to its client investors,[12] whose monies the manager has agreed to receive and invest.

ICGN's *Guidance on Investor Fiduciary Duties* provides a framework for deconstructing what asset managers owe to their beneficiaries and how this translates into an obligation to conduct proper stewardship.[13] It explores fiduciary duty across a range of dimensions, including ESG factors, time horizon, systemic risk and fiduciary duty in the investment chain. It also places emphasis on fundamental fiduciary duties for investors to consider. The fiduciary duties of asset managers, like those of company directors and officers, fall into two general categories—the duty of loyalty and the duty of care—with the latter commonly referred to in the asset management context as the duty to exercise prudence in the management of beneficiary assets.

Duty of loyalty

The duty of loyalty requires that all actions taken by asset managers with respect to client assets be for the sole benefit of their client investors. Investment decisions may not be made with the objective of furthering the interests of the manager or, for that matter, any other party. In the words of the *Kay Report*, the duty of loyalty 'require[s] that the client's interests are put first, that conflict of interest should be avoided, and that the direct and indirect costs of services provided should be reasonable and disclosed.'[14]

ICGN's *Model Disclosure on Conflicts of Interest* summarises key disclosures that investors can make to address their conflicts of interest. See Figure 1.2.

While clear enough in principle, applying the duty of loyalty is not without its practical challenges. It is all well and good to say that conflicts of interest should be avoided. But, in practice, the interests of asset managers and their client investors are not always perfectly aligned. For asset managers to perform their functions, they must charge their clients fees, which generates an unavoidable conflict of interest for the manager. Different fee structures are likely to have different potential outcomes for the client. *Ceteris paribus*, higher fees for the manager mean lower net returns for investor clients. The typical solution to the unavoidable conflict of interest around fees is fullest possible disclosure by the manager and informed consent from the client investors.

FIGURE 1.2 ICGN Model Disclosure on Conflicts of Interest

1. State that client/beneficiary interests come first
2. Identify forms of conflict of interest relevant to stewardship matters
3. Describe how conflicts are minimised and managed in normal circumstances
4. Clarify the escalation and oversight of particularly intense conflicts
5. Reveal specific case studies of how conflicts have been handled to reassure clients and beneficiaries that the processes are effective in practice
6. Address specific risks related to areas of stewardship conflicts
7. Review conflicts periodically and report to clients/beneficiaries

These principles are commonly reflected in regulatory regimes that require asset managers to fully explain their proposed fee structures and to disclose any adverse incentives these might generate around the manager's investment behaviour. A fee arrangement that provides for the sharing of potential upside between the manager and its clients ('performance compensation' or 'carried interest') may induce a manager to run a riskier portfolio than a fee calculated exclusively as a percentage of assets under management. It may be beyond the capacity of certain investors to properly evaluate complex fee structures and, therefore, impossible for them to give truly informed consent. Partially for this reason, certain fee structures are explicitly prohibited for retail fund management products in some contexts. For example, the US's Investment Advisers Act of 1940 largely prohibits performance fees for publicly offered mutual funds.

The business of asset management can present plenty of other types of conflicts of interest in addition to those related to compensation arrangements. Principals and employees of asset managers can sometimes have economic interests in assets that are potential investments for the funds they manage. Brokers and other service providers may offer fund managers discounts, research and other 'complimentary' benefits for directing business their way. An exhaustive treatment of the duty of loyalty of asset managers and how to identify, mitigate and manage various types of conflicts of interest is beyond the scope of this work.[15] However, potential conflicts that can arise in connection with investor stewardship, such as those around share voting, are discussed in later chapters.

One question often raised in the context of fund managers' duty of loyalty is whether a manager may take into account the interests of unaffiliated third parties when making investment decisions. For purposes of ESG, 'third parties' might be those who stand to benefit from attention to a specific ESG issue (eg workers, local communities, etc)—and not the investor client itself. Can a manager figure into the calculus of investment selection not just the likely risk and return to the investor client, but also the possible positive or negative impact on, for example, society and the environment?

Without an explicit mandate from the investor client, the short answer is no.[16] The duty of loyalty of the asset manager to its investor clients is an *exclusive* loyalty. The duty of loyalty requires that the asset manager serve only one master—its client investor. Its obligation to act in the best interest of its clients may not be diluted by considering the interests of any other party.[17]

Does what we have just said mean that consideration of environmental and social factors in investment decision-making somehow violates asset managers' duty of loyalty? The short answer to this question is, likewise, a resounding no. One thing we hope this book will convey is that consideration of social and environmental impact is fundamental to investment analysis. While pursuing environmental and social benefits for third parties goes against asset managers' duty to act in the exclusive interest of client investors, ignoring the environmental and social impact of a company's activities almost always means turning a blind eye to the risks these impacts imply for the company's own performance and sustainability. The challenge for institutional investors is to incorporate in their investment processes the identification and evaluation of the links between impacts on third parties and the performance of companies over time.

Similarly, the UK Law Commission's *Guidance on Fiduciary Duty of Investment Intermediaries* stresses adequate assessment of the risks to long-term performance of company failure to take into account ESG. It states:

> When investing in equities over the long-term, the risks will include risks to the long-term sustainability of a company's performance. These may arise from a wide range of factors, including poor governance or environmental degradation, or the risks to a company's reputation arising from the way it treats its customers, suppliers or employees. A company with a poor safety record, or which makes defective products, or which indulges in sharp practices also faces possible risks of legal or regulatory action.[18]

Ignoring material risks in the course of investment decision-making, especially those that may bring into question the sustainability of a potential investee company's business, at least arguably presents the potential for violation of asset managers' other category of fiduciary duty: the duty of prudence (care).

Duty of prudence (care)

It is not sufficient that an asset manager be loyal to its client investors. And loyalty does not compensate for carelessness or incompetence. An asset manager must also act with an adequate degree of professional effort and expertise. This obligation is analogous to the duty of care of corporate directors and officers to the company that we will discuss in Chapter 2. In the investment management context, this requirement is typically referred to as the duty of prudence and requires the asset manager to measure up to the degree of care, skill and caution expected of a professional managing the investments of another. This benchmark of professionalism can be referred to in legislation or regulation as the 'prudent person,' 'prudent expert' or 'prudent investor' standard. However articulated, the principle is that even a well-meaning, completely unconflicted asset manager does not have carte blanche to make investment decisions in any way it pleases. The information it considers, the degree of diligence it exercises in considering the risk and return potential of individual investments, and the process it follows to make investment and portfolio decisions must be comparable to those expected of a careful, professional investor.

Asset management is the business of allocating capital under uncertainty. Evaluation of risk is therefore central to every investment decision. Investment and portfolio decision-making requires every professional investor to devote resources to, and follow, sensible processes for collecting and analysing the information necessary to assess the potential risk-adjusted returns of alternative investments. All asset managers' resources are limited. A central challenge of successful investing is therefore determining how much time and money to devote to collecting and analysing data around different categories of risk. Each institutional investor will make a different determination, depending on its unique set of characteristics, including its particular asset class, investment objective, risk appetite, investment style and the experience and expertise of its team.

As we hope this book's discussion of stewardship will make increasingly clear, failing to devote some level of resources to understanding the ESG and sustainability risks of potential investments—namely, excluding consideration of ESG risks in portfolio construction and management—is hard to square with asset managers' duty of prudence. The amount of information available to investors on the ESG performance of companies has grown exponentially in recent years. Standards, benchmarks and analytical tools to identify and estimate the potential risks these present for investors have developed alongside this tsunami of data. Not to seek ways to improve investment and portfolio decisions by tapping into these informational and analytic resources may amount to a violation of the duty of prudence. If nothing else, it is certainly unwise.

5. INVESTOR GOVERNANCE AND STEWARDSHIP

ICGN's GSP reflect the conviction that effective stewardship is only possible when the internal governance of an asset owner or asset manager incentivises and supports it. Principle 1 states 'Investors should keep under review their own governance practices to ensure consistency with the aims of national requirements and the ICGN GSP and their ability to serve as fiduciary agents for their beneficiaries or clients.' As the Principle implies, for the investor's approach to stewardship to remain effective, its governance structures and practices around ESG integration cannot be static. They must be amenable to periodic review and updating in response to developments in corporate sustainability, expectations of beneficiaries and clients, and the learning that comes from the investor's own stewardship experience.

Of course, the same overarching principles that apply to the governance of corporates and other complex enterprises also apply to institutional investors, including a long-term focus on value creation, accountability and independent oversight, and standards of ethical conduct that are reinforced by the tone at the top of the organisation and robust processes for detecting and penalising any lapses in behaviour. However, investor governance also needs to be especially attuned to issues that are particularly relevant to stewardship, including conflicts of interest, institutional capacity and expertise, and remuneration and incentives of staff charged with implementing the institution's stewardship policies.

All institutional investors should have in place policies and procedures to minimise the potential for conflicts of interest to arise, and to identify and manage conflicts of interest when they inevitably occur. With respect specifically to stewardship, investors may face a conflict of interest when the firm or one of its affiliates (many institutional investors are part of larger financial groups) provide services or financial products to a company whose securities are held in the portfolios of the funds they manage. In such cases, an investor may fear loss of business from the company if it votes the funds' shares against management proposals at the shareholders meeting, or if it criticises the company's behaviour publicly or in private interactions with the company's management.

In addition, individual executives of the investor may have personal relationships with company executives or may have personal account investments in company securities with a shorter expected holding period than the fund's holdings in such company. In these cases, the funds' beneficiaries' interest in effective stewardship and the investor staff member's interest in not rocking the boat can diverge. Board members and senior management have a direct responsibility to beneficiaries and clients to ensure that the institutional investor's conflict of interest policies and procedures specifically identify the types of conflicts that may arise around stewardship and how the investor will mitigate the potential negative impact on the effectiveness of its stewardship efforts.

Certain items that today fall under the rubric of sustainability or ESG have long been considered relevant to investment decision-making. For example, at least since the European revolutions of 1848, investors have been aware of the potential risk to operations of inequality or poor labour relations. But many sustainability topics, and by extension issues to be addressed through investor stewardship, are more novel. Understanding them requires a continuous effort to expand the base of knowledge, skills and experience available to the institutional investor beyond those traditionally associated with fund management professionals.

The board and senior management need to be attentive to the skills required to execute the investor's stewardship strategy effectively and to ensure that the firm's hiring and training programmes keep up with it. As underlined in the commentary to ICGN's *Global Stewardship Principle 1*,

> this includes devoting time and training to decision makers along all parts of the investment chain, particularly coordinating with fund managers [portfolio managers], to exercising stewardship and fiduciary duties. It can also include, delegating to governance specialists to guide governance policies and voting.

An institutional investor is more likely to achieve its stated stewardship objectives if it establishes incentives that encourage both the firm as a whole and responsible personnel to accord them the priority and effort such objectives deserve. Sub-principle 1.7 of ICGN's GSP asserts that investors should reinforce their obligations to act fully in the interests of beneficiaries or clients by setting fee and remuneration structures that provide appropriate alignment over relevant time horizons. Investors should disclose to their beneficiaries or clients an explanation of how their remuneration structures and performance horizons for individual staff members advance alignment with the interests of beneficiaries or clients.

Setting fee structures and establishing remuneration policies for senior executives and other personnel are core responsibilities of the board and senior management of asset owners and asset managers. The asset management industry is doubtless in the early stages of working out how to appropriately reflect the importance of stewardship in fee structures and individual compensation packages. But it is incumbent on board members and senior management to keep up with industry experience in this area and especially to analyse carefully how well, or poorly, existing fee and compensation arrangements incentivise effective stewardship.

6. ICGN *GLOBAL STEWARDSHIP PRINCIPLES*

ICGN's policy work on stewardship dates back to its 2003 *Statement on Institutional Shareholder Responsibilities*. ICGN's GSP[19] were first put forward for consultation among ICGN members in 2015 and subsequently ratified by ICGN members at its 2016 annual general meeting (AGM). They were most recently revised in 2020, following an ICGN member consultation.

The ICGN GSP consist of seven principles:

1. Internal governance: foundations of effective stewardship.
2. Developing and implementing stewardship policies.
3. Monitoring and assessing investee companies.
4. Engaging companies and investor collaboration.
5. Exercising and protecting voting rights.
6. Promoting long-term value creation and integration of ESG.
7. Meaningful transparency, disclosure and reporting.

The GSP were developed to provide an international standard of reference for investors, regulators and standard setters. ICGN is quick to emphasise that these are *principles* of stewardship and not intended to compete for attention and priority with stewardship codes in other jurisdictions. ICGN encourages domestic investors to adhere to their own national codes before adopting any additional global best practices as expressed in the GSP. However, the GSP do reflect a global investor perspective and can be used as a resource or benchmark by both asset owners and asset managers as they develop their own in-house stewardship policies.

The GSP are also used by some institutional investors with global holdings as an international 'passport' to present a global stewardship credential in markets where they may not be a signatory to a local stewardship code. As of January 2022, 55 of ICGN's investor members, representing over US$28 trillion in assets under management, have formally endorsed ICGN's GSP.[20] The GSP have also been used by regulators in many markets as a global benchmark as they develop or update their own stewardship codes.

The GSP should be read on their own and merit attention by all stewardship professionals. Each individual principle has several sub-principles that are relevant for both asset owners and asset managers. They are broadly self-explanatory, but we add here a bit of perspective on each principle.

Principle 1: internal governance: foundations of effective stewardship

Resulting from strong feedback from an ICGN member consultation, a conscious decision was taken by ICGN to make investors' *own* governance the starting point of the GSP. The premise is that, if investors cannot achieve satisfactory internal governance themselves, then stewardship itself may easily fail to achieve its intended objectives. This begins with an explicit recognition of investor fiduciary duty to act in the interests of clients and end beneficiaries. ICGN's *Guidance on Investor Fiduciary Duties*[21] provides a framework for deconstructing what asset managers owe to their beneficiaries and how this translates into a duty to conduct proper stewardship. We will explore this in greater detail in Chapter 5.

Many stewardship codes focus on conflicts of interests, which are certainly very important to avoid or mitigate, and these are addressed in the GSP; for example, particular care should be taken in voting and engagement activity when the investor is an interested party. But the ICGN GSP address governance more broadly than this—in addition to covering independent governance structures, they assert the importance of buy-in by the chief executive and chief investment officers, adequate resourcing and, more generally, a tone from the top that is ethical and reflects appropriate values.

Principle 2: developing and implementing stewardship policies

A coherent policy framework is a fundamental cornerstone of stewardship; otherwise objectives will not be achieved, and stewardship will likely become haphazard or a matter of form over substance. An important initial consideration is scope, including questions of client preferences, geographic jurisdiction and asset class. The initial focus of stewardship has traditionally been on listed equities, which is certainly a logical starting place, particularly given investor ownership rights. This book focuses primarily on stewardship for listed equities, taking the perspective of a long-term institutional investor (reflecting the fact that much institutional investment is related to pension plans or long-term insurance policies). But stewardship is a relevant concept across all asset classes, including fixed income, private equity, infrastructure and real estate. It is important for investors to consider the breadth of their stewardship programme in a policy framework based on their own capabilities and building from client requirements. In Chapter 6, we address the role of the creditor in stewardship and examine the alignment between creditor and shareholder engagement.

Policies should also reflect the time horizon of the investor and end beneficiaries, particularly given that many beneficiaries are pensioners or long-term savers. Stewardship policies should frame key themes and priorities, including strategy, risk, shareholder rights, board effectiveness, remuneration, ethics, stakeholders, ESG and corporate responsibility. They should also relate to key components of the investment process such as investment analysis and decision-making (including the integration of ESG factors), engagement and voting. Chapters 5 and 6 will address how investors can develop a methodology to address stewardship through processes that encompass inputs, analytical tools and outputs/actions/decisions.

Principle 3: monitoring and assessing investee companies

Monitoring is a question of investors keeping track of an investee company's financial, strategic and operational matters—and includes assessment of how ESG factors are integrated in company operations and reporting. It also calls for investors to develop an understanding of executive management leadership and the quality of board oversight, and to monitor any company explanations about non-adherence to voluntary governance codes. This may seem like an obvious thing to do, but achieving this can be easier said than done, particularly for investors such as index funds with large numbers of individual holdings to track.

As will be discussed in Chapter 5 on ESG and investment decision-making, monitoring involves first deciding what information to track and collect relating to financial, strategic and ESG issues. The great challenge is to pull together these diverse factors and integrate them with investment research and the decision-making process—including into risk or valuation models. Monitoring can also help in the process of prioritising companies and sectors for engagement and identifying issues that are relevant to AGM votes.

Principle 4: engaging companies and investor collaboration

Engagement is a core component of stewardship. In a stewardship context, engagement effectively is a fancy term meaning dialogue. The goal is to build mutual understanding of needs to guide both companies and investors in a hopefully constructive, two-way conversation. Engagement can take many forms, including face-to-face meetings, letters, emails and telephone conversations. It can also involve differing levels in the company hierarchy, including both its executive management and the board. There can be cultural resistance in some markets to non-executive directors meeting with investors, but this is changing and becoming more commonplace. This will be explored in detail in Chapter 6 on effective stewardship in practice.

An investor's engagement policy and methodology should encompass how companies are prioritised for engagement in terms of risk, holding size or other factors, including ESG factors. The type and intensity of engagement must be consistent with an investor's investment strategy and style. There should be a framework for escalation, and escalation policies should exist to make clear how investors handle difficult situations that require resolution. This can include making public statements, filing resolutions or making portfolio decisions about individual holdings.

Collective engagement, where investors join forces to engage as a group with companies, can be possibly the most influential form of engagement. Investors should be prepared to collaborate when an engagement message is most effectively or efficiently achieved in a larger group context—both with individual companies and in a public policy context. But collective engagement can also be elusive. It can be a challenge, and sometimes costly, to bring investors together, and in some markets (Germany, for example), investors are concerned about breaching concert party rules that limit certain forms of investor interaction.

Principle 5: exercising and protecting voting rights

Voting is a fundamental ownership right. It is the vehicle through which control over a company is applied by investors to its managers and board in shareholders meetings—including matters such as capital raising, director elections, auditor appointments and executive pay. Voting can be both mundane and hugely important. The mundane part is that it can be a costly, high-volume and time-consuming process, and for some investors this can involve voting at thousands of AGMs per year, often involving small percentages (less than 1%) of a company's shares, with limited impact on the vote outcome. However, voting is a critical stewardship activity, and the ICGN GSP state that voting should cover all shares held, and this should be reflected in an investor's voting policy.

Voting policies provide direction on when to support or vote against (or abstain on) management or shareholder resolutions. Policies should also address how investors that engage in stock lending practices deal with the voting of lent shares. Investors should not only be prepared to vote against management resolutions or support shareholder resolutions when justified, but should also endeavour to communicate with the company the reasoning behind their voting decisions.

The protection of voting rights is also a critical criterion, particularly as dual class share structures serve to water down, if not marginalise, the power of minority shareholders in voting at shareholder meetings. This suggests a stewardship need for investors to discourage the issuance of dual class shares in engaging with regulators, stock exchanges and individual companies—or at least call for protections, such as sunset clauses.

Given the important role that proxy advisors play, investors should disclose how they use proxy advisor services in the voting process and should make appropriate use of proxy advisors—rather than rely blindly on their judgement and voting recommendations. Other voting issues relate to the quality of the 'plumbing' in the voting process—ensuring that all votes made are received, counted and, ideally, confirmed by companies. These issues will also be addressed in Chapter 6.

Principle 6: promoting long-term value creation and integration of ESG factors

A distinguishing feature of the GSP when compared with most national stewardship codes is its emphasis on ESG integration as a core principle of stewardship.[22] This reflects both economics and ethics. ESG integration builds awareness of what an investee company's interface is with its stakeholders and society more generally. ESG factors are fundamental drivers of long-term risk and opportunity for companies, economies and markets and are critical considerations for sustainable value creation. From a stewardship perspective, the imperative for investors is to identify those ESG factors that are material for a company's long-term performance—and to integrate these into stewardship activities such as investment analysis, voting and engagement. This calls for investor understanding and application of ESG data.

The 17 United Nations *Sustainable Development Goals* (SDGs) identify systematic risks where investors and the private sector can contribute to broader long-term economic and financial stability. Through its Taxonomy, the European Union provides further definition to environmental sustainability for investors by outlining six overarching objectives: climate change mitigation, climate change adaptation, sustainable use of water and marine resources, transition to a circular economy, pollution prevention and the restoration of biodiversity and ecosystems.[23]

Investors should engage with companies to adopt integrated reporting practices (see Chapter 7 on sustainability governance and reporting for companies) that provide appropriate ESG disclosure and linkage to financial performance. There is also the macro dimension—investors' growing focus on systemic risks, such as those relating to the financial system, climate risk, income inequality, human rights or corruption. These are axiomatically linked to ESG factors. Both public policy engagement and engagement with individual companies on ESG factors can contribute to systemically stable economies and markets.

Principle 7: meaningful transparency, disclosure and reporting

Meaningful investor reporting on stewardship is fundamental to the credibility of the stewardship process and is a way to express investor accountability to direct beneficiaries, regulators and the public generally. It is clearly important that investment clients and beneficiaries receive reports on how their capital is being managed, including stewardship, governance arrangements, company engagement and how the client's equity shares have been voted. The broad base of reporting audiences beyond beneficiaries is important to help build public understanding of how stewardship can positively impact individual companies and markets—and to monitor where stewardship may be working and where it is not. This includes academics seeking to build an evidence trail on stewardship through research.

The GSP encourage investors to communicate their commitment to a relevant national stewardship code and/or endorse the ICGN GSP themselves. In many cases, stewardship codes call for investor signatories to signify their commitment to a national stewardship code by reporting annually on their stewardship activities along the code's various parameters. Early experience with stewardship reporting evidenced instances of superficial reporting along the lines of a marketing document or, in the worst of cases, 'greenwashing.' This led the UK's Financial Reporting Council (FRC) to implement a tiering system in 2016 for UK *Stewardship Code* reporters, to differentiate between the quality and seriousness of the reports. This has progressed to an application system with would-be signatories assessed on the quality of the reports. The FRC has rejected the applications of several prominent investors whose disclosures may have been long on policy statements but weak on evidence of outcomes.[24] In Europe, the EU's Sustainable Finance Disclosure Regulation (SFDR) lays down sustainability disclosure obligations for institutional investors, particularly with regard to the integration of sustainability considerations in investment product creation, investment decision-making and investor stewardship.[25]

Stewardship reporting involves disclosure of the stewardship policy framework as well as reporting on actual stewardship policies and activities as inputs to the stewardship process. While this is a useful foundation, it may lack meaning if it is not linked to practical *outcomes*, in particular reporting on its effectiveness and the practical impacts of stewardship. As a new profession, stewardship presents challenges to auditors or other third parties who may seek to offer independent assurance. Although this may test comfort zones, particularly with traditional audit firms, forms of assurance tailored to the nature of stewardship will ultimately be an important governance element in ensuring rigour and building confidence in the process. This topic will be explored further in Chapter 7.

ICGN 2020 Global Stewardship Principles revisions

ICGN reviews and updates its core policy documents—its *Global Governance Principles* (GGP) and the GSP—on a regular basis. The project to revise the GSP for the first time since their 2016 launch began in 2019 with an internal review and feedback from ICGN's Board and Shareholder Responsibilities Committee, followed by a membership consultation. The revised GSP were ratified by ICGN members at its 2020 AGM. While ICGN believes the 2016 Principles remained robust and fit for purpose, it made a number of specific changes or additions to reflect changes in market practice and regulation and ongoing thinking about stewardship. The main changes in the 2020 GSP include:

- More emphasis placed on fiduciary duty and the 'soft,' but real, issues of culture and values by institutional investors. Not only does good stewardship require policies and processes, but it is essential that investors embrace its underlying principles and adapt these within their organisations.

- An explicit link between fiduciary duty and long-term value creation, which is in turn directly linked to sustainable benefits for the economy, environment and society. Particularly for investors whose beneficiaries are pensioners and individuals saving for retirement, a long-term perspective is fundamental to stewardship. In turn, sustainable value creation for long-term savers is a social good with broad social and economic benefits.
- The use of ESG factors in investment decision-making as a critical part of stewardship. ESG factors are clearly linked to long-term company performance and should be considered not only in the context of engagement and voting, but also in investment decisions relating to valuation and the buying or selling of financial assets.
- Greater focus on systemic risks relevant to institutional investors. It is important for investors to recognise that systemic risks, including those relating to pandemics, climate change, wealth inequality and corruption, can affect the sustainable value creation of individual companies as well as the health of economies and financial markets. For investors seeking to develop an approach to portfolio construction that is aligned with the 2016 Paris Agreement objectives, this suggests a stewardship engagement strategy for investors to encourage companies to commit their business models to achieve a 'net zero' target by no later than 2050.
- More emphasis on the application of stewardship to asset classes beyond listed equities. Institutional investors invest in a wide range of assets on behalf of their beneficiaries. While listed equities are a logical starting point because of their unique investor ownership rights, the broad principles of stewardship are relevant to other classes, including corporate and public sector debt, private equity, real estate and infrastructure.
- Identifying capital allocation as an important topic for engagement for both creditors and shareholders. Sustainable companies must recognise and respect the different requirements of both providers of corporate capital. Creditors generally seek a stable and predictable credit risk profile, and shareholders have a focus on upside potential and risk-adjusted returns on capital. Effective capital allocation seeks to achieve a sustainable (but necessarily dynamic) equilibrium between these potential tensions.
- Protecting voting rights against dual class shares and other forms of differential ownership which have the practical effect of marginalising stewardship and the accountability of companies to minority shareholders by diluting their voting rights. Differential ownership stands in sharp contrast to the ambition of stewardship to empower shareholders, through voting and engaging, to exercise their voice in direct proportion to their economic stake in a company.
- Encouraging investors to disclose more information about stewardship activities and outcomes. Stewardship has the greatest meaning when it directly relates to practical outcomes, and not just a policy framework. Beneficiaries should have a clear understanding of how stewardship provides meaningful benefits.

7. THE INVESTMENT CHAIN AND THE STEWARDSHIP ECOSYSTEM

While stewardship focuses on the activities of asset owners and asset managers, the broader stewardship ecosystem includes a range of actors that can influence the quality of corporate governance and financial markets. Applied in an investment and capital markets context, institutional investors are the agents, or stewards, acting on behalf of assets owned by the end beneficiaries of stewardship. These beneficiaries include individual savers, pension contributors, retirees and holders of long-term insurance policies. They rely on institutional investors as their agents, which include both asset owners and asset managers, to act in the interests of beneficiaries.

Institutional investors invest in a range of assets, including the equity and debt of listed companies, to produce investment returns for their beneficiaries. Particularly for pension funds and insurance companies funding annuities, the perspective of institutional investors is typically long-term. Both institutional investors and their beneficiaries therefore have a strong interest in ensuring that investee companies are successful and sustainable over time. This has broader systemic implications in terms of promoting healthy capital markets and economic development as well as positive environmental and social outcomes.

One way to look at these relationships is as links in the 'investment chain'—the flow of capital from providers of capital (investors) to users of capital (companies) and the broader flow to the financial markets, real economy and society.

As Figure 1.3 suggests, the investment chain involves a complex set of interactions between many different actors and third-party influencers, including regulators, stock exchanges, governance and stewardship codes, investor associations, information providers, proxy and rating agencies, investment consultants, plaintiff law firms, investment bankers, process agents and company advisors. As we introduce stewardship in this chapter, it is worth emphasising two fundamental points:

1. For providers of capital, who are often individuals or members of pension plans, the priority is to generate adequate risk-adjusted returns—particularly to build long-term savings to support retirement incomes. For companies as users of capital, the objective is to generate value and economic growth. Asset owners, asset managers and their influencers are means to these ends, and not ends themselves.
2. Each of these actors or influencers in the chain has proprietary self-interests, as individual entities or as sub-industries in some cases. These commercial interests can conflict with the interests of clients they are supposed to serve. The integrity of a financial system ultimately depends on the actors in the chain, including asset owners and asset managers, serving the end of the investment chain, namely users and providers of capital—prioritising their clients' interests over their own. This has close links to investor fiduciary duty and helps to put into context the importance of an investor's own governance system to ensure that these conflicts are managed as part of its own stewardship obligations.

While stewardship codes are most fundamentally a statement of investor responsibilities, the effective implementation of stewardship activities requires constructive co-ordination of many market participants. The GSP recognise that these participants have differing agency roles throughout the investment chain for the successful application of stewardship. The success of stewardship implementation also relies

FIGURE 1.3 The investment chain

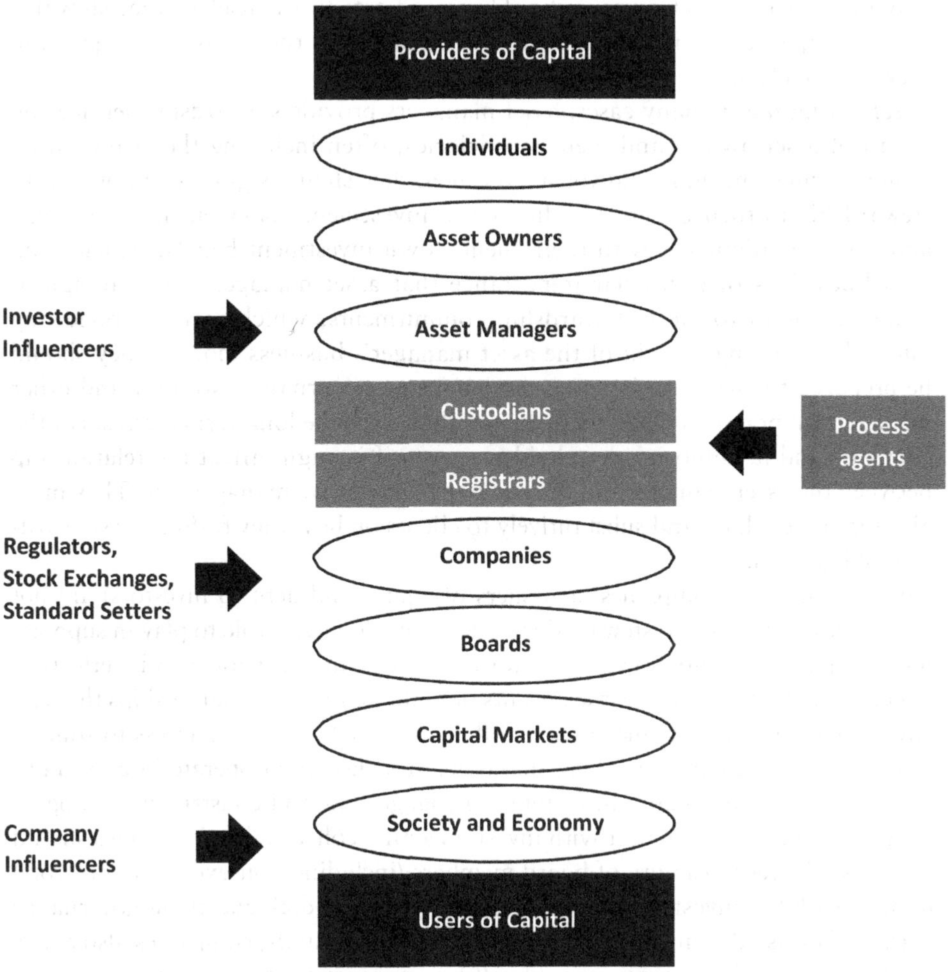

on participants understanding their roles and working in good faith to contribute positive outcomes.

These links extend along the investment chain from the end provider of capital to the user of capital and include specific roles for asset owners and asset managers, companies, regulators and service providers to play in making stewardship a reality.

- *Asset owners*: asset owners invest capital to preserve and enhance the value of assets held for beneficiaries. They articulate investment beliefs, allocate assets, award mandates to asset managers, develop and disclose investment strategies, and monitor and measure performance of asset managers whom they incentivise to act on their behalf. One of the main applications of the ICGN GSP is to serve as a guide for asset owners and their trustees in terms of monitoring an asset manager's adherence to stewardship practices. Many asset owners have limited in-house capacity to implement all aspects of stewardship; where this may be the case, asset owners should instead satisfy themselves that stewardship principles are being implemented adequately by their asset managers and service providers.

- *Asset managers*: in many cases, asset managers provide stewardship services on behalf of asset owners and their beneficiaries, often including the heavy lifting of monitoring, engaging and voting. As such, they should signify commitment to stewardship to their clients by adhering to investment management agreements and ensuring alignment with their clients' own investment beliefs, policies and guidelines. It is of particular importance that asset managers dedicate appropriate resources to meet stewardship commitments, which includes reviewing internal resourcing in light of the asset manager's business model. They should be prepared to challenge investee companies on governance, strategy and other management practices when these do not align with the long-term interests of the company and its minority shareholders—even if it might affect the relationship between the asset manager and the company's executive management. They must also report regularly and substantively to clients on how they fulfil their stewardship obligations.
- *Companies*: while companies (as issuers of equity and debt to investors) are not themselves signatories to stewardship codes, they do have a role to play in supporting the spirit and ambitions of a stewardship code in order for it to be effective. Companies should recognise the benefits of building investor relationships that can strengthen trust and enhance financial flexibility by broadening access to sources of cost-effective capital. In doing so, companies should co-operate in good faith with investors, particularly in facilitating engagement and constructive dialogue, including willingness to meet with investors acting collectively. Companies should recognise the responsibility of board members (including non-executive directors) to meet with key investors to build understanding and dialogue about governance matters. For listed companies with their own pension funds, companies also act as asset owners, and companies should call for appropriate stewardship practices in corporate pension funds.
- *Regulators*: regulators can play an important role in championing stewardship in the markets they oversee and should seek to support the ability of investors to exercise stewardship, for example, by facilitating effective enforcement of minority shareholder rights and collective engagement on ESG matters. Regulators wishing to promote the concept of stewardship in any market have a primary role in developing, publishing and requiring reporting against a national stewardship code. The GSP offer an internationally recognised framework for regulators to support and guide the development and ongoing revisions of national codes. Regulators often play the same role with regard to corporate governance codes in their markets.
- *Investment consultants / advisors / service providers*: investment consultants and advisors can assist asset owners and asset managers with developing and implementing their responsibilities as part of their advisory services. Such consultants and advisors provide research and voting services that can assume

stewardship responsibilities, and they can play an influential role. This includes, among others, proxy voting agencies, data and rating services and custodians. Though not issuers or investors, these service providers should seek to understand their role in the investment chain and to provide services in the interests of their clients and ultimate beneficiaries to support good stewardship practices.

Pre-conditions of effective stewardship

The preconditions of effective stewardship in a given market include the existence of a critical mass of investors (principally, but not exclusively, institutional investors) willing to commit to and adopt stewardship and the willingness of companies to engage with investors in good faith. Asset owners play a particularly important role in ensuring that stewardship responsibilities are built into investment management mandates as a standard feature of asset management practices. It can also be very important to have regulatory encouragement for stewardship activities to take place.

A stewardship code can play a critical role in providing a market-based system for investors to hold companies to account for their corporate governance practices. The risk of an overly prescriptive approach to a stewardship code would be to encourage a counterproductive 'tick box' compliance mentality of investors—which is not what lies behind the intent of the GSP or stewardship more generally. In this context, it is important to highlight the intangible qualities of tone and culture as critical components to a stewardship code's success in any market.

Effective stewardship within a 'comply or explain' context

Investors play a critical role in ensuring the effectiveness of a 'comply or explain' corporate governance framework, discussed in greater detail in Chapter 2. 'Comply or explain' provides companies with flexibility to refrain from adhering to particular provisions of a corporate governance code, without legal or regulatory sanction. This reflects recognition that not all aspects of a corporate governance code may be relevant for an individual company to apply to be well governed. But this approach also carries the obligation for companies to explain the reasoning why specific governance practices recommended in the code have not been adopted.

For a 'comply or explain' system to be effective, a company's explanation of non-compliance with corporate governance code recommendations needs to be monitored by interested parties to ensure that a company's explanations are robust. While regulators must be able to monitor company compliance with hard law and regulation, they may be insufficiently resourced and less well placed to make sometimes subjective judgements as to the quality of a company's explanations. This is where institutional investors have a role to play to be proactive in engaging with companies whose explanations are unsatisfactory.

TABLE 1.1 Legitimate needs of actors in the stewardship ecosystem—and distortions

Actor	Executive managers	Boards	Shareholders	Stakeholders
Legitimate needs	• Remuneration that fairly incentivises and rewards good performance over the long term	• Need full support of company management, including adequate information and advisory services • Adequate remuneration reflecting the importance of the job (but without incentive structures that could skew independent judgement)	• Sustainable and economic risk-adjusted returns to capital	• Protection of basic rights of employees, customers, supply chains, communities—including broad social and environmental interests
Potential distortions or self-interests	• Excessive remuneration based on inappropriate incentive structures • Short-term profit motivations reduce attention to ESG performance and stakeholder relations • Entrenchment and limited accountability to shareholders	• Lack of independence (even for nominally independent directors) • Lack of teeth (under-resourced or ill-informed) • Lack of effort (overcommitted boards)	• Undue pressures on companies to adopt business models and capital allocation strategies that prioritise short-term performance and threaten long-term company success	• Disproportionate awards or protections that affect the company's competitive position or have negative cost implications for shareholders

In the event that company explanations are inadequate, it is the role of institutional investors to use ownership rights to challenge companies when necessary. Collaborative engagement with other investors sharing similar views can be both an efficient and an effective way for investors to engage with companies on key issues. Without the active monitoring of explanations by investors, a 'comply or explain' system would lack an ultimate means of enforcement or influence.

8. GOVERNANCE, SUSTAINABILITY AND STEWARDSHIP: HOW DO THEY COME TOGETHER?

At a micro level, the key actors in the stewardship universe—executive managers, boards, investors and stakeholders—all come together, at least normatively, to support a company's long-term success and sustainable value creation. The sustainability dimension links this mission to ESG performance as a way to both manage risk and create opportunity, and to produce social outcomes that are either positive or, on balance, at least neutral.

Healthy companies need to have managers, boards, investors and stakeholders that are aligned and mutually supportive. All these actors have basic needs that must be satisfied if the company is to be successful and sustainable over time. Conversely, if any of these groups are inappropriately disadvantaged relative to others, the company faces a potential disequilibrium or disruption that could impact its long-term performance and success.

Getting the balance right is the endgame. This requires mutual sensitivity to what the legitimate needs of these individual actors are. It also requires awareness of the private motivations of each party and how, taken to extreme, these self-interests could distort the company's performance negatively or threaten its sustainability.

Table 1.1 presents the main actors that come together in corporate governance and investor stewardship. It presents their legitimate interests, but also identifies where self- or proprietary interest could challenge alignment with the other actors or threaten the long-term success and sustainability of the individual company.

Looking systematically at a company in this way, this is ultimately a question of governing the company to achieve a sustainable multiple equilibrium—in the 'trilectic' sweet spot where company, investor and stakeholder interests are aligned. Advocates of shareholder primacy may be concerned that this multiple equilibrium approach diminishes the authority of shareholders as providers of capital. But a company can still seek to maximise its returns to shareholders as long as it can do so while paying sufficient heed to the legitimate interests of its executives and stakeholders.

The diagram in Figure 1.4 borrows from the Japanese philosophy of '*ikigai*,' which seeks to achieve a sustainable balance of potentially conflicting tensions. The normative, if not aspirational, vision that builds from the alignment of interests between companies, investors and stakeholders has both micro and macro dimensions. The micro dimension reflects the needs of the individual actors: supporting the company's own success, generating fair and economic returns for investors and protecting the legitimate interests of the company's key stakeholders. At a macro level, this plays out in a broader social context, contributing to sustainable value creation, economic growth and social welfare, including environmental issues.

Another way to look at this is to think in terms of the philosopher John Rawls's 'veil of ignorance.' If this metaphorical veil were put over our eyes, such that we did not have a particular side to take to bias our interests, it is likely that we would also arrive at a solution that seeks to achieve a sustainable multi-equilibrium between these interdependent members of the stewardship ecosystem. The Rawls formulation is grounded in the concepts of fairness and social justice, which we believe are fundamental to a healthy and sustainable capital market system.

FIGURE 1.4 Stewardship and sustainability: players and objectives

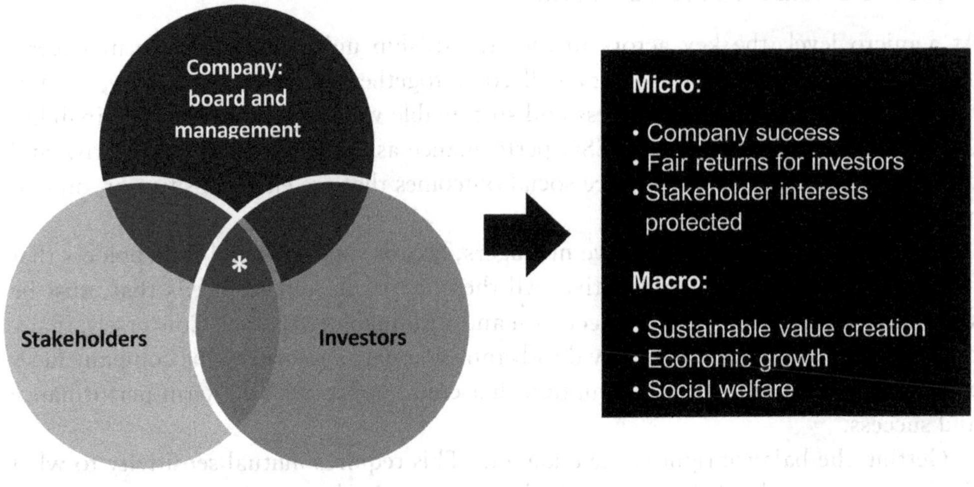

Good corporate governance and responsible investor stewardship are necessary elements to making this aspirational vision a reality. This is why it is important to know how to do it.

NOTES

1. ICGN, *Statement on Institutional Shareholder Responsibilities,* 12 December 2003.
2. United Nations, *Sustainable Development Goals*, 2015: https://sdgs.un.org/goals
3. Sifma, *Capital Markets Factbook*, 2021: www.sifma.org/wp-content/uploads/2021/07/CM-Fact-Book-2021-SIFMA.pdf
4. An activist investor is defined in Investopedia as 'an individual or group that purchases large numbers of a public company's shares and/or tries to obtain seats on the company's board to effect a significant change within the company': www.investopedia.com/terms/a/activist-investor.asp. 'Activists' should not be confused with 'active owners' or 'active ownership' investors, whose strategies revolve around using stewardship and engagement to effect typically longer-term improvements in the ESG practices of investee companies.
5. David Walker, *A Review of Corporate Governance in UK Banks and Other Financial Industry Entities*, 26 November 2009: https://ecgi.global/sites/default/files/codes/documents/walker_review_261109.pdf
6. EU High Level Expert Group on Sustainable Finance, *Financing a Sustainable European Economy: Final Report*, 2018: https://ec.europa.eu/info/publications/sustainable-finance-high-level-expert-group_en
7. Khan, Serafeim and Yoon (2015) found that portfolios weighted for corporate social responsibility factors outperformed by an average return of 3.1–8.9% per year over 20+ years; Corporate Sustainability: First Evidence on Materiality, *The Accounting Review*, vol 91, no 6, pp. 1697–1724: papers.ssrn.com/sol3/papers.cfm?abstract_id=2575912
8. EY, *Sustainable Investing: The Millennial Investor*, 2017: https://assets.ey.com/content/dam/ey-sites/ey-com/en_gl/topics/financial-services/ey-sustainable-investing-the-millennial-investor.pdf
9. See Chapter 5 for a discussion of screening.
10. It also warrants noting that the term ESG has become pejoratively politicised in some quarters as representing a political agenda that is not linked to mainstream interests. Other commentators have begun to question whether this term remains fit for purpose, and some are replacing the term 'ESG' with the term 'sustainability' or other descriptors of environmental and social risk factors.

11. Investopedia defines a social licence to operate as 'the ongoing acceptance of a company or industry's standard business practices and operating procedures by its employees, stakeholders, and the general public.'
12. ICGN's *Model Disclosure on Conflicts of Interest*, 2018.
13. ICGN, *Guidance on Investor Fiduciary Duties*, 2018: www.icgn.org/sites/default/files/2021-06/ICGN%20Guidance%20on%20Investor%20Fiduciary%20Duties.pdf
14. *Kay Review of UK Equity Markets and Long-Term Decision-Making. Final Report*, July *2012*: https://assets.publishing.service.gov.uk/government/uploads/system/uploads/attachment_data/file/253454/bis-12-917-kay-review-of-equity-markets-final-report.pdf
15. For example, in the case of pension funds, or asset managers providing investment services on behalf of pension funds, the time horizon is certainly long-term—and theoretically infinite. This brings into question the issue of intergenerational fairness. If a company's management and board provide a governance model for long-term corporate sustainability, what does this imply with regard to the fiduciary duty of occupational pension funds to consider future beneficiaries who are not yet in the workforce—or who might not even yet be born?
16. As discussed in Chapter 5, impact investors do receive explicit mandates to take into consideration particular third-party benefits in investment decision-making.
17. Max M. Schanzenbach and Robert H. Sitkoff, Reconciling Fiduciary Duty and Social Conscience: The Law and Economics of ESG Investing by a Trustee, 2020, *Stanford Law Review*, vol 72, p. 381: https://papers.ssrn.com/sol3/papers.cfm?abstract_id=3244665
18. Law Commission (UK), *Is It Always about the Money? Pension Trustees' Duties when Setting an Investment Strategy: Guidance from the Law Commission*, 1 July 2014. Para. 1.16: www.lawcom.gov.uk/app/uploads/2015/03/lc350_fiduciary_duties_guidance.pdf
19. ICGN, *Global Stewardship Principles*, 2020: www.icgn.org/sites/default/files/2021-06/ICGN%20Global%20Stewardship%20Principles%202020_1.pdf/www.icgn.org/sites/default/files/2021-06/ICGN%20Global%20Stewardship%20Principles%202020_1.pdf
20. ICGN, *Stewardship Principles* endorsers: www.icgn.org/icgn-global-stewardship-endorsers
21. ICGN, *Guidance on Investor Fiduciary Duties*, 2018: www.icgn.org/sites/default/files/2021-06/ICGN%20Guidance%20on%20Investor%20Fiduciary%20Duties.pdf
22. See ICGN GSP, sub-principle 6.4.
23. European Commission, *EU Taxonomy for Sustainable Activities*, 2020: https://ec.europa.eu/info/business-economy-euro/banking-and-finance/sustainable-finance/eu-taxonomy-sustainable-activities_en
24. Attracta Mooney, *Big Asset Managers Missing from Revamped UK Stewardship Code*, *Financial Times*, 2021: www.ft.com/content/1094e923-9e52-4cc7-986e-538d045c9779
25. European Union, *Regulation of the European Parliament and of the Councils on Sustainability-Related Disclosures in the Financial Services Sector*, 27 November 2019: https://eur-lex.europa.eu/legal-content/EN/TXT/?uri=celex%3A32019R2088

FURTHER READING

William Burckart and Steve Lydenburg, *21st Century Investing: Redirecting Financial Strategies to Drive Systems Change*, Berrett-Koehler, 2021: www.tiiproject.com/21st-century-investing/

European Commission, *EU Taxonomy for Sustainable Activities*, 2020: https://ec.europa.eu/info/business-economy-euro/banking-and-finance/sustainable-finance/eu-taxonomy-sustainable-activities_en

ICGN, *Global Stewardship Principles*, 2020: www.icgn.org/sites/default/files/2021-06/ICGN%20Global%20Stewardship%20Principles%202020_1.pdf/www.icgn.org/sites/default/files/2021-06/ICGN%20Global%20Stewardship%20Principles%202020_1.pdf

Corporate Reporting Dialogue, *The Sustainable Development Goals and the Future of Corporate Reporting*, 2019: www.integratedreporting.org/wp-content/uploads/2019/02/The-Sustainable-Development-Goals-and-the-future-of-corporate-reporting-1.pdf

UK Financial Conduct Authority, *Building a Regulatory Framework for Effective Stewardship*, January 2019: www.fca.org.uk/publication/discussion/dp19-01.pdf

EU High Level Expert Group on Sustainable Finance, *Financing a Sustainable European Economy: Final Report*, 2018 https://ec.europa.eu/info/publications/sustainable-finance-high-level-expert-group_en

Roger M. Barker and Iris H.y. Chiu, *Corporate Governance and Investment Management: The Promises and Limitations of the New Financial Economy*, 2017.

Stephen Davis, Jon Lukomnik and David Pitt-Watson, *What They Do with Your Money—How the Financial System Fails Us and How to Fix It*, Yale University Press, 2016.

Principles for Responsible Investment, *Fiduciary Duty in the 21st Century*, 2015: www.unepfi.org/investment/fiduciary-duty/

United Nations, *Sustainable Development Goals*, 2015: https://sdgs.un.org/goals

John Kay, *Kay Review of UK Equity Markets and Long-Term Decision-Making. Final Report*, July 2012: https://assets.publishing.service.gov.uk/government/uploads/system/uploads/attachment_data/file/253454/bis-12-917-kay-review-of-equity-markets-final-report.pdf

Sir David Walker, *A Review of Corporate Governance in UK Banks and Other Financial Industry Entities*, 26 November 2009: https://ecgi.global/sites/default/files/codes/documents/walker_review_261109.pdf

Chapter 2

Basic principles of corporate governance: Investor expectations and corporate realities

DOI: 10.4324/9781003307082-2

In the broad context of economic history, it was not until relatively recently—roughly over the past 30 years or so—that corporate governance developed from a somewhat arcane term to a growing area attracting the attention of companies, investors, regulators, stakeholders and academics. In the investment world, governance is increasingly regarded as a fundamental risk factor by institutional investors. It influences investment decisions, valuation models and how investors engage with companies and vote at shareholder meetings.

To some extent, there are dismal underpinnings to this growing interest in corporate governance, as it has been fed by high-profile corporate failures, both large and small in magnitude, in markets all over the world. Company failures and poor corporate governance are not new. The roots go back to the Renaissance and the formation of the modern corporate structure. Prominent early collapses include the once-mighty House of Medici bank in 15th-century Florence, the bursting of the Dutch South Sea Company's bubble in the early 1700s, and numerous further examples of greater and lesser proportion since then. The spectacular collapse of the once-mighty Enron Corporation in the early 2000s was a lightning rod moment in the US and stock markets around the world—serving effectively as a monument to poor corporate governance and the damage that can bring.

In a world in which man has harnessed electricity, travelled to the moon, split the atom and developed vaccines for infectious diseases, it seems remarkable that the seemingly simpler question of how to achieve good corporate governance in companies remains elusive. As we have just made historical references, we can also add the name of Sir Isaac Newton to help explain why this is so. Though one of history's great geniuses, Newton was himself also a victim of bad corporate governance, having lost a fortune in the South Sea Bubble of 1720. In so doing, the eminent physicist presciently, if unwittingly, identified one of the key dimensions of corporate governance when, in response to his losses in the Bubble, he claimed 'I can account for the motion of celestial bodies, but not the madness of people.' It is the human factor at the core of corporate governance: how to bring out the best in human nature—and how to avoid the worst.

This challenge has led to the development of corporate governance as a profession and a complex ecosystem of professionals, including not only investors, boards and companies, but also a growing number of service providers to both boards (board evaluations, remuneration, risk management, proxy solicitors) and investors (proxy voting, data, ratings and analytics).

1. WHAT IS CORPORATE GOVERNANCE AND WHY IS IT IMPORTANT?

This chapter starts with definitions of corporate governance and considers why this is a topic worth studying. It explores the differing approaches to governance in diverse markets globally, considering the relevance of shareholder- and stakeholder-based models of governance, as well as the critical role that ownership structure plays in shaping governance practices in both developed and emerging markets. We focus primarily on governance at the individual company level, and in particular on ICGN's Global Governance Principles (GGP) as a global benchmark of good governance practice from an investor perspective. But the chapter also reviews country-specific factors (including law, regulation and ownership structure) that influence governance standards and practice in individual jurisdictions. A critical survey of the academic literature on corporate governance in Chapter 3 will offer guidance on the relative importance of these factors as uncovered by empirical evidence.

Definitions

Corporate governance is a commonly used term, yet it often means different things to different people, depending on how they are affected by corporate governance and how governance is reflected in laws and regulations in different jurisdictions around the world. So it is useful to start this chapter with a few examples of how corporate governance has been defined, both to help us get a handle on the concept and to show how varied the definitions can be. There are many that can be chosen from, but we begin with five.

We start with Sir Adrian Cadbury's 1992 definition crafted for the introduction to 1992's *Report of the Committee on the Financial Aspects of Corporate Governance*,[1] a report issued after a series of scandals in the UK that led to the formation of what is now the *UK Corporate Governance Code*:

> Corporate governance is the system by which companies are directed and controlled. Boards of directors are responsible for the governance of their companies. The shareholders' role in governance is to appoint the directors and the auditors and to satisfy themselves that an appropriate governance structure is in place. The responsibilities of the board include setting the company's strategic aims, providing the leadership to put them into effect, supervising the management of the business and reporting to shareholders on their stewardship. The board's actions are subject to laws, regulations and the shareholders in general meeting.

Thirty years after its publication, the UK's Financial Reporting Council (FRC) still retains this wording in the *UK Corporate Governance Code*, labelling it as the core definition of governance under the Code.[2] It places most emphasis on the role of the board and shareholders.

A somewhat broader definition is the Organisation for Economic Co-operation and Development's (OECD) *Principles of Corporate Governance*, first published in 1999 (today the *G20/OECD Principles*). The *G20/OECD Principles* frame corporate governance in a global context and are a common standard of reference for investors, companies and regulators. In the 2015 version of its *Principles*, the OECD stated that:

> Corporate governance involves a set of relationships between a company's management, its board, its shareholders and other stakeholders. Corporate governance also provides the structure through which the objectives of the company are set, and the means of attaining those objectives and monitoring performance are determined.[3]

Compared with the Cadbury definition, the *G20/OECD Principles* stress a company's multiple relationships, in particular including stakeholders as well as shareholders. It also extends more deeply into setting company objectives and strategy and monitoring performance as part of corporate governance.

Legal experts and economists also develop their own definitions of corporate governance, which can be crafted to complement scholarly research in individual disciplines. For example, an academically inspired definition in the financial/economic research literature is:

> Corporate governance deals with the ways in which suppliers of finance to corporations assure themselves of getting a return on their investment.[4]

This definition frames governance narrowly, in a strict financial context, and is so general and abstract that it is of limited use for practitioners.

Definitions of governance also may differ significantly around the world, reflecting differing economic norms and cultural traditions. As an example, Japan's *Corporate Governance Code* builds from a distinctive corporate culture and takes a broader definition of governance from what we see in the UK, placing stakeholder interests alongside those of shareholders. This definition also does not explicitly reference the role of the company's boards of directors:

> Corporate governance means a structure for transparent, fair, timely and decisive decision-making by companies, with due attention to the needs and perspectives of shareholders and also customers, employees and local communities.[5]

Another distinctive approach to corporate governance is found in South Africa's corporate governance code, *King IV*, which places strong emphasis on ethical performance—suggesting that the scope of good governance is not simply a financial matter. It defines corporate governance as:

> the exercise of ethical and effective leadership by the governing body towards the achievement of the following governance outcomes:
>
> - Ethical culture
> - Good performance
> - Effective control
> - Legitimacy.[6]

While we could review many more definitions of governance by corporate governance codes, academics and practitioners, this brief sampling shows that the same term can generate varying interpretations. If there is a common thread between the varying definitions of governance, it would lie within the broad purview of how a board or governing body promotes the mission and objectives of the company. But it is not always clear how or for whose benefit.

At the same time, the interdisciplinary nature of corporate governance defies its being pigeonholed in an individual academic field. In addition to law and finance, governance touches a broad range of disciplines, including management and strategy, ethics, psychology, political science, sociology and even anthropology. Each field brings its own perspectives, and all address in some shape or form the challenges that human nature brings to the governance of organisations.

What is the purpose of finance—and corporate governance?

In approaching the purpose of corporate governance, at least in a financial context, it can be useful to take a step back and think first about the purpose of finance more generally. In a broader social or economic landscape, finance has limited intrinsic meaning. Its function is to serve as a conduit of capital from providers of capital (savers) to users of capital (corporations). In this context, financial markets are where providers of capital can find users of capital, so that users can employ this capital to generate sustainable value, both for the business and for its providers of capital—shareholders and creditors.

This approach was articulated by the economist John Kay in his 2012 *Review of UK Equity Markets*, which he undertook on behalf of the UK government. Kay states that the core purposes of the equity markets are 'to enhance the performance of UK companies and to enable savers to benefit from the activity of these businesses through returns to direct and indirect ownership of shares in UK companies.'[7] The *Kay Report* framed this approach to finance in a long-term context and focused on the problem of short-termism in equity markets.

If we use the *Kay Report* as a jumping-off point, the purpose of corporate governance in a financial context can be presented as how a governing body promotes success and sustainable value creation in companies as users of capital. This is linked with the parallel goal of also producing fair returns for providers of risk capital, both shareholders and creditors. However, while providers of capital, including institutional investors, are critical to corporate governance—particularly given ownership and voting rights for shareholders—the purpose of corporate governance extends beyond financiers.

Taking a systemic perspective—and not just looking at individual companies and shareholders—the broader economic purpose of corporate governance is to contribute to the efficient production of the goods and services society demands and healthy and efficient financial markets, providing pension incomes for beneficiaries, creating jobs for employees and generating taxable income for governments and growth for economies in a sustainable way. The word 'sustainable' is fundamental here and suggests both the assumption of a long-term perspective as well as sensitivity to the social and environmental impacts of companies and how they treat their stakeholders. If it is not promoting positive social impact, it at the very least, on balance, seeks a neutral impact. It is this approach to the purpose of corporate governance that will lie at the core of this book.

The corporate form and agency theory

Corporate governance inevitably focuses on the corporate form as a legal construct. Like the corporate form, it has a history of innovation—one of co-evolution of numerous checks and balances embedded in legal, regulatory and other norms. This can include company law, corporate statutes, securities regulation, audit and accounting standards, and channels of communication between companies, financial markets, shareholders and other stakeholders.

Linked to these legal foundations, an important underlying governance construct of modern corporations—where ownership and control are separated—is agency theory. This concept was articulated by the academics Berle and Means in a classic 1932 treatise on the foundations of US corporate law.[8] To address this separation of ownership (by often small shareholders) and control (by company managers), the owners of a company—its shareholders—elect directors as their agents to represent their interests vis-à-vis the company's management.[9] This helps to guard against managerial abuse such as self-dealing. Within this framework, it is the role of the board to hold management to account, and it is the role of shareholders to hold the board to account. Among other things, this means that a board should ensure that company strategies, policies and operations are undertaken in the interests of the company's long-term success and, ultimately, that of its shareholders and stakeholders—and not the private interests of a company's executive management.

This is why the board of directors is of fundamental importance and at the centre of a company's governance system. It is the formal link between the company's management and its owners. However, as logical as the agency construct is, it does not always work in a straightforward fashion and can be complicated by differing types of ownership structures, particularly when there are controlling owners whose personal interests may differ from those of minority shareholders.

This book will explore in detail the fiduciary duty of investors as stewards of capital on behalf of beneficiaries. Company directors also have fiduciary duties—towards the company itself. For example, Section 172 of the revised UK Companies Act (2006) explicitly establishes the duty of directors to support the long-term success of the company. While the focus in the first instance is to benefit shareholders, these fiduciary duties encompass stakeholder and environmental issues in its litany of matters that directors are expected to take into account in the conduct of their duties. It establishes stakeholder relations as matter of fiduciary duty for directors.

2. SHAREHOLDER VERSUS STAKEHOLDER PRIMACY: A FALSE DICHOTOMY?

Balancing the interests of shareholders and stakeholders economically and equitably is a huge issue relevant to both corporate governance and investor stewardship. This has energised a renewed debate about corporate purpose. It also links with the emergence of so-called stakeholder capitalism as a direct challenge to the traditional model of shareholder primacy that has been established as a governance orthodoxy in many markets. So it is important to spend a bit of time on this. We build from agency theory.

Agency theory typically presumes a governance model anchored by shareholders and supported by the concept of shareholder primacy. This has a legal grounding particularly in the common law jurisdictions, such as the US, UK, Australia and Canada, and is based on the premise that the company is run first and foremost in the interests of its owners—the shareholders—whose objective as providers of capital is to see their investments yield returns. This perspective was famously captured by the economist Milton Friedman in his 1970 *New York Times* article titled 'The Social Responsibility of Business Is to Increase Its Profits.'[10] His conclusion:

> there is one and only one social responsibility of business—to use its resources and engage in activities designed to increase its profits so long as it stays within the rules of the game, which is to say, engages in open and free competition without deception or fraud.

Friedman's caveat of 'rules of the game' does reflect his as awareness of business as a social entity and is an important nuance that can be missing from superficial or simplistic interpretations of Friedman's philosophy—by both his supporters and detractors.[11] Yet Friedman remains an icon for the shareholder primacy camp.

Other stakeholders, including employees and customers, are obviously critical to the success or failure of a company, but under a strict shareholder primacy model these stakeholder interests are secondary to those of shareholders. This is often referred to as the Anglo-Saxon model of corporate governance and has traditionally dominated the debate among financial economists.

However, there are alternative approaches to why companies exist. The most prominent alternative to the shareholder primacy model would be a *stakeholder-based* model—one that would regard shareholders as one group among several key stakeholders, alongside employees, customers, communities and broader societal interests. The stakeholder focus, which is more common in markets such as Continental Europe or Japan, emphasises the company's role in a social context, and not just as an engine for shareholder returns. The objectives of the company in a stakeholder system may be multivariate and not only focused on shareholder value. This broader stakeholder-oriented definition of governance may have greater resonance with management scholars or academics in non-legal or non-financial disciplines:

> the objectives of the firm should be derived by balancing the conflicting claims of the various 'stakeholders' in the firm: managers, workers, stockholders, suppliers, vendors.[12]

Even in a stakeholder system, shareholders typically have unique ownership rights—in particular the rights to vote at general meetings and elect/fire a company's board. Yet, while shareholders are clearly important in a stakeholder model, they are just one of several stakeholders. In this model, the desire of shareholders to maximise profits might be tempered with the social role and impact of the company, particularly to provide a source of employment and to contribute to growth and investment to support broader macroeconomic performance.

In recent years, the debate on shareholder versus stakeholder primacy has intensified, particularly with regard to greater attention to company purpose and the importance of stakeholders. This has been stimulated by a range of factors, including the growing interest in ESG issues and how these link to a company's stakeholder relations and its broader social and environmental impact. For example, as a counterpoint to Milton Friedman's advocacy of profit maximisation, Oxford University Professor of Management and Finance Colin Mayer has articulated an alternative view that companies should be guided in the first instance by purpose, not profit, and that this purpose is defined as creating (profitable) solutions to the problems and needs of individuals and societies.[13]

A similar, but different, challenge to the shareholder model has been an enthusiastic embrace by some of what is known as *stakeholder capitalism*. The World Economic Forum's (WEF) *Davos Manifesto 2020* brought renewed focus to this term and proclaimed that business should serve the interests of all society, not just shareholders. In this

FIGURE 2.1 Whose company is it?

A 1995 research project by the Japanese academic Masaru Yoshimori asked two basic questions of executives domiciled in five developed economies. The first question is 'whose company is it?' The second poses a less abstract question about shareholder/stakeholder priorities relating to dividend cuts versus job cuts in a time of corporate stress. In both cases, the outcomes show striking differences between the Anglo-American approach versus the more stakeholder-focused societies in Japan, Germany and France.

This is a snapshot of another era. If we were to repeat this research project today, how do you think it would be different after over 25 years? Do you think there is now greater convergence?

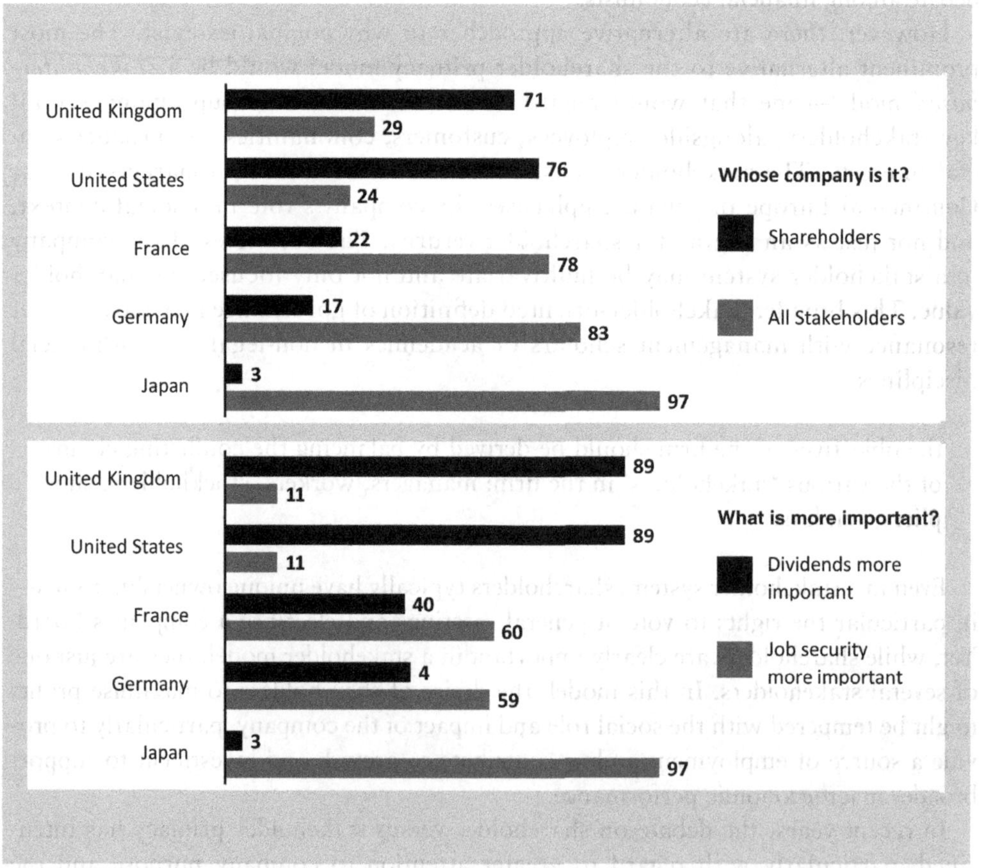

Source: Masaru Yoshimori, Whose Company Is It? The Concept of the Corporation in Japan and the West, 1995, *Long Range Planning*, vol 28, no 4, pp. 33–4.

articulation, stakeholder capitalism has been hailed by the WEF as a solution—'a way of addressing the world's greatest challenges, from societal divisions created by income inequality and political polarisation to the climate crisis we face today.'[14]

This stakeholder focus has also found a possibly unlikely ally in the US business elite, traditionally a politically and socially conservative group—and not one to mix capitalism with a broader social purpose. But, in August 2019, the Business Roundtable (BRT), a body representing chief executives of major US companies, issued its *Statement on the Purpose of a Corporation*.[15] In a conscious step away from articulating corporate purpose in shareholder-centric terms, the BRT statement redefines the purpose of a corporation as being to foster 'an economy that serves all Americans.' This stakeholder agenda complements the growing investor focus on social and environmental issues, in keeping with the WEF campaign on stakeholder capitalism. To some, the BRT Statement is regarded as a progressive initiative: according to Mohamed El-Erian, economic advisor at Germany's Allianz Group, it is an important shift reflecting an 'emerging consensus about the importance of a more inclusive capitalism.'[16]

Stakeholder capitalism: too good to be true?

But not everyone is convinced. Some are sceptical about the motivation lying behind the seemingly noble expression of public purpose in the BRT Statement, sensing this is in part a public relations exercise to give companies a better image in an environment of diminishing trust and increasing concentration of wealth and corporate power. Former US Treasury Secretary Larry Summers offers a cynical interpretation of this nature, suggesting that the BRT's rhetorical embrace of stakeholders is in part a 'strategy for holding off necessary tax and regulatory reform.'[17]

The US investor association, the Council of Institutional Investors (CII), offers a similarly sceptical view of the BRT statement, claiming that it undercuts managerial accountability. CII argues that 'accountability to everyone means accountability to no-one,' and that the net effect of this BRT statement would be to diminish shareholder rights and marginalise shareholders' voices, without establishing alternative mechanisms to hold management accountable.[18]

The BRT letter and the broader movement towards stakeholder capitalism are also facing academic challenge. In their 2020 paper, The Illusory Promise of Stakeholder Governance, Harvard Law School professors Lucian Bebchuk and Roberto Tallarita conduct an economic and empirical analysis of stakeholderism and its expected consequences. They conclude that stakeholder capitalism would have the practical ill effects of increasing the insulation of corporate leaders from shareholders, reducing their accountability and hurting economic performance.[19]

As the debate now stands, there remain differing schools of thought at intellectual loggerheads about company purpose and the primacy of shareholders versus stakeholders. This is a fascinating intellectual debate, and there is a temptation to pick a side—to embrace one extreme or the other. Yet, one must be wary of buying into a possibly false dichotomy. If nothing else, the word 'primacy' itself may be too emotive and unfit for purpose, whether it is shareholder or stakeholder primacy.

This discussion also can be a bit academic and rarified for practitioners—and divorced from practical realities. For example, even a red-blooded advocate of shareholder primacy (such as Milton Friedman) would recognise the fundamental importance of positive stakeholder relations to long-term company performance—as witnessed by shareholder support for companies and their stakeholders during the Covid-19 crisis.[20] Moreover, an increased emphasis on stakeholders need not diminish the important anchoring role that shareholders play, given their distinctive rights afforded in corporate charters to hold management to account, most notably through the exercise of voting rights.

Is there a third way?

A dialectic approach to the shareholder/stakeholder debate would seek to establish a workable synthesis between the thesis of the shareholder and antithesis of the stakeholder. This effectively is what Harvard Business School academics Joseph Bower and Lynn Paine propose in their 'company-centric' model, which focuses fundamentally on the core health and sustainability of the enterprise as a whole, rather than its distinct shareholder/stakeholder audiences.[21] Similarly, section 172 of the revised UK Companies Act (2006) also defines director duties in the first instance as promoting the sustainable success of the company itself for the benefit of its shareholders—but, in the process, it requires directors to have appropriate 'regard for' the interests of key stakeholders.

Ultimately shareholders and stakeholders may have distinct interests and priorities, but they are united by the company that brings them together. Both also need one another and share a long-term interest in the success and sustainability of the company whose shares they own, which employs them, and which makes products that customers want and need. It is a symbiotic relationship. So, while the tensions of the shareholder/stakeholder debate create risks for outcomes that might disproportionately favour or disfavour shareholders relative to other stakeholders, the process of good governance should seek to understand these tensions and find sustainable ways to balance the potentially conflicting interests of shareholders and stakeholders.

The objective is effectively one of seeking a sustainable multi-equilibrium—or a constrained optimisation.[22] For shareholders, this should mean that the company should normally be managed to generate risk-adjusted economic profits that cover the company's cost of capital. For stakeholders, this should mean adequate protections and safeguards and positive social outcomes. These objectives are not intrinsically incompatible, and, particularly from a long-term perspective, sustainable companies will require these 'win–win' outcomes, similar to the concept of '*ikigai*' discussed in Chapter 1. This is also compatible with the concept of 'enlightened shareholder value,' which recognises that sustainable value creation requires positive treatment of company stakeholders, including social and environmental performance.

3. DIFFERING MODELS OF GOVERNANCE: IN SEARCH OF A 'TRUE NORTH'

Just as there are many different definitions of corporate governance, there are also differing governance models. The main differentiator tends to be regional or jurisdictional—this can build from a range of factors, including a country's legal structure, prevailing ownership patterns, the state of development of capital markets and the size of the public sector. It can also reflect historical and social factors as well as cultural differences.[23]

Another important dimension is time frame and the life cycle of the company, where governance requirements for companies may vary on the basis of their own state of development or maturity. For example, a small or medium-sized business that is just getting off the ground will not need the same governance structures as a large and mature multinational.[24]

These observations suggest that corporate governance is dynamic (if path-dependent) and can be subject to change and differing influences. This can reflect a company's own development and needs for capital. It can also change because of tensions, both positive and negative, when shareholders from one jurisdiction are owners of equity of companies domiciled in a different jurisdiction. Governance preferences and expectations can and do differ across markets. The search for a single governance structure that is valid for all companies globally at every stage of development has been unsuccessful and is very likely futile. So, is corporate governance therefore simply endogenous to individual companies, or are there governance features that may strike a more universal chord?

The OECD asked a similar question as it began to develop a globally applicable framework in 1998. Noting the diversity of governance systems around the world, it concluded that there are 'fundamental parameters' that should have relevance in all companies, no matter how big or small, no matter where they are based.[25] These parameters are fundamentally *principles*, not rules, and were summarised as follows:

- *Fairness*: protecting the rights of investors providing a company's risk capital.
- *Responsibility*: operating in a way that is sensitive to a company's social impact and its relationships with key stakeholders, including employees, customers, suppliers and related communities.
- *Accountability*: ensuring that a company's management and board can be held to account by shareholders and regulators.
- *Transparency*: allowing investors and stakeholders to have timely and accurate accounts of company performance.

We believe these four principles do have universal relevance to serve as a guiding 'north star' that brings us all together. They constitute a reliable lens through which corporate governance can be assessed at both a macro (country) and micro (company) level in a wide range of jurisdictions. Many corporate governance failures, including those discussed in this book, have stemmed from some form of breakdown in one or more of these guiding principles. In many ways, this puts moral leadership at the core of good corporate governance.

Codes of corporate governance

The UK's *Cadbury Code*, cited above, became the first national corporate governance code in 1992, prompted in part by crises in the early 1990s in visible UK listed companies such as Maxwell Communication Corporation, Polly Peck and the bank BCCI. Their downfall was fundamentally linked to corporate governance failures, with fraud at the core.

The *Cadbury Code* was the first in a series of codes in the UK that came together to constitute what is now the *UK Corporate Governance Code*, overseen by the UK's FRC. It is a 'soft law' voluntary framework of what is regarded as best corporate governance practice, at least in a UK context. The current version of the Code (2018) breaks up corporate governance into fundamental elements, including board leadership and company purpose; division of responsibilities; composition, succession and evaluation; audit risk and internal control; and remuneration.[26]

Since the launch of the *Cadbury Code* in 1992, national corporate governance codes have been developed in close to 100 jurisdictions, all over the globe[27]—in many cases motivated by local governance failures. Corporate governance codes tend to stem from a framework of broad principles and have a common focus on the role of the board and its effectiveness. But they can differ significantly in the details—reflecting differing governance preferences, including between a shareholder or stakeholder orientation.

The benefit of codes is that they can advocate specific governance practices at a fairly granular level without establishing such practices as hard and fast legal requirements or rules. There are many aspects of what is assumed to be governance best practice that are not supported by a rigorous base of empirical evidence. Examples include common governance code provisions calling for a separate CEO and chair or for majority board independence. The lack of definitive evidence supporting code provisions does not mean that these provisions are a bad idea. It may simply reflect the challenges of research design to meaningfully capture qualitative aspects of governance, such as board effectiveness or independence. But the absence of a convincing body of evidence may also suggest that rigid adherence to a code's rules is not always the best practice.

In some cases, individual recommendations of a code may be accorded priority. For example, the German *Corporate Governance Code* breaks down its provisions into 'shall' versus 'should' recommendations; the former are indicated by 'shall adhere' and are more prescriptive and less voluntary; the *Code* requires companies to disclose where and why their governance policies may differ. On the other hand, German *Code* recommendations that are indicated with the word 'should' are taken more in the context of best practice suggestions, where non-adherence does not require explanation.[28]

Codes are fundamentally recommendations based on overarching governance principles. Because there is no 'one-size-fits-all' approach to corporate governance, codes provide companies with both guidance as to which governance practices are regarded as most appropriate in a given market and important flexibility and discretion to adopt the governance framework that they feel best meets their own specific needs. This means that it can be legitimate for companies not to adhere to all of a code's provisions. To maintain the integrity and meaningfulness of codes, however, it is important for companies to be able to clearly and publicly justify departures from their national governance code's recommended practices.

Comply or explain

A common disclosure requirement in many codes is a 'comply or explain' mechanism, which provides a basis for companies to justify code non-compliance.[29] 'Comply or explain' requirements therefore provide a form of discipline to ensure that a company's departures from its prevailing code are clearly disclosed. And the onus is on companies to provide convincing explanations. But explanations to whom? Who reads 'comply or explain' statements, and what do they do with them? At one level, a regulator may monitor disclosures of this nature, with a view to assessing which statements may be more, or less, convincing. But it can be very challenging for a regulator to assess the quality and legitimacy of a non-compliance statement. If code compliance is ultimately a matter of company discretion by law, there may be limited, if any, channels of regulatory enforcement for code non-compliance.

Therefore, for many observers, the 'soft law' of codes and 'comply or explain' suggest the need for monitoring through the financial markets, and investors in particular. If the onus is put on a company to produce a credible statement of non-compliance, this would suggest a further burden is put on the markets, and ultimately a company's shareholders, to assess the merit and quality of a company's response. In cases where such explanations are weak or suggest significant governance vulnerabilities, it would seem logical to expect that shareholders will wish to use ownership rights, including voting rights, and the ability to engage with companies to advocate reforms in governance practice. Weak compliance could also affect investor perceptions and investment decisions—and ultimately valuations. The case for investor stewardship in many ways builds from the importance of investors using their ownership rights to promulgate good governance practices. Otherwise, corporate governance might look good on the surface, but be toothless in practice.

Do all shareholders monitor code compliance and carefully assess 'comply or explain' statements? The mixed answer is that some do, and some do not. Or, if they do, they will do so selectively, and different investors will focus on different information. Particularly for large institutional shareholders with highly diversified portfolios of individual investment holdings, it may not be feasible for them to assess each and every company they own shares in—particularly if the individual stake is relatively small. It is fair to say that some companies demonstrating poor or superficial adherence to code provisions may be able to fly under the radar and avoid serious repercussions.

4. IMPORTANCE OF OWNERSHIP STRUCTURE

A company's ownership structure will fundamentally influence its governance framework, in particular the differences between controlled and widely held companies.[30] A particular problem of a 'comply or explain' system comes with a controlling ownership structure. If a controlling owner chooses to adopt substandard, or non-code-supported, governance practices, it can do so, even if minority shareholders express clear differences in preference. This is another way in which the soft law of a code-based system may demonstrate practical weaknesses.

Understanding a company's ownership structure is a critical first step to appreciating its governance requirements—and potential tensions. Although there can be several variations of ownership structure, the most basic split is the difference between companies that are widely held and those that have defined control. Neither structure is intrinsically good or bad; however, both structures have vulnerabilities to poor governance.

There is much literature relating to governance of widely held companies, particularly in the US market, where this is a common feature of large publicly listed companies (and where research is facilitated by ready access to corporate financial data). In this context, the main governance risk is that a diffuse ownership base may be ill positioned to hold company management to account, notwithstanding the existence of a board of directors. This has been branded the 'ownerless company' in that no single investor may hold a critical mass of shares to exert meaningful market discipline on the company's executive management or its board.

The risk in widely held companies is of management self-dealing or pursuing private benefits that are not shared by the shareholder base, particularly in the event that the board proves to be non-independent or weak in its company oversight. However, when an effective board is in place, a widely held structure can have positive advantages—in particular the absence of a single controlling shareholder whose interests have the potential for the pursuit of private benefits of control at the expense of minority shareholders.

Apart from Anglo-American markets, controlled ownership is the norm globally, particularly in Continental Europe and in emerging markets.[31] It poses a particularly relevant risk in country environments where rule of law and regulatory quality are weak, as minority shareholders may have limited legal redress to challenge the actions of controlling owners.

At the same time, a shareholder who can exercise effective controlling voting power (which can range from 20% to over 50% depending on the overall shareholding structure) has the potential to provide the most robust oversight of the company and its board and will usually heavily influence board composition and key decisions made by executive management. If a controlled company is governed with appropriate attention to the interests and rights of its minority shareholders, the controlling owner might be regarded as a form of *'benign dictator'*—some would argue this is the best of all worlds. But, sometimes, even benign dictators can morph into simply being dictators—taking advantage of their own private interests at the expense of the company and its other shareholders.

5. MACRO/COUNTRY INFLUENCES ON CORPORATE GOVERNANCE

The governance of companies is significantly influenced by their country (or countries) of domicile. Country factors set the scene for philosophies and systems of governance. This comes from a range of sources. According to the 'Law and Finance' approach to comparative corporate governance,[32] the most fundamental influence is a country's legal system, which can differ significantly from market to market. This provides a foundation for company law and regulation—as well as for stock exchange listing rules, corporate governance codes, board structures and attitudes towards investors. Country factors also influence a market's informational infrastructure and the standards of transparency and disclosure that are expected of companies. For companies that are listed on stock markets outside their home jurisdiction, multiple country influences may apply—including law, regulations and listing standards in the markets where a company is listed.

Country influences can differ notably in terms of the degree to which they support good governance—or allow for bad governance. The consulting firm McKinsey & Company sought to demonstrate this relationship in an investment context in an investor survey first published in June 2000. They asked investors if they would pay a premium for investing in a company with good board practices, as defined by a range of indicators, including a majority of outside directors, true independence and responsiveness to investor requests.[33] The investor response clearly affirmed the notion that well-governed companies warrant a premium relative to other companies. It also suggests the opposite interpretation, namely that poorly governed companies warrant a discount.

As this McKinsey study was fundamentally a perception study, it did not lend itself well to empirical study of actual investor behaviour. But it does clearly suggest that

FIGURE 2.2 Rule of law scores

Country	Rule of Law
Germany	91.4
Japan	90.9
United Kingdom	90.4
United States	88.5
France	88.0
South Korea	84.6
Italy	60.6
India	54.3
China	52.9
South Africa	49.5
Brazil	48.1
Russia	22.6

Source: World Bank, Governance Indicators, 2020.

country factors can strongly influence perceptions of governance, and most likely governance realities as well. A more contemporary picture of how macro governance influences may differ can be pieced together with a range of country governance indicators, many of which are freely accessible in the public domain. A non-exhaustive list would include rule of law and regulatory quality indicators from the World Bank; the Transparency International Corruption Perception Index; sovereign credit ratings from Fitch, Moody's and S&P Global; the Yale Environmental Protection Index; the United Nations Development Programme's Human Development Index; and the Heritage Foundation Economic Freedom Index. While quantitative metrics relating to these broad issues have inherent limitations, it is nonetheless useful to produce a bespoke index of indexes to provide at least an indicative snapshot of how countries may differ. We present such an index in Chapter 5 to place some of the world's leading developed and emerging markets in context.

Rule of law is one important indicator of governance at the country level. It reflects both the quality of written law and regulation, as well as their enforcement by public authorities. For minority investors, rule of law is fundamental to the protection of shareholders and their ownership rights. The chart in Figure 2.2 looks at six developed economies (lighter shading) and six emerging markets (darker shading) in the World Bank's 2018 governance indicators.[34] These indicators are compiled by the World Bank using a systematic methodology to provide a rough assessment of one country's rule of law in both absolute and relative terms.

While we always need to be mindful of the potential for subjectivity in rankings of this nature, these outcomes have largely been consistent over time—and if nothing else suggest that rule of law is a major differentiator in terms of country risk between developed and emerging markets. But this is not automatic, and some of the relativities may be surprising. For example, South Korea has often been regarded as an emerging market, but its rule of law ranking is only slightly below the US and France and well ahead of a 'developed' market such as Italy. This macro perspective sets the stage for assessment of risks at the individual company level.

6. GOVERNANCE AT THE COMPANY LEVEL: THE ICGN GLOBAL GOVERNANCE PRINCIPLES

As noted earlier, corporate governance codes can provide companies, boards, investors and stakeholders with a framework to promote best governance practices in individual companies.

While there are many corporate governance codes in circulation focused on individual jurisdictions, ICGN's contribution to this global dialogue comes through its own *Global Governance Principles* (GGP), a global framework of reference that has been developed in consultation with, and ratified by, ICGN members. In a global context, the ICGN GGP and the G20/OECD *Principles of Corporate Governance* are regarded as the two leading authoritative global frameworks relating to corporate governance. The OECD *Principles* are intended in the first instance for regulators, policymakers and standard setters; this complements the focus of the ICGN GGP on the perspective of investors as institutional owners. Both the ICGN GGP and the OECD *Principles* were recognized as authoritative global frameworks in the European Union's Corporate Sustainability Reporting Directive.[35]

The GGP focus primarily on board effectiveness and shareholder rights in listed companies along a range of dimensions—taking the perspective of institutional investors with both equity and debt stakes in companies. The GGP are meant to complement, not supersede, individual country corporate governance codes, and part of the value of the GGP lies in serving as a global basis of comparison for companies, investors, regulators and other standard setters (including corporate governance code developers).

We encourage governance and stewardship professionals to read the GGP and their sub-principles themselves. They consist of ten basic principles of corporate governance to guide board effectiveness and protect the rights and interests of investors. Some of the key features of the GGP are presented below.

Principle 1: board role and responsibilities

> The board should promote the long-term best interests of the company by acting on an informed basis with good faith, care and loyalty, for the benefit of shareholders, while having regard to relevant stakeholders.

This principle emphasises the board's fiduciary role as supporting the long-term success and sustainability of the company itself, accountable to investors as providers of risk capital, as well as to its key stakeholders. It also presents the purview of the board's role relative to company purpose, strategy, finance, risk oversight and sustainability, including ESG practices, executive remuneration and the appointment of (and succession planning for) the chief executive. The board's purview is not constrained by its focus on a company's financial capital; rather, it must consider the dimensions of a company's human and natural capital as well.

Board members need to ensure that their other commitments will not interfere with their ability to provide diligent oversight. This also requires the board to have regular access to senior management, and it also calls for the board—and particularly independent non-executive directors—to establish appropriate communication channels with shareholders, creditors and other stakeholders.

Principle 2: leadership and independence

> Board leadership requires clarity and balance in board and executive roles and an integrity of independent process to protect the interests of shareholders and relevant stakeholders in promoting the long-term success for the company.

Governance is ultimately about people and the quality of leadership to steer a company to achieve its purpose and obligations to shareholders and stakeholders. This principle focuses on the critical importance of board leadership and independence. It calls for a balance of leadership roles, including an independent chair—separate from the chief executive. While board independence remains a difficult concept for outsiders to monitor and measure in practice, the GGP embrace the importance of independence and call for majority independence on company boards, both widely held and controlled. However, particularly for controlled companies, majority independence may be aspirational. A minimum one-third independence in controlled companies may be a more modest investor expectation.

Principle 3: board composition and appointment

> The board should comprise a sufficient mix of directors with relevant knowledge, independence, competence, industry experience and diversity of perspectives to generate effective challenge, discussion and objective decision-making in alignment with the company's purpose, values and relevant stakeholders.

Independence alone does not make for a good board member or for a good board in aggregate. Board effectiveness also requires the appropriate mix of expertise and skills required to provide oversight of company executive management. This will typically require differing degrees of industry and financial expertise, as well as knowledge of different markets, technologies or specific risks, including ESG-related issues. It also calls for diversity, equity and inclusion (gender, ethnic, geographic, cognitive) to ensure balanced oversight and decision-making.[36]

Good practice includes the development of a skills matrix to identify needs and gaps in board composition, as well as an independently led nomination committee to lead the board nominations process. Regular board evaluations (both internal and external) can be valuable tools to guide a nomination committee, and the board as a whole, with regard to the board's performance and potential weaknesses. This will include monitoring of director tenure and ensuring that there is an appropriate balance between institutional knowledge and 'new blood'. The board should ensure that shareholders are able to nominate candidates for board appointment, subject to an appropriate threshold of share ownership.

Principle 4: corporate culture

> The board should instil and demonstrate a culture of high standards of business ethics and integrity aligned with the company's purpose, vision, mission and values at board level and throughout the workforce.

Effective governance requires a supportive corporate culture, based on ethics and shared values, to guide behaviour and decision-making. Culture starts at the top and sets a tone, hopefully a positive one, for the entire organisation. To be meaningful, it cannot simply be a code of conduct sitting in isolation. It should link to strategy, operations and risk management, including anti-corruption and whistleblowing mechanisms to provide cultural safeguards and controls. Healthy stakeholder relations reflect a positive corporate culture.

Principle 5: remuneration

> Remuneration should be designed to fairly and effectively align the interests of the CEO, executive officers and workforce with a company's strategy and purpose to help ensure long-term, sustainable value preservation and creation. Aggregate remuneration should be appropriately balanced with the payment of dividends to shareholders and retention of capital for future investment, and the level of quantum should be defendable relative to growing social concerns relating to inequality.

Overseeing executive remuneration and related performance incentives is a fundamental board responsibility.[37] This is best achieved through an independently led remuneration committee. The board is responsible for ensuring that remuneration is reasonable and equitable in both structure and quantum and is determined within the context of the company's values, internal reward structures and competitive drivers, while being sensitive to the expectations of stakeholders and societal norms. Increasingly, board remuneration committees, and the board as a whole, will need to justify the level of executive pay, and not just the remuneration policy.

Pay structures and practices should be transparent and link clearly to the company's long-term strategy for value creation. Companies should include provisions in their incentive plans that enable the company to withhold or reduce the payment of any sum before it is paid ('malus') or recover sums that have been paid ('clawback') in the event of serious misconduct or a material misstatement in the company's financial statements.

Binding or advisory votes on pay plans provide an important tool for shareholders to send signals on remuneration. Since the introduction of say on pay votes in some markets, only rarely has a majority of shareholders voted against a pay plan. But it does happen. For example, in the 2020–21 voting season in the US, 15 companies listed in the S&P 500 (3%) had failed say on pay votes, including well-known firm NCR Corporation's remuneration plan only having 16% shareholder support.[38] Even when a pay package is formally approved, a significant 'protest' vote in excess of 20% (such as the 35% vote against the pay package of the UK's Wm Morrison in 2020) sends a clear signal that the board and management ignore at their peril.

Investor interest in sustainability has been a factor in the growing inclusion of ESG metrics in executive incentive plans. ICGN encourages executive remuneration structures to include ESG factors—as long as they are reliably measured and material to the company's business model and financial performance.[39] However, this is not always easy to do, and the risk is that ESG metrics can be chosen more on their measurability than materiality. This is what the academic Alex Edmans calls 'hitting the target but missing the point.' Moreover, there may be many possible ESG metrics that have strategic relevance, but their relative importance might also shift over time.[40]

Principle 6: risk oversight

> The board should proactively oversee the assessment and disclosure of the company's key risks and approve the approach to risk management regularly or with any significant business change and satisfy itself that the approach is functioning effectively.

Board oversight of risk has traditionally been within the purview of audit committees (and in many cases still is), but risk oversight is coming into its own as a critical board function, and stand-alone risk committees are increasingly common. Whatever the structure, ultimate accountability for risk oversight rests with the board as a whole.[41]

A very basic first step is for boards to agree a risk culture that is linked to the company's purpose, business model, strategy and capital allocation. Traditional risk management focused on financial risks, which remain as relevant as ever. But there is also scope for risk oversight to be more comprehensive with regard to operational or enterprise-wide risks which can include material ESG issues that may be less readily quantifiable or audited. With regard to ESG factors, the risk perspective should take 'double materiality' into consideration: both the risk that ESG factors pose to the company specifically, but also the risks that arise from negative social or stakeholder impacts.

Principle 7: corporate reporting

> Boards should oversee timely and reliable company disclosures for shareholders and relevant stakeholders relating to the company's financial position, approach to sustainability, performance, business model, strategy, and long-term prospects.

The board should present a balanced and understandable assessment of the company's position and prospects in the annual report and accounts in order for shareholders and other stakeholders to be able to assess the company's financial performance, business model, strategy and long-term prospects. Company financial reports should present a true and fair view of the company's position and prospects.

It is important for the company to make a clear statement of its approach to capital allocation. It should seek to clarify how a sustainable balance of capital allocation is achieved among different and competing company, shareholder, creditor and stakeholder interests.

As will be discussed in detail in Chapter 7, boards must increasingly focus on 'non-financial' reporting, which can include material ESG factor key performance indicators (KPIs) that integrate financial and narrative reporting. Boards should ensure that companies are disclosing the most relevant non-financial information that matches their sector, business model and geographical operations. Companies should be encouraged to adopt ESG and non-financial reporting metrics that mesh with establish global standards. ESG disclosures should link to the company's management of its natural and human capital. ESG reporting should also seek to address 'double materiality,' which includes reporting on the company's social and environmental impacts as well as on how ESG factors may impact the company's own financial performance.

Principle 8: internal and external audit

> The board should establish rigorous, independent and effective internal and external audit procedures, to ensure the quality and integrity of corporate reporting.

Board audit committees play a key role in the governance process, and it is important that such a committee is fully independent to ensure the quality and integrity of the board's financial oversight for investors, stakeholders and other users of financial information. In addition to traditional financial statements, the company's annual report should also include a statement on the company's capital allocation policies and practices. The audit committee should take the lead responsibility for the relationship with the company's auditor, including auditor selection and ensuring that relevant financial accounting policies are prudent and appropriate for the company and its business model. Accounting policies should not encourage short-term behaviours that expose the company to longer-term risks. To ensure objectivity, non-audit fees from the auditor ideally should be minimal, or at least less than the audit fee itself. Independent third-party assurance should be encouraged for non-financial reporting.

Principle 9: shareholder rights

> Rights of all shareholders should be equal and must be protected. Fundamental to this protection is ensuring that a shareholder's voting rights are directly linked to its economic stake, and that minority shareholders have voting rights on key decisions or transactions which affect their interest in the company.

In most cases, institutional investors are minority shareholders in the companies whose equities they hold. This can make them vulnerable to the vested or private interests of company managers and controlling shareholders. Robust protections should safeguard shareholder rights and guard against potential abuse. Related party transactions and other conflicts of interest, both in controlled and widely held companies, require independent scrutiny and protocols to protect minority shareholder interests.

A fundamental shareholder right is the right to vote at shareholder meetings, and companies should facilitate the participation of institutional investors voting by proxy through establishing efficient, low-cost, accessible voting procedures. But companies also need to fundamentally protect the integrity of the shareholder vote. Dual class shares in particular create a separation of economic rights and voting control in a way that is problematic. Defenders of differential ownership argue this can protect a company from being captured by the short-term orientation of shareholders and financial markets by removing the threat of being taken over by activist shareholders.

But, in doing so, dual class shares can effectively turn a widely held company into a controlled company (but a controlled company where the dominant shareholder bears only a minority of the economic risk)—with many potential negative outcomes, including entrenching existing executive managers or controlling shareholders, limiting external accountability and marginalising the voice of minority shareholders. Most institutional investors object to dual class shares for these reasons.[42] Although dual class share structures are increasingly allowed in many world equity markets, investors have lobbied against the use of dual class shares, and, where they exist, they encourage protections such as sunset mechanisms to be in place to wind down the differential ownership structure over time.[43] However, there are academic arguments that dual class shares do bring benefits.[44]

In addition to shareholder rights, boards must also consider creditor rights and protections and how these balance with shareholder interests, as both are providers of risk capital. This links more broadly to capital allocation—where corporate finance meets corporate governance. As a protection of both creditors and shareholders, boards should actively define and disclose their approach to capital allocation, and how the company proposes to manage its capital base sustainably.

Principle 10: shareholder meetings and voting

> Boards should ensure that meetings with shareholders are efficiently, democratically and securely facilitated to enable constructive interactivity and accountability for the company's long-term strategy, performance, and approach to sustainable development upon which voting decisions may be influenced.

Shareholder meetings are a critical part of the corporate governance process. They allow shareholders to both exercise their voting rights and engage with the company's executive management and board. Even though institutional investors attend AGMs in person fairly rarely, they play a critical role in ensuring the accountability of the board to those shareholders who elect them. Shareholder meetings came under scrutiny during the Covid-19 pandemic in 2020, given that physical meetings in a period of lockdown or quasi-lockdown were not a possibility. As a result, many shareholder meetings shifted to virtual meetings, sometimes offering little or no opportunity for shareholders to engage directly with companies. As a result, this new principle has been added to the GGP.

While many companies might prefer virtual-only meetings going forward, even once the pandemic passes, shareholders will likely prefer the option of having in-person meetings to underscore the board's direct accountability to shareholders. So, in a post-Covid-19 environment, shareholder meetings should allow for the physical presence of participants, including provision for voting electronically by proxy, and ensure live interaction is possible between shareholders and the board and management. Hybrid formats, which allow for both the physical and virtual presence of participants, enable 'live streaming' of the AGM proceedings, accessible via the internet, and should be encouraged. For most investors, the hybrid format is arguably the best solution. Virtual-only meetings should only be held in extraordinary circumstances. And, even if it might be legally permissible in some jurisdictions, audio-only recorded meetings should be strongly discouraged.

2021 revisions to the ICGN Global Governance Principles

During 2020 and 2021, ICGN conducted a periodic review of its GGP as a standard practice to keep them up to date and reflecting the latest in governance thinking globally. Since the 2017 GGP were published, there has been considerable societal change, including the disruptive effects of Covid-19 on public health and economic activity, ethnic and social tensions and the growing concerns about climate change. The role and purpose of corporations have faced renewed scrutiny, and stakeholder capitalism has emerged as a challenge to the model of shareholder primacy that prevails in many markets.

In the context of this debate, ICGN's position has been, and remains, to focus on the sustainable success and value creation of the company itself, which involves meeting legitimate shareholder needs for returns on capital, while maintaining positive and effective relations with key stakeholders, including employees, customers, supply chains, communities and civil society more broadly. These factors were taken into consideration in the most recent periodic review of the GGP, which were approved by ICGN's members at its 2021 AGM, following an extensive member consultation process.

Against this background, there are many changes in this latest 2021 version of the GGP, reflecting a wide range of corporate governance issues, as outlined below. But it is clear that one of the key themes of these revisions is to reflect the need for a greater focus on corporate purpose, improving stakeholder relations and ensuring that sustainability issues are a meaningful part of board oversight and the governance process. Both investors and companies need to focus not only on preserving and building a company's financial capital, but also on its human and natural capital. Reflecting these considerations, many of the changes to the text reflect emphasis on the following factors:

- *Company purpose*: encouraging the board and management to articulate and disclose the company's purpose to justify the company's social licence to operate and ensure this is embedded within strategy and operations.
- *Director fiduciary duty*: emphasising that directors have a fiduciary duty to act in good faith, with due care and loyalty, to promote the long-term success of the company for sustainable value creation.
- *Controlled or group companies*: emphasising that the fiduciary duty of directors is not compromised in controlled companies, and that directors on boards of subsidiary companies owe allegiance to the subsidiary as a separate legal entity and not to the group holding company.
- *Governance of sustainability*: clarifying the responsibility of the board to take ownership of the governance of sustainability in the company and its integration with company strategy, operations and risk oversight, including the effectiveness of the company's policies and practices as related to human and natural capital. We provide a greater focus on the governance of sustainability in Chapter 7, 'Company perspective: sustainability governance and reporting.'
- *Board diversity*: stressing the strategic urgency of addressing diversity, both at the board level and in the workforce as a whole, to ensure effective and inclusive decision-making in alignment with the company's purpose.
- *Stakeholder relations*: holding the board accountable to understand legitimate stakeholder needs and support healthy and sustainable stakeholder relations linked to the board's oversight of the company's human and natural capital management.
- *Systemic risks*: ensuring that boards and committees identify, address and report on relevant systemic risks to the business, particularly those identified in the UN Sustainable Development Goals.
- *Climate change*: assessing and disclosing the impact of climate change on the company business model and how it will be adapted to meet the needs of a net zero economy as part of a long-term strategy.

- *ESG data and frameworks*: encouraging the board to make use of established ESG reporting standards and frameworks to facilitate consistency and comparability of reporting and to contribute to the global consolidation of ESG standards.
- *Board independence*: introducing tighter independence standards recommending majority board independence in companies with both widely held and concentrated ownership structures, including fully independent audit and remuneration committees, as well as an emphasis on true independence of mind (versus nominal independence).
- *Capital allocation*: ensuring the board articulates and discloses a clear approach to capital management and how the company seeks to achieve a sustainable balance of capital allocation among different and competing company, shareholder, creditor and stakeholder interests.
- *Executive remuneration*: incorporating material ESG metrics into incentive plans, determined within the context of the company's values, internal reward structures and competitive drivers while being sensitive to the absolute quantum of pay relative to the expectations of shareholders, stakeholders and societal norms.
- *Shareholder meetings*: when practicable, as the challenges presented by the Covid-19 crisis are overcome, shareholder meetings should allow for the physical presence of participants, including provision for voting electronically by proxy, and ensure live interaction is possible between shareholders and the board and management. Hybrid formats should be encouraged, and virtual-only meetings should be discouraged if they cannot ensure constructive dialogue and interaction between the company and its shareholders.

NOTES

1. Sir Adrian Cadbury, *Report of the Committee on the Financial Aspects of Corporate Governance*, 1 December 1992, Gee, London, Section 3.2: www.frc.org.uk/getattachment/9c19ea6f-bcc7-434c-b481-f2e29c1c271a/The-Financial-Aspects-of-Corporate-Governance-(the-Cadbury-Code).pdf
2. Financial Reporting Council, *The UK Corporate Governance Code*, July 2018: www.frc.org.uk/getattachment/88bd8c45-50ea-4841-95b0-d2f4f48069a2/2018-UK-Corporate-Governance-Code-FINAL.pdf
3. G20/OECD, *Principles of Corporate Governance*, 2015: www.oecd.org/corporate/principles-corporate-governance/
4. Andrei Shleifer and Robert Vishny, A Survey of Corporate Governance, June 1997, *Journal of Finance*, vol 52, 737–83.
5. Tokyo Stock Exchange Inc., *Japan's Corporate Governance Code: Seeking Sustainable Corporate Growth and Increased Corporate Value over the Mid- to Long-Term*, 2015: www.jpx.co.jp/english/news/1020/b5b4pj000000jvxr-att/20180602_en.pdf
6. Institute of Directors of Southern Africa, *King IV Report on Corporate Governance for South Africa*, 2016: https://cdn.ymaws.com/www.iodsa.co.za/resource/collection/684B68A7-B768-465C-8214-E3A007F15A5A/IoDSA_King_IV_Report_-_WebVersion.pdf
7. John Kay, *The Kay Review of UK Equity Markets and Long-term Decision-making. Final Report*, July 2012: https://assets.publishing.service.gov.uk/government/uploads/system/uploads/attachment_data/file/253454/bis-12-917-kay-review-of-equity-markets-final-report.pdf
8. Adolf A. Berle, Jr. and Gardiner C. Means, *The Modern Corporation and Private Property*, 1932.
9. This is not universally a power exclusive to shareholders. The German corporate governance system, for example, has 50% of its Supervisory Board (*Aufsichtsrat*) elected by employees and comprised of employee representatives (note, only for companies that meet certain criteria).
10. Milton Friedman, The Social Responsibility of Business Is to Increase Its Profits, 13 September 1970, *New York Times Magazine*.

11. Alex Edmans, What Stakeholder Capitalism Can Learn from Milton Friedman, *Oxford Business Law Blog*, 13 November 2020: www.law.ox.ac.uk/business-law-blog/blog/2020/11/what-stakeholder-capitalism-can-learn-milton-friedman
12. Edward Freeman and David Reed, Stockholders and Stakeholders: A New Perspective on Corporate Governance, Spring 1983, *California Management Review*, vol 25, 88–106.
13. Colin Mayer, *Prosperity: Better Business Makes the Greater Good*, 2018, Oxford University Press.
14. World Economic Forum, *Stakeholder Capitalism: A Manifesto for a Cohesive and Sustainable World*, 14 January 2020: www.weforum.org/press/2020/01/stakeholder-capitalism-a-manifesto-for-a-cohesive-and-sustainable-world/
15. Business Roundtable, *Statement on the Purpose of a Corporation*, 19 August 2019: www.businessroundtable.org/business-roundtable-redefines-the-purpose-of-a-corporation-to-promote-an-economy-that-serves-all-americans
16. Richard Henderson and Patrick Temple-West, Group of US Corporate Leaders Ditches Shareholder-First Mantra, 19 August 2019, *Financial Times*: www.ft.com/content/e21a9fac-c1f5-11e9-a8e9-296ca66511c9
17. Ibid.
18. Council of Institutional Investors, *Council of Institutional Investors Responds to Business Roundtable Statement on Corporate Purpose*, 19 August 2019: www.cii.org/content.asp?contentid=277
19. Lucian A. Bebchuk and Roberto Tallarita, The Illusory Promise of Stakeholder Governance, 26 February 2020, *Cornell Law Review*: https://cornelllawreview.org/wp-content/uploads/2021/02/The-Illusory-Promise-of-Stakeholder-Governance.pdf
20. ICGN, *Governance Priorities During the Covid-19 Pandemic*, 23 April 2020.
21. Joseph Bower and Lynn Paine, The Error at the Heart of Corporate Leadership, May–June 2017, *Harvard Business Review*: https://cornelllawreview.org/wp-content/uploads/2021/02/The-Illusory-Promise-of-Stakeholder-Governance.pdf
22. A mathematical analogy is in linear programming—solving systems of equations subject to constraints to find optimal solutions. In this context, the shareholder primacy advocate might call for shareholder returns as the objective function to be maximised (as the 'left-hand side of the equation'). But, in a governance system where stakeholders and market pressures exist as realities (to 'have regard for', as per UK Companies Act 2006, sec. 172), these factors can be regarded conceptually as binding 'constraint functions' that first must be satisfied before a feasible solution relating to shareholder returns can be realised. This effectively amounts to optimising shareholder returns subject to these stakeholder and market constraints rather than simply maximising shareholder returns without constraint. In other words, long-term shareholders must realise that, if a shareholder model is to prevail, then companies cannot cut corners regarding stakeholder obligations and economic efficiency.
23. Raghuram Rajan and Luigi ZIngales, The Great Reversals: The Politics of Financial Development in the Twentieth Century, 2003, *Journal of Financial Economics*, vol 69, 5–50.
24. Igor Filatochev and Mike Wright (eds.), *The Life Cycle of Corporate Governance*, 2005, Edward Elgar, Cheltenham, UK.
25. OECD Business Sector Advisory Group on Corporate Governance, Ira M. Millstein, Chairman, *Corporate Governance: Improving Competitiveness and Access to Capital in Global Markets*, 1998.
26. UK Financial Reporting Council, *The UK Corporate Governance Code*, July 2018: www.frc.org.uk/directors/corporate-governance-and-stewardship/uk-corporate-governance-code
27. The European Corporate Governance Institute maintains a comprehensive listing of global corporate governance codes: https://ecgi.global/content/codes
28. Regierungskommission Deutscher Corporate Governance Kodex, *German Corporate Governance Code*, 7 February 2017: https://ecgi.global/code/german-corporate-governance-code-amended-february-7-2017-decisions-plenary-meeting-february-7
29. There is different wordsmithing in some markets reflecting nuances of the 'comply or explain' concept. For example, the *King III* Code in South Africa uses the term 'apply or explain,' suggesting a more definitive requirement.
30. Organisation for Economic Co-operation and Development (OECD): www.oecd.org/corporate/the-future-of-corporate-governance-in-capital-markets-following-the-covid-19-crisis-efb2013c-en.html, pp. 21–22, 50–51.

31. Organisation for Economic Co-operation and Development (OECD), *Owners of the World's Listed Companies*, 2019: www.oecd.org/corporate/Owners-of-the-Worlds-Listed-Companies.pdf
32. Rafael La Porta, Florencio Lopez-de-Silanes, Andrei Shleifer and Robert Vishny, Law and Finance, December 1998, *Journal of Political Economy*, vol 106, 1115–55.
33. McKinsey & Company, *Investor Opinion Survey*, June 2000: www.oecd.org/daf/ca/corporategovernanceprinciples/1922101.pdf
34. Daniel Kaufman and Aart Kraay, *Worldwide Governance Indicators, World Bank Group*, 2017: https://info.worldbank.org/governance/wgi/
35. Recital 44, European Union's Corporate Sustainability Reporting Directive, Proposal for a Directive of the European Parliament and of the Council, 1 April, 2021: https://data.consilium.europa.eu/doc/document/ST-10835-2022-INIT/x/pdf
36. For a more detailed discussion of board diversity from an investor perspective, see ICGN, *Guidance on Diversity on* Boards, 2016: www.icgn.org/sites/default/files/2021-06/ICGN%20Guidance%20on%20Diversity%20on%20Boards%20-%20Final.pdf
37. For a more detailed discussion of remuneration from an investor perspective, see ICGN, *Guidance on Executive Director Remuneration*, 2016: www.icgn.org/sites/default/files/2021-06/ICGN%20Guidance%20on%20Executive%20Remuneration%20%282016%29.pdf
38. Semler Brossy, *Say on Pay & Proxy Results*, 29 July 2021.
39. ICGN Viewpoint, *Integrating ESG into Executive Compensation Plans*, November 2020: www.icgn.org/sites/default/files/2021-06/ICGN%20Viewpoint%20Integrating%20ESG%20in%20Executive%20Compensation.pdf
40. Alex Edmans, Why Companies Shouldn't Tie Pay to ESG Metrics, *Wall Street Journal*, 27 June 2021.
41. For a more detailed discussion of risk oversight from an investor perspective, see ICGN, *Guidance on Corporate Risk Oversight*, 2015: www.icgn.org/sites/default/files/2021-06/ICGN%20Corp%20Risk%20Oversightweb.pdf
42. In a 2021 ICGN membership poll, 90% of ICGN members disapproved of differential voting right structures, and 58% believed that differential voting structures would impact stock valuations negatively. Sixty-six per cent of ICGN respondents indicated that the major share indices should exclude companies with dual class shares, and 93% believed that, where dual class structures exist, there should be a 'sunset clause' to provide a time limitation for a dual class structure in a company.
43. For more detail, see ICGN Viewpoint, *Differential Rights*, April 2015: www.icgn.org/sites/default/files/2021-06/Stewardship%20does%20not%20benefit%20from%20differential%20ownership%20rights.pdf. We also encourage you to read ICGN's 2020 comment letter to the UK's Hill Review on UK Listings. This articulates the ICGN position on dual class shares, including reference to related academic research: www.icgn.org/sites/default/files/26.%20ICGN%20Letter%20to%20UK%20Hill%20-%20Call%20for%20Evidence%20–%20UK%20Listings%20Review.pdf
44. A 2021 defence of dual class shares led by academics at the University of Georgia presents a more sympathetic case: Ugur Lel, Jeffry M. Netter, Annette B. Poulsen and Zhongling Qin, *Dual Class Shares and Firm Valuation: Evidence from SEC Rule 19c-4* (June 1, 2020). European Corporate Governance Institute—Finance Working Paper No 807/2021. Available at SSRN: https://ssrn.com/abstract=3729297 or http://dx.doi.org/10.2139/ssrn.3729297

FURTHER READING

Wolf-Georg Ringe, *Investor-Led Sustainability in Corporate Governance* (November 1, 2021). European Corporate Governance Institute—Law Working Paper No 615/2021. Available at SSRN: https://papers.ssrn.com/sol3/papers.cfm?abstract_id=3958960

International Organization for Standardization (ISO), *ISO 37000: Governance of Organizations: Guidance*, 2021.

Guido Ferrarini, *Corporate Purpose and Sustainability* (December 7, 2020). European Corporate Governance Institute—Law Working Paper No 559/2020, An edited version of this paper will be published as a chapter in Danny Busch, Guido Ferrarini and Seraina Grünewald (eds.), *Sustainable Finance*, Palgrave MacMillan (forthcoming). Available at SSRN: https://ssrn.com/abstract=3753594

Alex Edmans, *Grow the Pie*, Cambridge University Press, 2020

Lucian A. Bebchuk and Roberto Tallarita, The Illusory Promise of Stakeholder Governance, 26 February 2020, *Cornell Law Review*, vol. 106, pp. 91–178. https://cornelllawreview.org/wp-content/uploads/2021/02/The-Illusory-Promise-of-Stakeholder-Governance.pdf

World Economic Forum, *Stakeholder Capitalism: A Manifesto for a Cohesive and Sustainable World*, 14 January 2020: www.weforum.org/press/2020/01/stakeholder-capitalism-a-manifesto-for-a-cohesive-and-sustainable-world/

OECD, *Corporate Governance Factbook*, 2019.

OECD, *Owners of the World's Listed Companies*, 2019.

Business Roundtable, *Statement on the Purpose of a Corporation*, 19 August 2019: www.businessroundtable.org/business-roundtable-redefines-the-purpose-of-a-corporation-to-promote-an-economy-that-serves-all-americans

Colin Mayer, *Prosperity: Better Business Makes the Greater Good*, Oxford University Press, 2018.

George Dallas, Shareholder Primacy: Is This Concept Fit for Purpose? *Ethical Boardroom Magazine*, Winter 2018: https://ethicalboardroom.com/shareholder-primacy-is-this-concept-fit-for-purpose/

The Purposeful Company Task Force, *The Purposeful Company Policy Report*, Big Innovation Centre, February 2017: https://thepurposefulcompany.org/wp-content/uploads/2021/01/feb-24_tpc_policy-report_final_printed-2.pdf

Lucien Bebchuk and Assaf Hamdani, Independent Directors and Controlling Shareholders, *University of Pennsylvania Law Review*, vol 165, no 6, 2017.

Renee B. Adams, *Boards, and the Directors Who Sit on Them; The Handbook of the Economics of Corporate Governance*, European Corporate Governance Institute (ECGI)—Finance Working Paper No 515/2017, pp 1–7, 16–55, 30 June 2017: https://papers.ssrn.com/sol3/papers.cfm?abstract_id=3002219

Joseph L. Bower and Lynn S. Paine, The Error at the Heart of Corporate Leadership, *Harvard Business Review*, May–June 2017: https://hbr.org/2017/05/the-error-at-the-heart-of-corporate-leadership

Thomas Clarke, *International Corporate Governance: A Comparative Approach.* London and New York: Routledge, 2017.

ICGN, *Global Governance Principles*, 2017: www.icgn.org/sites/default/files/2021-11/ICGN%20Global%20Governance%20Principles%202021.pdf

David Larcker and Brian Tayan, *Corporate Governance Matters, third edition*, Pearson Education, 2021.

Financial Reporting Council, *The UK Corporate Governance Code*, April 2016: www.frc.org.uk/getattachment/ca7e94c4-b9a9-49e2-a824-ad76a322873c/UK-CorporateGovernance-Code-April-2016.pdf

G20/OECD, *Principles of Corporate Governance, 2015.*

Lucian Bebchuk and Michael Weisbach, The State of Corporate Governance Research, *Review of Financial Studies*, vol 23, 939–961, 2010.

Rafael La Porta, Florencio Lopez-de-Silanes, Andrei Shleifer and Robert Vishny, Law and Finance, *Journal of Political Economy*, vol 106, 1115–55, December 1998.

Andrei Shleifer and Robert Vishny, A Survey of Corporate Governance, *Journal of Finance*, vol 52, 737–83, June 1997.

Sir Adrian Cadbury, *Report of the Committee on the Financial Aspects of Corporate Governance*, Gee, London, Section 3.2, 1 December 1992: www.frc.org.uk/getattachment/9c19ea6f-bcc7-434c-b481-f2e29c1c271a/The-Financial-Aspects-of-Corporate-Governance-(the-Cadbury-Code).pdf

Milton Friedman, The Social Responsibility of Business Is to Increase Its Profits, *New York Times Magazine*, 13 September 1970.

Adolf A. Berle, Jr. and Gardiner C. Means, *The Modern Corporation and Private Property*, 1932.

Chapter 3

The case for stewardship and sustainability: Ethics and economics

DOI: 10.4324/9781003307082-3

Companies, investors and other practitioners live in a world in which practical decisions are taken daily with regard to corporate governance and sustainability. For investors, these include basic investment decisions and company valuations, decisions on how to exercise voting rights and decisions on which companies to engage on which issues. All of this begs the question of what good corporate governance and sustainability mean in practical terms—and whether our prevailing beliefs, assumptions and codes of practice have valid underpinnings. It is useful for practitioners therefore to step back periodically from the daily grind to think about governance and sustainability in a broader and more rigorous context.

This is where case studies and academic research can play an important role in helping practitioners to better understand how corporate governance and sustainability fit into a broader market context, and which commonly accepted practices are—or are not—substantiated by evidence linking corporate governance or stewardship to specific performance outcomes.

The case for stewardship and sustainability is a matter of both ethics and economics. Investor stewardship focused on sustainability can enhance long-term thinking and use the voice of capital to protect investor beneficiaries in a way that will also promote better markets, economies and societies. While the exercise of investor rights and other stewardship activities should ultimately serve the economic interests of long-term investors and their beneficiaries, there is also an ethical dimension to investor involvement in addressing systemic issues that have a broad impact on society (which also includes these beneficiaries).

It is important to begin with reference to the ethical case, because ethical concerns were a principal driver of important early efforts to take account of sustainability factors in investing and they remain a component of the motivation for analysis of ESG factors for many investors to this day. However, given the fiduciary obligations of most institutional investors to prioritise investment returns, we will focus primarily on the business case relating to governance, stewardship and sustainability—and what the economic or business case is for ESG. We will examine why both companies and investors should take sustainability seriously and will review the current, and continuously evolving, evidence trail relating both to corporate governance and sustainability research more generally.

1. ETHICAL CONSIDERATIONS

Ethical considerations can enter into an institutional investor's decision-making through at least three channels: (1) beneficiaries may include requirements for consideration of certain ethical issues in their investment mandates; (2) asset owners and asset managers should apply high standards of ethical business conduct to their own activities; and (3) failure to consider ethical issues at the company, industry and even national (or systemic) level may have negative consequences for long-term investment performance.

For investors who have been given a clear mandate to incorporate particular ethical considerations in portfolio construction and stewardship, a business case may not be needed for sustainable investing. The ethical dimension alone can be sufficient to steer such investors towards the use of ESG metrics or to justify portfolio exclusions on ethical grounds that might impact (at least near-term) financial returns. For example, the exclusion of cluster munitions manufacturers is a standard provision in the investment mandates of major pension funds and other asset owners. Many asset owners also require their managers to exclude companies in sectors such as fossil fuels, tobacco or military equipment.

To the extent that ethical investment portfolios involve exclusions of this nature, there is the risk that they are less technically 'efficient' compared with investment portfolios not subject to such constraints. From a financial theory perspective, limiting the investible universe decreases the ability to diversify; ethical investment portfolios are therefore subject to potentially lower returns and greater tracking errors relative to major indices.[1] While some individual socially minded investors may be willing to accept this trade-off, without a specific mandate from beneficiaries, most asset managers, particularly those investing pension fund assets, are not in a position to make this compromise for ethical reasons alone. Imposing one's own ethical preferences in a way that is not contemplated in the investment mandate amounts to a breach of fiduciary duty.

Systemic risks: linking the ethical and the economic

There is also a systemic dimension to ethical considerations—and this provides a link to the economic case. The immediate impact of the Covid-19 crisis—as a systemic risk—demonstrated the need for all elements of society, including investors and the capital they represent, to join forces in urgent situations to support the common good. Investors have a large stake in promoting the ongoing health and integrity of economies, markets and the financial system. While their beneficiaries and society do not bestow on institutional investors responsibility to serve as ethical guardians for society, they do implicitly (and sometime explicitly through their investment agreements) expect them to be good corporate citizens and to contribute to ethical and sustainable solutions to many critical systemic issues—or at least not to exacerbate existing injustices or externalities.

This systemic perspective brings in wider considerations, including those articulated in the 17 United Nations *Sustainable Development Goals* (SDGs), which articulate a role for the private sector to join forces with the public sector to address key risks affecting society generally. Covid-19 is a clear example of a systemic risk that has both an ethical and an economic imperative. In addition to pandemics, climate change, human rights, income inequality and anti-corruption are among the most pressing ethical issues that have relevance for governance or stewardship. Recognising that failure to address issues such as those identified in the SDGs raises grave consequences for societies and economies, an increasing number of institutional investors, particularly those with long-term investment horizons, see addressing these ethical concerns as fully consonant with generating sustainable investment returns.[2]

Consideration of systemic factors has also led to critical thinking about the use of traditional financial theory as a philosophical foundation to best investment practice. In their book *Moving Beyond Modern Portfolio Theory* (MPT), the authors Jon Lukomnik and James Hawley argue that 75–94% of investor returns are driven by systemic risk factors (market risk or 'beta') rather than individual company performance ('alpha'). But, while MPT simply accepts these systemic risks as exogenous givens, the authors argue that investors may be most productive with their stewardship efforts using their voice to address these systemic factors directly. They label this 'beta activism,' which focuses more on the macro than the micro dimension of stewardship.[3] An example of beta activism is the European investor body the Institutional Investors Group on Climate Change (IIGCC), whose mission is to mobilise capital for the low-carbon transition and which is engaging with policymakers and standard setters to encourage company financial statements and disclosures to be aligned with the Paris Agreement of 2015.[4]

Not all investors share the conviction that contributing to long-term solutions to systemic challenges provides sufficient justification for considering them in investment decision-making and stewardship. Even if sympathetic to ethical concerns, they may not accept it as their professional role to contribute to broader social solutions beyond serving their clients' immediate interests. For these investors, sustainability and stewardship would benefit from a clearer evidence trail, particularly with regard to their impact on company performance and investor returns. Moreover, others may doubt the linkage between sustainability factors and financial or economic outcomes. This is where the business case for sustainability comes in; it starts with the premise that poor ESG performance produces bad outcomes, and good ESG performance produces good ones. As much as we might like to believe this premise is self-evident, it needs to be tested.

2. BUILDING THE ECONOMIC CASE

The evidence base for governance, stewardship and sustainability research is in many ways still nascent—particularly with regard to research on sustainability (E and S) factors. As the evidence trail continues to develop further, it can give both academics and practitioners guidance on what works and does not work in terms of best practice. This can also provide practical guidance to support the resourcing of stewardship within investment institutions—as well as guide specific applications in investment analysis and decision-making, engagement and voting.

We have anecdotal evidence and case studies that suggest links to performance, but the relatively short history of stewardship means that there is relatively limited data for cross-sectional statistical analysis to shed light on exactly which stewardship approaches are the most effective or exactly which ESG factors may (or may not) have causal impacts on company financial performance and value creation. Empirical evidence is important to distinguish fact from dogma, and scholars can be quick to challenge the legitimacy of normative governance and sustainability standards if rigorous evidence is lacking. A sounder foundation of evidence can help to inform investors in terms of how they may wish to value stewardship resources internally and also guide how effective stewardship is implemented in practice.

Anecdotal evidence

Anecdotal evidence, typically in the form of case studies, can provide examples of how ESG factors can influence company results. Some economic historians go back to the Dutch East India Company in the early 17th century to cite cases illustrating how poor governance and ethical performance can affect a company and its investors.[5] Business history contains many examples of unethical or irresponsible behaviour, including more recently in the 20th and 21st centuries. The enormity of the collapse of the US energy giant Enron in the early 2000s was in many ways a modern turning point, providing a hugely visible and tawdry example of corruption and governance gone wrong. A trail of infamy has continued since Enron to the present day, with scandals in markets around the world that can be linked with poor governance and ESG. Cases abound in a range of jurisdictions. A non-exhaustive list of prominent examples in the 21st century include the following.

EUROPE

- *Germany*: A fraud perpetuated by the former blue-chip Wirecard surfaced in 2020, and the company is now in administration.
- *Germany*: Volkswagen's 'DieselGate' scandal of 2014 involved fraudulent emissions testing devices. We explore this case study in greater detail at the end of the book.
- *UK*: BP's Gulf of Mexico Deepwater Horizon explosion and oil spill in 2010.
- *UK*: A charismatic, and feared, CEO led the Royal Bank of Scotland to its demise though an overly aggressive expansion strategy with weak board oversight that blew up as the 2008 financial crisis began to kick in—effectively bankrupting RBS and requiring the bank to be bailed out by the UK government.
- *France*: A rogue trader at the bank Société Générale was convicted and imprisoned in 2008 for breach of trust, forgery and unauthorised use of the bank's computers, resulting in trading losses valued at €4.9 billion.
- *Italy*: In the food company Parmalat, a massive accounting fraud occurred in a family-controlled pyramid structure that bankrupted the company and negatively impacted creditors in 2003.[6]

AMERICAS

- *Brazil*: Vale's collapse of a tailings dam killing 270 people in 2019.
- *US*: Personal data were harvested from millions of Facebook profiles without consent and were manipulated by the firm Cambridge Analytica for political advertising and to influence the 2016 US presidential election.
- *Brazil*: The 'Lava Jato' (Operation Car Wash) investigation into corruption at the state-owned oil company Petrobras led to the construction firm Odebrecht and its executive management being convicted of bribery and corruption in 2015.
- *US*: Fraud-based collapse of Enron in 2001, one of the most highly valued companies in the US at the turn of the century.

ASIA-PACIFIC

- *Australia*: The mining company Rio Tinto ignored indigenous peoples' concerns about a 46,000-year-old sacred Aboriginal site and destroyed ancient rock shelters to expand an iron ore mine. In 2020, this resulted in a huge public backlash and forced the departure of the company's CEO, Jean-Sébastien Jacques.

- *Bangladesh*: Rana Plaza garment factory (part of the supply chain of several large Western clothing manufacturers) collapsed in 2013, killing 1134 and injuring 2500.
- *Australia*: James Hardie underfunded the foundation established to provide financial benefits to asbestos victims, and the High Court of Australia ruled that the company misled the Australian Securities Exchange as to the solvency of the asbestos victims' compensation fund (2012).
- *Japan*: Olympus's financial fraud surfaced in 2011 and had been perpetuated over decades and under numerous CEOs.
- *China*: Foxconn suicides in 2010–12 resulted from sweatshop conditions; the company manufactured technology products for Western clients, including Apple.
- *India*: The 2009 Satyam accounting scandal led to the demise of this once-prominent software firm.
- *South Korea*: The chairman and CEO of Hyundai Motor Company, Chung Mong-koo, was convicted of embezzlement and corruption and sentenced to 3 years in prison (subsequently suspended because he was 'too important for Korea's economy').

These negative examples certainly establish a base of anecdotal evidence relating to bad ESG performance resulting in bad outcomes. But are there cases of how good ESG can result in positive outcomes? This is less easy to observe, but positive examples exist here as well:

- *Pfizer*: One of the first US corporates to embrace good governance practices— and found in 2000 it helped bank investor goodwill in a key US$90-billion takeover of Warner-Lambert, saving money and months of litigation.
- *Marks & Spencer*: Its board installed risk functions, including supply chain rules against multistory buildings, that helped it dodge 2013 reputation damage from the Rana Plaza collapse.
- *Unilever*: Goodwill banked through board and CEO commitment to excellence in ESG indices helped fend off a 2017 US$143 billion takeover effort by Kraft.
- *Facebook v Starbucks*: Facebook has ten votes/share for insiders, an all-US board and poor crisis response, with its stock price falling 20% after the Cambridge Analytica scandal. Starbucks, with one vote per share and quick crisis response after a racial incident, saw its stock price fall only 5%.
- *Pirelli*: The Italian tyre manufacturer, with operations in 13 countries and a global sales presence, merged its enterprise risk management and sustainability units into the same department and developed an IT platform to integrate environmental and social data across its own operations and suppliers. Together, these initiatives allow for greater internal and external transparency of the company's impact on stakeholders.
- *Novo Nordisk*: The Danish healthcare and pharma company's charter commits 'to conduct its activities in a financially, environmentally and socially responsible way.' It established a team of finance and ESG specialists in the company who work across all operational units to develop oversight and control mechanisms for all material sustainability factors.[7]

Anecdotal evidence and its limitations

Anecdotal case studies, while a legitimate form of evidence, have limited predictive power. Indeed, the anecdote is regarded by some as an 'enemy of science.' So caution is merited. In extremis, cherry-picked anecdotal examples may lend themselves to misinterpretation or the generation of 'rationalised myths.'[8] Although anecdotal evidence may credibly suggest that very poor corporate governance or poor ESG performance destroys value, for many observers, a scientifically generalisable statement is not entirely warranted without rigorous empirical research involving econometric modelling and probabilistic point estimations.

In this context, academics and practitioners often look at similar issues, but it can seem at times like a parallel universe where each group is framing problems differently, with differing levels of supporting data and standards of proof—and often drawing different conclusions as well. For some practitioners, academic research can sometimes come across as arcane or possibly difficult to follow, and links to practical applications can be unclear. Nevertheless, serious practitioners should seek to maintain a degree of literacy through reading and interpreting the results of more rigorous empirical studies of both corporate governance and sustainability.

3. THE EMPIRICAL CASE FOR CORPORATE GOVERNANCE

Academics grounded in empirical quantitative perspectives can be quick to observe that corporate governance is a subject about which there may be more opinions than facts. This reflects either mixed or inconclusive evidence relating to the benefits or disadvantages of individual governance practices—for example, the combined CEO/chair role. Academics sometimes refer to practitioner acceptance of established governance codes and standards as little more than a leap of faith over reason. At the same time, practitioners need some grounding on which to deal with the world as it is, even if based on imperfect or incomplete information.

Academic research relating to corporate governance has focused primarily on traditional indicators such as ownership, board effectiveness, shareholder rights and remuneration. Compared with research on environmental and social factors, there is a longer track record of research in corporate governance itself—much of it focused on the US where a large amount of data is both standardised and readily accessible.

The nature of good corporate governance itself is multifaceted and to some extent conceptual. Governance is not directly measurable per se, which presents significant epistemological challenges for empirical researchers in corporate governance. Breaking governance down into structural features or indicators (number of independent directors, CEO/chair split, shareholder rights, etc) can allow for quantification, but the lack of conclusive evidence suggests that what is measurable about governance is not always worth measuring.

Just as behavioural finance[9] introduces a human dimension into what can otherwise be a very technical subject matter, the human dimension is also relevant in corporate governance in ways that are often not suited for direct measurement. This might include so-called 'soft' features, such as company culture or the actual independence (versus nominal independence) of the non-executive directors.

We do not propose to present here an exhaustive review of the corporate governance literature, but would like to highlight two academic studies that build from this literature. In her paper *Boards, and the Directors Who Sit on Them*, Oxford economist Renee Adams conducts a literature review on corporate boards and concludes that 'while conceptually appealing, the evidence that conventional measures of board independence matter is inconclusive.' It is less about board structure than 'the people who sit on them' in the first place.[10]

In their book *Corporate Governance Matters*, Stanford academics David Larcker and Brian Tayan also conduct a literature study of empirical research relating to boards, assessing what the weight of empirical evidence is suggesting about the relevance and materiality of individual governance factors.[11] For example, they cite no evidence suggesting that an independent chair produces better results, and there is moderate or mixed evidence on many governance features that are generally seen by investors as a good idea—such as having a lead independent director, outside directors, independent committees and board diversity. But there are also a few clear correlations, including that busy boards (where directors sit on several other boards) are less effective, having an accountant is good for the board—and maybe having a banker is bad!

In general, the evidence suggests positive correlations for aspects of corporate governance and value creation. But there remain many open questions. Establishing causality about which aspects of corporate governance create value is a more rigorous technical challenge. And, while we have anecdotal evidence from major scandals about how bad corporate governance can destroy value, it remains less clear how, or if, good corporate governance creates value.

Ultimately, there is no 'silver bullet' or one-size-fits-all approach to governance, as many aspects of good corporate governance will be endogenous or specific to the circumstances of the individual company. In many ways, governance codes may guide us logically and intuitively in terms of best practice, but they have their limitations; adherence alone by companies to particular code recommendations will not automatically produce desired results.

4. THE EMPIRICAL CASE FOR SUSTAINABILITY

Statistically based empirical research on the impact of ESG factors, particularly the 'E' and the 'S', has been handicapped in the past by lack of data and disclosure—and standards of disclosure more generally. And, these days, there is perhaps too much data, or at least too much that are not standardised and comparable. We will explore this topic in Chapter 4. This has affected data availability, reliability and consistency, all of which are required for research to be rigorously linked to statistical and probabilistic outcomes. Also, the qualitative nature of sustainability means that, like corporate governance, it is in many ways conceptual in nature and, as such, difficult to model. Epistemological challenges can emerge when measurable data points are used as proxies for these complex concepts. Among other things, the measurement of 'performance' as an independent variable is not consistently defined. Sometimes it can relate to financial performance; in other applications it can relate to engagement success or an improvement in terms of third-party ESG metrics.

We must remember that, while we often casually bandy about the term 'ESG', ESG itself is a somewhat abstract acronym, not a cohesive 'thing' or something that is directly measurable. Attaching these three elements together artificially can be a bit of a forced marriage—or possibly like creating an unstable molecule, where the individual E, S and G 'atomic bonds' may be subject to sudden changes. As a result, much of the research that seeks to bring these factors together is contextual in nature, and there are scholars who still question the rigorous link between ESG performance and company financial performance or valuation.

As with corporate governance, econometric modelling relating to sustainability also commonly has an endogeneity problem—when statistically significant correlations may be established without demonstrating causation. For example, even if we know that better-performing companies may also have better corporate governance and sustainability practices, it may be impossible to demonstrate conclusively that improving ESG performance therefore creates value. Causality could run the other way (value-creating companies improve their governance), or other factors cause firms both to implement better governance and generate more value.

A serious body of scholarship relating to stewardship and sustainability, produced globally by leading financial and legal academics, is growing.[12] ESG factors and the role of investors are increasingly being researched in the academic community, including prominent academic bodies such as the European Corporate Governance Institute.[13] It is still relatively early days, but the weight of evidence is building relating to the impact of governance and sustainability.

Two key meta-studies relating to sustainability in the mid-2010s provided an encouraging foundation to stimulate further research:

- Clark, Feiner and Viehs, *From the Stockholder to the Stakeholder: How Sustainability Can Drive Financial Outperformance* (2015), Oxford University:[14] a meta-study of 200 of the highest-quality academic studies and sources on sustainability to assess the economic evidence relating to the impact of ESG factors. Their findings suggest:
  - companies with strong sustainability scores show better operational performance and are less risky;
  - investment strategies that incorporate ESG issues outperform comparable non-ESG strategies; and
  - active ownership creates value for companies and investors.
- Nyenrode University/Deloitte, *Good Governance Driving Corporate Performance?* (2016) meta-study: 'Dozens of empirical studies concluded a positive correlation between governance variables and corporate performance, measured in both financial metrics as well as non-financial metrics.'[15]

A more recent meta-study was published in early 2021 by researchers at the New York University Stern School of Business and Rockefeller Asset Management. It focused on over 1000 research papers from the period 2015–20 and reported a positive relationship between ESG and financial performance for 58% of the studies, 13% showing a neutral impact, 21% mixed results and only 8% showing a negative relationship. The study drew six overarching conclusions:[16]

- Improved financial performance due to ESG becomes more marked over longer time horizons.
- ESG as a broad investment strategy seems to perform better than negative screening approaches.
- ESG investing appears to provide downside protection, especially during a social or economic crisis.
- Sustainability initiatives in corporations drive better financial performance owing to mediating factors such as improved risk management and more innovation.
- Managing for a low-carbon future improves financial performance.
- ESG disclosure on its own does not drive financial performance.

Stewardship itself is still a young discipline subject to academic research, and meta-studies may be premature at this point for a full weighing of the evidence. But scholarship has emerged in recent years, particularly focusing on the impact of engagement on the practice of stewardship. The pool of research on sustainability continues to expand, but initial evidence is encouraging. As examples, we present short synopses of some representative academic papers that have been published in recent years relating to stewardship and engagement:

- *Engagement on ESG Matters Improves Governance and Performance, and Encourages a Longer-Term Perspective* (Dimson, Karakas and Li, 2021).
- *ESG Engagement Can Benefit Shareholders by Reducing Firms' Downside Risk* (Hoepner et al, 2020).
- *Engagement Had a Significant Influence on Trading Decisions by the Asset Manager and Contributed to an Informational Advantage, which in Turn Contributed to Alpha* (Becht, Franks and Wagner, 2019).
- *Engagement on ESG Matters Linked to Higher Financial Returns and Better ESG Ratings* (Barko, Cremers and Renneboog, 2018).
- *Engagement Can Inhibit Entrenchment and Pursuit of Value Destroying M&A Activity* (Schmidt and Fahlenbrach, 2017).[17]

Further research into the impact of corporate governance and sustainability is needed, both to reinforce—and to challenge—the business case. The stronger the business case, the greater the focus by both companies and investors. Investors should monitor academic research and consider how research on corporate governance and sustainability informs what they do, including their decisions, practices and outcomes. However, they should make use of academic research with care and not simplistically 'cherry-pick' research results that confirm their own individual biases. Similarly, practitioners can also help to shape and interpret academic research in a practical context and can inform the academic community in terms of considering areas and needs for governance research.

NOTES

1. In modern portfolio theory, 'unsystematic risk' (or diversifiable risk) is a technical term of art that refers to disproportionate exposure to the unique risks of investing in an individual company or set of companies. This risk is reduced or minimised through portfolio diversification. But, if the potential scope of diversification is limited by ethical preferences, this creates the potential for portfolio underperformance relative to portfolios without these constraints.
2. Steve Lydenburg, *Systems-level Considerations and the Long-Term Investor*, 2017, The Investment Integration Project: www.tiiproject.com/wp-content/uploads/2017/09/Systems-Level_Considerations_and_the_Long-Term_Investor.pdf
3. Jon Lukomnik and James P. Hawley, *Moving Beyond Modern Portfolio Theory: Investing That Matters*, 2021.
4. Institutional Investors Group on Climate Change, *Investor Expectations for Paris-Aligned Accounts*, November 2020: www.iigcc.org/download/investor-expectations-for-paris-aligned-accounts/?wpdmdl=4001&masterkey=5fabc4d15595d
5. See Paul Frentrop, *A History of Corporate Governance*, 2003, Deminor; Paul Frentrop, Joost Jonker and Stephen Davis, *Shareholder Rights at 400 : Commemorating Isaac Le Maire and the First Recorded Expression of Investor Advocacy*, 2009, APG.
6. Standard & Poor's assigned an investment grade credit rating to Parmalat until a week before its collapse in 2003. This inspired an S&P managing director to display a Parmalat milk carton on his desk as a constant reminder to junior (and senior) analysts to remain diligent.
7. Sources: Pfizer et al. from Stephen Davis, Harvard Law School; Pirelli and Novo Nordisk examples from R.H. Herz, B.J. Monterio and J.C. Thomson, *Leveraging the COSO Internal Control—Integrated Framework to Improve Confidence in Sustainability Performance Data*, 2017.
8. In a corporate governance context, a 'rationalised myth' can be defined as popular acceptance of a governance practice (or practices), regardless of whether there is evidence of its actual validity.
9. Behavioural finance takes into consideration how human psychology can affect the behaviour of investors and other economic actors. It can challenge traditional views of the 'rational economic man.'
10. Renée B. Adams, Boards, and the Directors Who Sit on Them, 30 June 2017, in *The Handbook of the Economics of Corporate Governance*, 2017, European Corporate Governance Institute (ECGI)—Finance Working Paper No 515/2017: https://bit.ly/39QXvLK
11. David Larcker and Brian Tayan, *Corporate Governance Matters, third edition*, 2021, Pearson Education, pp 140–1.
12. The website of the Principles for Responsible Investment includes a page with an Academic ESG Review tool. It is a repository of a wide range of research papers relating to ESG themes and includes a search function and hotlinks to the papers themselves: www.unpri.org/academic-research/academic-esg-review/5024.article
13. European Corporate Governance Institute is an international forum led by academics, focusing on research and debate on corporate governance topics: https://ecgi.global
14. Gordon Clark, Andrea Feiner and Michael Viehs, *From the Stockholder to the Stakeholder: How Sustainability Can Drive Financial Outperformance*, 5 March 2015.
15. Deloitte and Nyenrode Business University, *Good Governance Driving Corporate Performance? A Meta-analysis of Academic Research & Invitation to Engage in the Dialogue*, December 2016: www2.deloitte.com/content/dam/Deloitte/nl/Documents/risk/deloitte-nl-risk-good-governance-driving-corporate-performance.pdf
16. Tensie Whelan, Ulrich Atz and Casey Clark, CFA, *ESG and Financial Performance: Uncovering the Relationship by Aggregating Evidence from 1,000 Plus Studies Published between 2015–2020*, NYU Stern Center for Sustainable Business, February 2021: www.stern.nyu.edu/sites/default/files/assets/documents/NYU-RAM_ESG- Paper_2021.pdf
17. C. Schmidt and R. Fahlenbrach. 2017. Do Exogenous Changes in Passive Institutional Ownership Affect Corporate Governance and Firm Value? *Journal of Financial Economics*, vol 124, no 2, pp. 285–306.

FURTHER READING

Jon Lukomnik and James P. Hawley, *Moving Beyond Modern Portfolio Theory: Investing That Matters,* 2021.

Tensie Whelan, Ulrich Atz and Casey Clark, CFA, *ESG and Financial Performance: Uncovering the Relationship by Aggregating Evidence from 1,000 Plus Studies Published between 2015–2020*, NYU Stern Center for Sustainable Business, February 2021: www.stern.nyu.edu/sites/default/files/assets/documents/NYU-RAM_ESG-Paper_2021.pdf

Elroy Dimson, Oğuzhan Karakaş and Xi Li, *Co-ordinated Engagements*, European Corporate Governance Institute (ECGI)—Finance Working Paper No 721/2021, January 2021: https://papers.ssrn.com/sol3/papers.cfm?abstract_id=3209072

David Larcker and Brian Tayan, Corporate Governance Matters, *third edition*, Pearson Education, 2021.

Andreas G.F. Hoepner, Ioannis Oikonomou, Zacharias Sautner, Laura Starks and Xiao Y. Zhou, *ESG Shareholder Engagement and Downside Risk*, 16 April 2020: https://ecgi.global/sites/default/files/working_papers/documents/hoepneroikonomousautnerstarkszhoufinal.pdf

Marco Becht, Julian R. Franks and Hannes F. Wagner, *Corporate Governance through Voice and Exit* (1 October 2019), European Corporate Governance Institute, Finance Working Paper No 633/2019. Available at SSRN: https://papers.ssrn.com/sol3/papers.cfm?abstract_id=3456626

Tamas Barko, Martijn Cremers and Luc Renneboog, *Shareholder Engagement on Environmental, Social, and Governance Performance*, European Corporate Governance Institute (ECGI) Finance Working Paper No 509/2017, August 2017: https://ecgi.global/sites/default/files/working_papers/documents/5092017_1.pdf

Deloitte and Nyenrode Business University, *Good Governance Driving Corporate Performance? A Meta-analysis of Academic Research & Invitation to Engage in the Dialogue*, December 2016: www2.deloitte.com/content/dam/Deloitte/nl/Documents/risk/deloitte-nl-risk-good-governance-driving-corporate-performance.pdf

Mozaffar Khan, George Serafeim and Aaron Yoon, Corporate Sustainability: First Evidence on Materiality, *The Accounting Review*, November 2016.

Gordon Clark, Andrea Feiner and Michael Viehs, *From the Stockholder to the Stakeholder: How Sustainability Can Drive Financial Outperformance*, 5 March 2015.

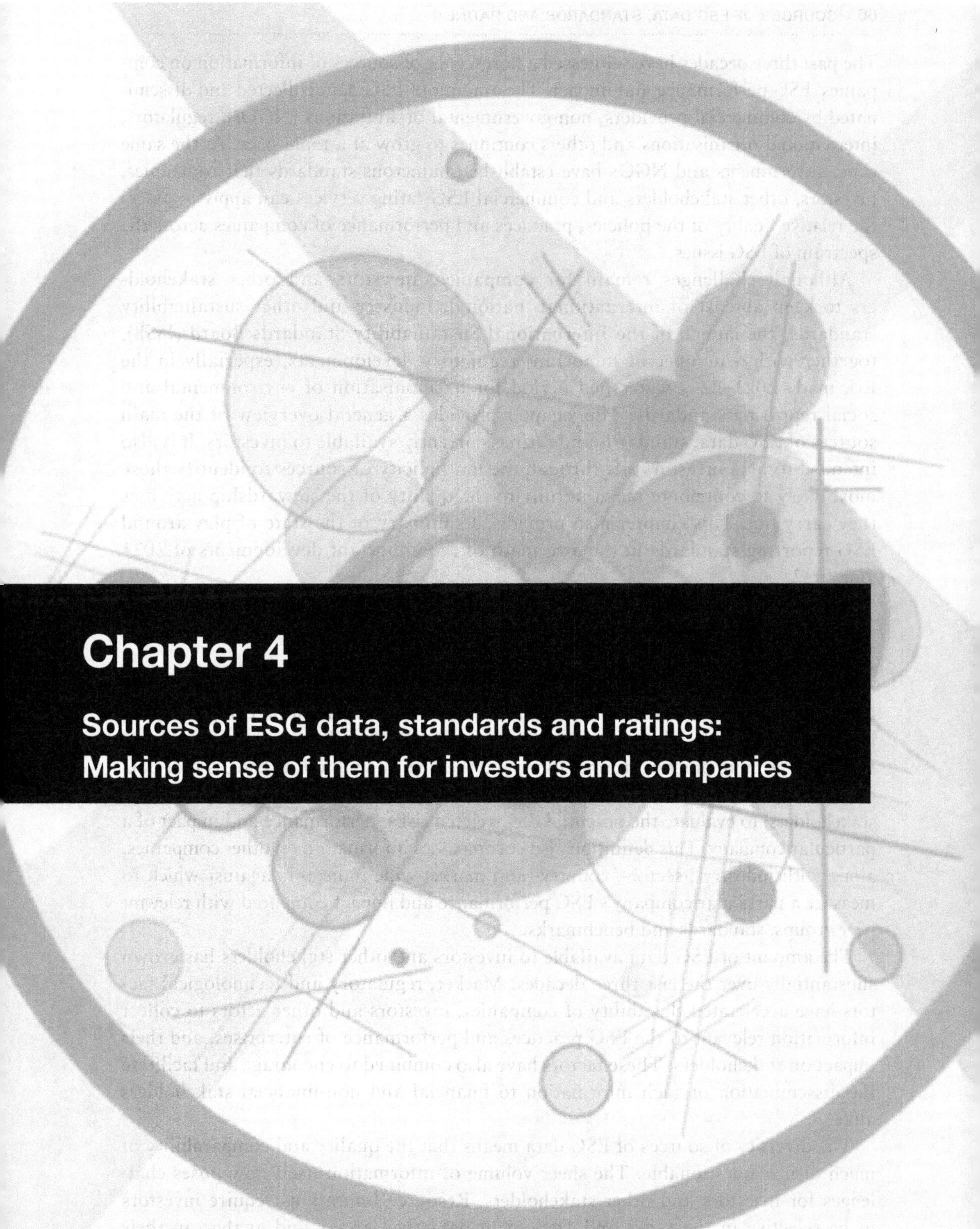

Chapter 4

Sources of ESG data, standards and ratings: Making sense of them for investors and companies

DOI: 10.4324/9781003307082-4

The past three decades have witnessed a florescence of sources of information on companies' ESG performance and impact. The amount of ESG data collected and disseminated by commercial providers, non-governmental organisations (NGOs), regulators, international organisations and others continues to grow at a rapid pace. At the same time, governments and NGOs have established numerous standards that companies, investors, other stakeholders and commercial ESG rating services can apply to assess the relative quality of the policies, practices and performance of companies across the spectrum of ESG issues.

Although challenges remain for companies, investors and other stakeholders to keep abreast of international, national, industry and other sustainability standards, the launch of the International Sustainability Standards Board (ISSB), together with a number of important regulatory developments, especially in the EU, made 2021–22 a watershed period for harmonisation of environmental and social reporting standards. This chapter provides a general overview of the main sources of ESG data, standards and ratings currently available to investors. It is also intended to help investors sift through the multiplicity of sources to identify those most likely to contribute meaningfully to the quality of the stewardship activities they carry out. This chapter also provides a summary of the state of play around ESG reporting standards in the aftermath of the important developments of 2021 and 2022.

1. WHAT ARE ESG DATA?

If one adopts a broad definition of ESG, much of the information on companies that is not narrowly financial or operational in nature probably falls within the category of ESG data. A more practical formulation, and the one we will follow here, is that ESG data include any information that can potentially assist investors (along with other stakeholders) to evaluate the potential ESG-related risks, performance and impact of a particular company. This definition also encompasses information on other companies, along with industry-, sector-, country- and market-wide indicators against which to measure a particular company's ESG performance and impact compared with relevant peer groups, standards and benchmarks.

The amount of ESG data available to investors and other stakeholders has grown substantially over the last three decades. Market, regulatory and technological factors have accelerated the ability of companies, investors and other actors to collect information relevant to the ESG practices and performance of enterprises, and their impact on stakeholders. These factors have also combined to encourage and facilitate the dissemination of such information to financial and non-financial stakeholders alike.

The diversity of sources of ESG data means that the quality and comparability of much of it is questionable. The sheer volume of information itself now poses challenges for investors and other stakeholders. Resource limitations require investors to be selective in the types and amount of data they access and analyse in their decision-making processes. Reliance on inaccurate or immaterial data translates into wasted resources, faulty assessment of ESG risk, and incorrect company valuations or risk assessments. But, at the same time, the tsunami of ESG information that arrives in the market each day also presents clever investors with opportunities. Those who can narrow down the types and sources of quality ESG data most relevant to the sustainable performance of the sorts of companies they invest in, and focus their analysis on such data, have an undeniable edge over those who remain adrift in an ocean of undifferentiated and unprioritised information on ESG factors that may be of only theoretical or marginal relevance.

2. SOURCES OF ESG DATA

Information on the ESG risks, performance and impact of a company may originate from the company itself (usually released through reporting to securities holders, stakeholders, government or others) or from external sources. However originated, investors access ESG data through channels provided by various commercial and non-commercial sources. To gauge its reliability, investors and other users of ESG data must develop an understanding of how the ESG information they consume gets from its originator to them. Limitations and biases in the content and presentation of the information the investor or other stakeholder ultimately receives are inevitably introduced by how the data are generated, defined, collected, marketed and disseminated and by whom. 'Consider the source' is the wise ESG data user's mantra.

As long ago as 2016, the Global Initiative for Sustainability Ratings identified no less than 125 providers of ESG data. There were probably significantly more then, and there certainly are many more today.[1] ESG data are available to investors and other stakeholders through various channels, including:

- Listed companies' prospectuses, periodic and material event reports, and other public securities filings
- Company filings with other government agencies, such as environmental and labour regulators
- Company press releases, interviews and other contact with media
- Investor relations and public relations communications
- Government agencies' own publications and communications
- Stock exchanges
- General and specialised news media
- ESG data service providers and ratings providers (eg MSCI, Bloomberg, FTSE, RepRisk, S&P's Trucost, Moody's Vigeo Eiris Diligent, Morningstar's Sustainalytics, Glass Lewis)[2]
- NGOs that collect and disseminate data relevant to the issues for which they advocate

- Academics and think tanks
- Advisory and consulting firms (including executive search firms)
- Investor associations
- Industry associations
- Securities analysts.

Investors and their agents may also collect proprietary ESG data themselves as part of their research and due diligence, including through interviews, surveys and questionnaires. Private equity investors and firms that focus on emerging markets and/or lesser-known companies, in particular, may rely to an extent on investigative research firms, some of whom specialise in ferreting out information on companies' ESG track records.

Key distinctions between corporate governance and environmental and social data and analysis

The sets of environmental and social issues that companies face are determined to a large extent by their sector and industry. As discussed later in this chapter, most ESG reporting frameworks and disclosure standards are, in practice, organised along sectoral lines. The activities a company engages in naturally drive its potential impacts, for good and for ill, on society and the environment.

In contrast, the nature of the corporate governance challenges presented to investors is driven more by ownership and control patterns (especially the degree of concentrated versus dispersed control), the structures of the capital markets they operate in, and local corporate laws and regulations.[3] The major exception to this general rule is the financial industry. Responding to the risk-management-centric nature of the business and the systemic implications of failure, most financial institutions are subject to more exacting and industry-specific corporate governance rules.

Chapter 2's discussion of corporate governance principles emphasised the importance of considering ownership structure to understand the differences in corporate governance challenges across markets. Many, if not most, markets are characterised by distinctive ownership patterns or sets of ownership patterns, including variations in the degree of concentrated versus dispersed control.[4] Legal frameworks, market practices and investor expectations have also typically co-evolved with such ownership patterns. In recognition of these factors, most governance codes are designed with application to specific national markets. Thoughtful corporate governance analysis takes into account considerable country-specific governance data and analysis.

Data on the corporate governance of companies, whether collected by data service providers, proxy advisors, corporate governance advocacy groups, academics or others, are typically organised along the broad outlines found in individual corporate governance codes or international frameworks such as the ICGN *Global Governance Principles* (GGP) or the G20/OECD *Principles of Corporate Governance*. A key focus is on board effectiveness, including its structure, composition and responsibilities. As discussed in Chapter 2, other governance factors include the rights and equitable treatment of shareholders, the control environment, transparency and disclosure, and relations with stakeholders.

Technology and ESG

Technological progress is a key driver of the massive increase in available data on the environmental and social practices and impact of companies. Today's communications, information dissemination, and data gathering and analysis technologies provide management, boards, investors and other stakeholders with windows into the impact of company activities, and the risks inherent in them, that simply did not exist just a few decades back.

It is no exaggeration to state that, well into the late 20th century, many very large enterprises faced limits to how far back into their supply chains they could track even essential inputs. Mid-century manufacturers bought much of their raw materials and finished inputs through commodity dealers and subcontractors, with few questions asked. Tyre producers were not expected to, nor as a practical matter could they, track the rubber used in their products back to the individual plantations in South America and South East Asia where the rubber trees were tapped. It was even less realistic to expect them to be able to assess with precision the labour conditions or environmental impact of the plantations' production methods, or for investors, governments or others to know enough about the supply chain to pressure them to do so.[5]

Today's communications and information flows make supply chains and the impacts of a company's activities on others (externalities) increasingly more traceable, allowing companies to understand at an increasingly granular level the impact of, and the risks inherent in, any production process. Access to this tracing technology and much of the information that it gathers is not restricted to corporates. Increasingly, investors, governments, consumers and others can employ it to independently estimate the totality of impacts and risks that a company's activities present to its own operations and externalities.[6] In recent years, innovative companies have popped up to develop and apply new technologies to trace the environment and social impacts of activities up and down supply chains. Their objective is to make it easier for supply chain participants (particularly global players at the apex of supply chains) and investors to understand such impacts, act on them and provide transparency to stakeholders (including regulators).

For example, today, North American and European consumers of Icelandic salmon, cod and haddock can track 'the complete journey of every fish, from sea to pan' through Niceland Seafood's website.[7] On a broader scale, Know the Chain, an international NGO, helps companies and investors track and address forced labour risks in global supply chains.[8] The sorts of technologies behind these and a multitude of similar tools mean that investors and other stakeholders, individually and collectively, can undertake their own efforts to identify and evaluate environmental and social risks on company-specific and cross-portfolio levels.

Technology also has the potential to become an important driver in the evolution of how data are analysed. Emerging technologies, including in the field of 'big data' and artificial intelligence (AI), may come to play an important role in how investors and other stakeholders make practical use of the ever-increasing stocks and flows of information on companies' ESG policies, practices and outcomes.[9] Big data involves sets of information, often from myriad sources, that are too large and complex for the application of standard analytical methods. AI and machine learning techniques can provide means for extracting actionable information for investors and other stakeholders from these masses of data originating from different sources.

Most of this chapter focuses on 'structured' ESG data—information provided in a reasonably consistent and searchable format on behalf of companies, either voluntarily or in compliance with legal or regulatory requirements. But, like most of the world's electronic data, an enormous and increasing portion of information relevant to the ESG policies, practices and performance of companies is 'unstructured'—originating from innumerable public and private sources, in all sorts of formats, with many different audiences and purposes in mind and very difficult to search through.[10]

Data collection and analytics firms are currently working with big data and AI technologists to access the increasing mass of potentially ESG-relevant information out there, sift out the 'garbage data' and develop algorithms that can extract useful information. Description of the various strategies currently being experimented with is beyond the scope of this book. And it is not our intention here to make judgements about which approaches are likely to prove most fruitful and for what purposes. But investors who are serious about integrating considerations of ESG factors in decision-making clearly should follow developments in the application of big data and AI technologies to ESG data with an eye towards how they can contribute to their investment processes as more evidence about their potential utility emerges.

3. ESG CORPORATE REPORTING: MANDATES, FRAMEWORKS, STANDARDS AND GUIDELINES[11]

Although the authors are optimistic about the prospects for the newly established ISSB, discussed below, as of this writing no single, universally accepted standard for companies to apply to collect, prioritise and present ESG-related information to investors and other stakeholders is currently in place. Indeed, the ISSB itself has stated that '[c]ompanies should continue using the [existing] voluntary frameworks and guidance as appropriate.'[12] For the moment, what is available is a rather large set of different supporting tools intended for ESG-related disclosure, developed over the past two decades for a variety of purposes. Although these tools may indeed be invaluable for certain applications, their multitude and diversity have until now generated a certain degree of confusion among companies and investors. Reconciling different approaches and key performance indicators with respect to ESG disclosure has therefore emerged as one of the key challenges in the ESG space, together with the additional complexities that are associated with assurance and audit of the content.

MANDATES, STANDARDS, FRAMEWORKS AND GUIDANCE

Mandates: legal and regulatory requirements that oblige a company to report general or specific ESG information. Mandates may be imposed for the purpose of increasing transparency around ESG issues, or may have been designed with other objectives in mind but have the side effect of providing investors and other stakeholders with information about a company's ESG risks, performance and impact.

Principal characteristics of most-cited standards and frameworks

	IIRC (VRF)	FASB (US GAAP)	SASB (VRF)	TCFD	CDSB
Type of guidance	Framework	Financial Accounting Standards	Standards	Framework	Framework
Coverage	Global	US	US; Global Aspirations	Global	Global
Topics	Value creation; use of capital in all forms (financial, human, natural)	Financial accounts	Environmental, social and human capital, business model and innovation, leadership & governance	Climate-related risks and opportunities, financial impacts and scenario analysis	Environmental information and natural capital
Target audience	Providers of financial capital	Investors	Investors	Investors	Investors

	GRI	IFC	IASB (IFRS Fndn)	ISSB (IFRS Fndn)
Type of guidance	Framework	Framework	Financial Accounting Standards	Standards
Coverage	Global	Focus on emerging markets	Global	Global
Topics	Economic, environmental and social activities and impacts	Strategy, governance and performance	Financial accounting	Sustainability metrics
Target audience	Multiple stakeholders	All stakeholders; investors prioritised	Current/potential capital providers (financial markets)	Investors and other capital market participants

Key: IIRC: International Integrated Reporting Council; SASB: Sustainability Accounting Standards Board (IIRC and SASB merged in June 2021 to form the Value Reporting Foundation – VRF); TCFD: Task Force on Climate-Related Financial Disclosures; CDSB: Climate Disclosure Standards Board; GRI: Global Reporting Initiative; IFC: International Finance Corporation; IASB: International Accounting Standards Board; ISSB: International Sustainability Standards Board (IASB and ISSB are both under the umbrella of the International Financial Reporting Standards Foundation – IFRS Foundation)

Standards: norms, or sets of norms, that lay out what ESG topics are deemed material for particular sectors and industries and what metrics should be disclosed to indicate a company's ESG risks, performance and impact. The Global Reporting Initiative (GRI) and the Sustainability Accounting Standards Board (SASB) are the providers of the two best-known comprehensive sets of standards for ESG disclosure.

(Continued)

Frameworks: principles-based norms for how companies should organise and present information related to their ESG risks, performance and impact. Frameworks provide issuers leeway to select for themselves which standards they should rely on to determine what topics to cover and what indicators and metrics to include in their disclosures. Some frameworks are intended to be comprehensive, while others focus on how to organise and present topic-specific information (eg climate, labour, supply chain).

Guidance: Recommendations, generally principles-based, for how companies should go about the selection and application of reporting standards and frameworks. Stock exchanges in particular have been active in the development of practice guides to assist listed companies in their efforts to provide greater and more intelligible disclosure around ESG issues.

Mandatory disclosures

Mandated disclosures are those required pursuant to legal and regulatory provisions for the reporting of specific or general ESG information imposed by governments. Specific reporting mandates tend to be more rule-based and narrower in their scope and intended beneficiaries than general mandates. For example, some securities law regimes require listed companies engaged in mining to report accidents, violations of health and safety laws, fines and settlements for deaths and injuries.[13] Others may require disclosure of employment law claims against the company.[14]

The European Union is arguably demonstrating global leadership in ESG reporting at present, reflecting in part its strategic emphasis on sustainability and sustainable finance. At the national level, Article 173 of France's Energy Transition Law set an earlier example in 2016, imposing mandatory disclosure requirements on both companies and investors relating to carbon emissions.[15]

But the most prominent example of ESG disclosure mandates is probably the EU's principles-based Non-Financial Reporting Directive (NFRD), which came into effect in 2018, and its progeny, as well as the national legislation that EU member states were required to approve to implement the NFRD. The NFRD is designed with a broad set of stakeholder interests in mind and so applies a correspondingly broad understanding of ESG risk materiality.

The NFRD instructs member states to require each listed company and significant enterprise (labelled 'public-interest entity') to publicly disclose its policies, the outcomes of such policies (including key performance indicators) and the risks associated with the company's operations in the areas of: environmental matters, social and employee aspects, respect for human rights, anti-corruption and bribery issues, and diversity on the board of directors. However, the NFRD does not prescribe integrated reporting. Approximately 6,000 European companies are subject to the NFRD. The NFRD will be succeeded by the Corporate Sustainability Reporting Directive (CSRD), which will expand its scope to all large companies and all companies listed on regulated markets (except for listed micro-enterprises) and introduces more detailed reporting requirements. Chapter 7 provides a more comprehensive discussion of the current and proposed EU sustainability reporting framework.

Approximately 60% of the 1,000 companies whose NFRD disclosures were analysed by the Alliance for Corporate Transparency (ACT) in 2019 integrated key ESG information into their annual reports, with the remainder publishing separate ESG or sustainability reports.[16] Furthermore, the NFRD does not require companies to follow a particular reporting framework, which obviously gives rise to challenges with respect to comparability. (See the explanation of reporting frameworks and standards in the box on 'Mandates, standards, frameworks and guidance' and the discussion below.) What companies must do is specify which domestic or international framework(s) they follow. The most frequently employed frameworks, according to the ACT study, include the GRI, the UN SDGs, the OECD *Due Diligence Guidance for Responsible Business Conduct*, the Carbon Disclosure Project and International Labour Organization standards.

ACT's 2019 analysis of NFRD implementation paints a mixed picture of its completeness thus far. Although over 80% of the companies surveyed disclosed their policies in the five categories, only 35% included targets, and only 28% reported on outcomes. About half of the companies surveyed by ACT provided disclosure on at least one strategic sustainability-related risk, but only 7.2% described how these risks are reflected in their core business strategies. Not surprisingly, companies whose disclosures were reviewed by ACT reported best on 'traditional' risks that today have come to be classified under the ESG rubric. For example, 99% of companies provided disclosure with respect to employees.

ACT analysed corporate reporting in the areas covered by the NFRD; it did not have access to the actual workings of the internal ESG risk management systems of reporting companies. It is therefore risky to extrapolate from corporate disclosures the true quality of companies' ESG risk management systems. Their ESG risk management practices, performance and impacts may be substantially better in reality than they appear from the public reporting. Or the reporting may succumb to marketing temptations and overstate their quality.[17]

The results of the ACT survey at least point to the possibility that European companies are better at identifying potential ESG risks than at incorporating consideration of them into strategic direction, setting KPIs and measuring outcomes. We suspect this is likely to be true of companies in most jurisdictions. Interestingly, ACT found a positive correlation between companies that reported ESG targets and those that secured some sort of assurance on the information included in their ESG disclosures. This would be consistent with boards and management seeking to have greater confidence around information that they judge may have a direct impact on corporate strategy and performance.

Reporting standards

Reporting standards lay out what specific ESG topics are deemed material for particular sectors and industries and what metrics should be disclosed to indicate company performance. The two comprehensive ESG reporting standards most frequently cited by investors are those issued by GRI and SASB. They both aim to allow for quantitative and like-for-like comparisons between companies and for potentially third-party assurance through an audit. To be credible, standard setters consult widely and seek consensus around the topics deemed material and the key performance metrics to be reported.

GRI was established in 1997 to develop standards for commercial and non-commercial organisations (including listed and unlisted firms, not-for-profits and other entities) to report ESG information for the benefit of a broad range of stakeholders. It has taken a modular approach, incrementally releasing standards over time as particular ESG issues gained salience. Companies employing GRI standards in their reporting are encouraged to upload them to the GRI website, which now catalogues disclosures from over 14,000 organisations. The GRI standards are set by the independently operated Global Sustainability Standards Board (GSSB), consisting of 15 members representing a range of expertise and multi-stakeholder perspectives on sustainability reporting. GRI standard setting involves regular stakeholder consultation, public notice and comment procedures. The GSSB's meetings are open to the public and made available online.

SASB started as an initiative largely focused on US companies and the US securities market, but in recent years has seen significant uptake also from non-US companies and investors, with approximately 50% of SASB reporters domiciled outside the US since 2019. As of February 2022, there were 1334 unique SASB reporters (year 2021 to date), with 598 reporters in the S&P Global 1200.[18] (SASB tracks over a 2-year period, recognising that many entities publish sustainability reports biennially.) Of the 42 global institutional investors surveyed for Morrow Sodali's 2021 Institutional Investor Survey, 53% recommended SASB as the best standards for companies to communicate their ESG information.[19] As of February 2022, more than 323 entities, including institutional investors, licensed SASB standards for use in operations. Its Investor Advisory Group numbers 61 members from 12 countries, representing US$52 trillion in assets under management.[20] As described in more detail later on in this chapter, SASB combined with IIRC in June 2021 to form the Value Reporting Foundation (VRF). As of this writing, VRF is in turn in the process of combining with the International Financial Reporting Standards (IFRS) Foundation in conjunction with the establishment of the ISSB.

SASB's governance structure and standard-setting process are similar to those of the internationally recognised bodies that set disclosure standards for the benefit of investors, such as the FASB and the IASB. SASB's standards are developed and revised under the guidance of its Standards Board and a Standards Advisory Group for each of the 11 SASB sectors. Members of the advisory groups include industry representatives, investors, technical experts, legal and accounting professionals, academics and others who engage with the Standards Board with the goal of settling on standards and metrics that are practical and fit-for-purpose.

SASB's standard setting takes place in accordance with a fully transparent six-stage process, progressing from project screening through research, standard-setting agenda, comment period, update and post-implementation review phases. The standard-setting agenda and comment period phases of the process in particular are designed to ensure that new standards and revisions 'are developed based on extensive feedback from companies, investors, and other market participants as part of a transparent, publicly-documented process.'[21] SASB has also established an Investor Advisory Group of leading asset owners and asset managers to encourage companies to participate in SASB's ongoing standards development process, so that outcomes reflect both issuer and investor viewpoints. GRI's GSSB similarly commits itself to 'due process' and multi-shareholder engagement and input in setting GRI standards, the main differences arising from the GRI standards' broader set of intended beneficiaries.

While usually cited as the most comprehensive ESG disclosure standards, SASB and GRI differ importantly with respect to their audiences, and thus their definitions of materiality. SASB is first and foremost a set of accounting standards for investors to consider in allocating capital, whereas GRI's definition of materiality takes into account the broader interests of non-financial stakeholders and societal impacts. Reflecting these differences and the potential confusion in the marketplace relating to these reporting standards, GRI, SASB and other standard setters have collaborated to help clarify for companies and stakeholders how their respective standards operate, where the key similarities and differences lie, and even how they can be used in combination. (See discussion below.)

Reporting frameworks

Reporting frameworks, such as the International Integrated Reporting Council's (IIRC) '<IR>' framework for comprehensive reporting, and the Task Force on Climate-Related Financial Disclosures (TCFD) framework for climate-related disclosures, are examples of principles-based recommendations for how companies should organise and present ESG-related information. Both these frameworks accord issuers significant leeway to select for themselves which standards they should rely on to determine what topics to cover and what indicators and metrics to include in their disclosures.

As its name implies, the IIRC was established as a coalition of regulators, investors, companies, standard setters, the accounting profession and NGOs that promotes the presentation of financial, ESG and other information in a consolidated fashion, tailored to each company's own value creation thesis. Consistent with this goal, the <IR> framework does not prescribe which topics, metrics or KPIs should be included in a company's (integrated) reports. In the IIRC's view, companies (with input from their stakeholders) are best positioned to decide which of these are most relevant (material) to value creation.

Instead, the <IR> framework lays out a structure for presenting the categories of information required to be included in an integrated report. The 'content elements,' which are fundamentally linked to each other and are not mutually exclusive, are stated in the form of questions to be answered in a way that makes the relationships between them apparent.[22] In June 2021, the IIRC merged with SASB to form the VRF, which in turn is in the process of combining into the IFRS Foundation as of this writing. That was a significant step in the consolidation of global sustainability standards. The benefits and challenges of integrated reporting will be covered in greater depth in Chapter 7.

Some companies choose to organise the presentation of all or part of their ESG reporting along the lines of principles or best practices that may not have been conceived of as reporting frameworks when they were first issued. Aspirational objectives, such as the SDGs, or recommendations for operational best practices, such as the OECD *Due Diligence Guidance for Responsible Business Conduct* and its complementary sector-specific guidance, fall into this category.

The OECD *Due Diligence Guidance* supports the implementation of the OECD *Guidelines for Multinational Enterprises* and 'help[s] enterprises avoid and address adverse impacts related to workers, human rights, the environment, bribery, consumers and corporate governance that may be associated with their operations, supply chains and other business relationships.'[23] Together with its complementary sector-specific due diligence guidance for the minerals, agriculture, and garment and footwear supply chains, and good practice reports for the extractives and financial sectors, the OECD *Due Diligence Guidance* provides companies with guidance for identifying and assessing potential adverse impacts of their operations, supply chains and business relationships and examples of practical actions for managing the risks that these present for both the companies and others. Seventeen per cent of respondents to the recent ACT survey of compliance with the NFRD cited the OECD *Due Diligence Guidance* and its complementary sector-specific guidance among the frameworks employed for reporting the ESG-related information required by the Directive and national implementing legislation.

Climate reporting

Given the particular urgency of the global climate crisis, climate-related risk has received considerable emphasis in recent years, arguably more so than many other ESG factors facing companies (at least until the outbreak of Covid-19). The clear systemic nature of climate risk is very much on the radar screens of high-level global governance bodies, including the Group of 20 (G20) finance ministers and central bank governors and the Financial Stability Board (FSB). This prompted specific global developments in climate reporting, notably the recommendations by the TCFD, an organisation that was set up in 2015 by the FSB as a means of co-ordinating disclosures among companies impacted by climate change. As explained in greater detail later on in this chapter, the obvious urgency around the climate crisis is the motivation for the climate-first priority of the new ISSB.

As illustrated in Figure 4.1, TCFD is a principles-based framework. For example, TCFD recommends that every company include in its non-financial reporting an explanation of how its strategic planning process takes into account greenhouse gas emissions. Seventy-five per cent of the respondents to Morrow Sodali's *2021 Institutional Investor Survey* named TCFD as the preferred ESG reporting framework for climate-related disclosures.[24]

The latest AI review of the reporting of 1126 companies from 142 countries and eight industries, conducted by TCFD, found that the percentage of companies disclosing information aligned with each of its recommendations increased between 2016 and 2018. The average number addressed by companies out of the 11 recommended disclosures grew from 2.8 recommendations in 2016 to 3.1 in 2017 and to 3.6 in 2018. Seventy-eight per cent of the companies in the review disclosed information aligned with at least one of the Task Force's recommendations in 2018, up from 70% in 2016. However, climate-related disclosure remains patchy, and 'only around 25% of companies disclosed information aligned with more than five of the 11 recommended disclosures and only 4% of companies disclosed information aligned with at least 10 of the recommended disclosures.'[25]

FIGURE 4.1 Core elements of recommended climate-related financial disclosures

Governance
The organisation's governance around climate-related risks and opportunities

Strategy
The actual and potential impacts of climate-related risks and opportunities on the organisation's business, strategy and financial planning

Risk management
The processes used by the organisation to identify, assess and manage climate-related risks

Metrics and targets
The metrics and targets used to assess and manage relevant climate-related risks and opportunities

Source: Task Force on Climate-Related Financial Disclosures

The TCFD framework has received support in many markets around the world. The endorsements of TCFD around the launch of the ISSB at the COP26 meeting in Glasgow, Scotland, in November 2021 and the inclusion of the TCFD in the ISSB's Technical Readiness Working Group mean that the TCFD approach will be reflected in the ISSB's eventual climate-related disclosures standards.

The relative simplicity of this structure (say, compared with the <IR> framework and its six forms of capital) has an intuitive appeal, and this has prompted interest in expanding the TCFD framework to other areas of sustainability, including social, ethical or other environmental issues. For example, the large asset manager BlackRock, in seeking to encourage consolidation of ESG reporting standards and platforms, has pushed for a standardised framework for investors involving SASB data and the TCFD reporting framework.[26] Similarly, in the UK, the FRC encourages companies to report against the TCFD framework, together with the use of SASB sectoral metrics. It is also positive to see that the TCFD framework has emerged as a foundational standard and common denominator in the 2022 sustainability reporting initiatives of the ISSB, EFRAG and the SEC.[27]

In our discussion of sustainability governance and reporting in Chapter 7, we explore in greater detail the ongoing dynamics of climate reporting and accounting.

Practice guides

Disclosure practice guides are intended to help companies navigate the sea of disclosure standards and frameworks. They typically reflect market expectations and offer recommendations around the application of more detailed tools to help companies on their journey towards greater and more meaningful ESG transparency. Stock exchange initiatives intended to encourage public company disclosure of ESG information generally fall into the category of practice guidelines. We cite two examples here, one in the US, the other in Japan.

In the US, NASDAQ's *ESG Reporting Guide* is designed to help companies listed on its exchanges to identify suitable reporting methodologies appropriate for their activities as well as to 'help both private and public companies navigate the evolving standards on ESG data disclosure.'[28] In parallel, NASDAQ has established an ESG Reporting Platform to facilitate the distribution of listed companies' ESG information to users, including data services, ESG rating services and index providers. NASDAQ also maintains a team of ESG experts available to work with client companies to 'analyse, assess and action ESG programs with the goals of attracting long-term capital and enhancing value creation.'[29]

In early 2020, Japan Exchange Group and the Tokyo Stock Exchange (TSE) released their *Practical Handbook for ESG Disclosure*. The *Handbook* is intended to help Japanese listed companies respond in a meaningful way to demands for quality ESG information from investors. It advocates a step-by-step approach, encouraging boards and management to begin by gaining an understanding of market expectations around ESG disclosure and identifying the ESG issues relevant to the company's operations. Companies should then articulate how these issues feed into the formulation of the company's strategy. Once the links between ESG issues and strategic direction are clear, the company can '[p]ut in place an internal structure for oversight and implementation of

ESG issues and set metrics/targets, to enable steady progress on ESG activities.'[30] Finally, in dialogue with investors and other stakeholders, the TSE *Handbook* suggests that the company should be in a position to determine what existing disclosure frameworks and standards best communicate the company's approach to ESG risk and how it fits into the company's business model, value proposition and overall risk management system.

4. THE QUESTION OF MATERIALITY

A particular framework's or set of standards' definition of materiality is central to understanding its utility, and its limitations, as a tool for communicating the nature and quality of a company's ESG practices. What matters to one set of stakeholders may be of only minor interest or irrelevant to others. For example, SASB's definition of materiality is narrower than GRI's. SASB focuses on what is relevant to investors—how ESG factors impact financial performance—in a way analogous to public company accounting and financial reporting standards in the US. GRI's definition takes into account much more of what non-financial stakeholders might deem relevant to their interests and decision-making.

One way to see this expressed is in the amount of disclosure. GRI reporting can be expected to be longer and cover more topics than SASB disclosure. IIRC's <IR> framework promotes reporting that tells the story of how financial and non-financial factors combine to achieve a company's objectives. The IIRC definition of materiality focuses on value creation. Companies should select what information to report based on whether it can be expected to impact the value the company will create for its stakeholders over time.

As noted in the discussion of mandatory reporting above, the NFRD in the European Union is designed with a broad set of stakeholder interests in mind and so applies a correspondingly broad understanding of ESG risk materiality. A core feature of the NFRD is its concept of 'double materiality.' Double materiality recognises that the audience for non-financial (ESG) reporting should include both financial and non-financial stakeholders, and the information needs of the two groups do not entirely overlap. It features prominently at the core of the proposed European Sustainability Reporting Standards.

Double materiality is not only intended to address the question of how ESG factors affect the company and its ability to create value; it also requires examination of how the company's ESG performance might impact its stakeholders and society more broadly, even when there is likely to be limited financial impact on the company itself. The application of double materiality places pure externalities (negative impacts of a company's activities on other parties that have no predictable financial consequences for the company) in the category of material risks. National legislation for EU countries implementing NFRD must reflect this multi-stakeholder approach to materiality, providing impetus for the adoption by European companies of reporting frameworks and standards that meet the needs of financial and non-financial stakeholders alike.

Table 4.1 compares the materiality definitions of five major ESG disclosure frameworks and standards (four currently in existence, plus the incipient IFRS Sustainability Disclosure Standards to be issued by the ISSB; see below). Their diversity reflects differences in the purposes for which each was developed and their intended audiences.

SASB applies its materiality definition on a sector and industry-by-industry basis. The topics and standards deemed material for each industry and sector are presented

TABLE 4.1 Materiality standards of prominent frameworks and standards

IIRC (VRF)	SASB (VRF)	TCFD	GRI	ISSB
Substantively affect the organisation's ability to create value over short, medium and long term	Substantial likelihood that disclosure of the omitted fact would alter the 'total mix' of information available for the reasonable investor	Companies should determine materiality consistent with how they determine it for other information included in their financial filings	Reporting covers topics that reflect the reporting organization's significant economic, environmental and social impacts, or substantively influence the assessment and decision of stakeholders	High-quality, comprehensive baseline of sustainability disclosures focused on the needs of investors and financial markets

in tabular format in a materiality map accessible on the SASB website.[31] An example is provided in Figure 4.2. The map lays out what sustainability issues SASB believes are likely, possible and unlikely material for companies in each industry and indicates these through shading of the boxes.

In contrast, while clearly recognising that some ESG risks and corresponding standards are of greater relevance to some sectors and industries than others, GRI organises and presents its standards on a more topic-by-topic basis. This reflects its broader definition of materiality and the resultant absence of a single value, such as SASB's financial materiality, against which to determine materiality on an industry-by-industry basis.

Of course, the set of ESG risks that are material to a company in a particular industry and to its investors and other stakeholders is never static. With the passage of time, new risks can be expected to emerge, some risks that were present all along may be 'discovered' through painful experience, and other risks may be effectively eliminated by new technologies. As investor and customer sentiments have real effects on the cost of capital and sales, changes in perception of risks can affect their materiality.

Companies, investors, stakeholders and standard setters should therefore take into account the emerging concept of 'dynamic materiality' to anticipate and prepare for changes in awareness and impact of ESG risks. Dynamic materiality relates in part to how ESG factors that may not have a clear link to financial impacts today might lead to financial impacts tomorrow.[32]

How companies, investors and standard setters 'keep their ears to the ground' on potentially material ESG risks is one of the main challenges this book addresses. The specific set of material ESG risks for individual companies is typically endogenous, reflecting both sectoral and regional influences particular to the company itself. While we continue to make progress in our understanding of ESG risks, a generalisable model that fits all companies remains aspirational. But we are on the case. However, we do note that there are some indications that big data and AI technologies can help detect shifts in the mix of material ESG risks that companies and investors should be looking out for.

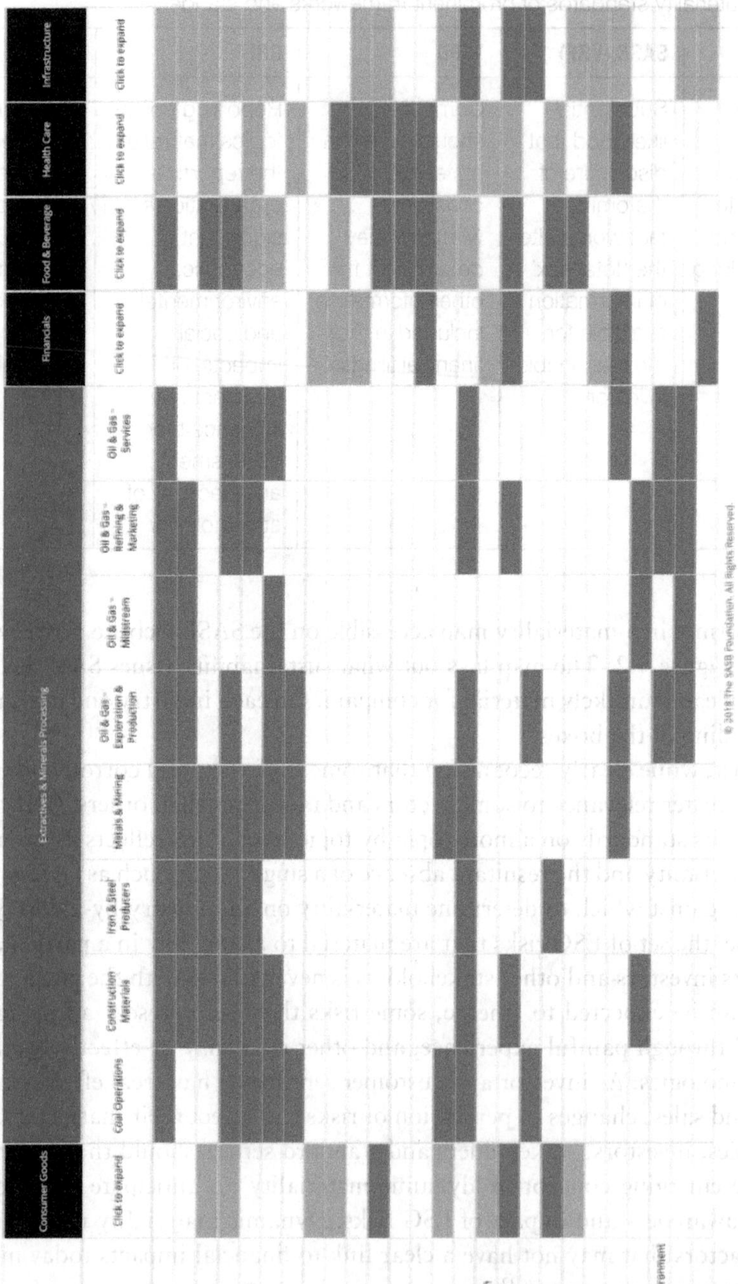

FIGURE 4.2 SASB materiality map

Source: Value Reporting Foundation

5. IFRS SUSTAINABILITY DISCLOSURE STANDARDS: HARMONISATION AND CONVERGENCE OF STANDARDS AND STANDARD SETTERS

The establishment of the ISSB is the most significant attempt to date at harmonisation and convergence of the plethora of ESG standards issued over the past few decades by governments, regulators, industry and investor associations, NGOs and other standard setters. The endorsement, on 3 November 2021 (at the COP26 meeting in Glasgow, Scotland), by the International Federation of Accountants (IFAC) and the International Financial Reporting Standards (IFRS) Foundation of a new global sustainability standard setter (to exist alongside the IASB) was the outcome of a series of efforts by other standard setters to build towards a comprehensive, consistent and workable set of global standards for reporting the ESG performance of companies.[33] These efforts responded to a growing consensus among companies, investors, securities regulators and other stakeholders that the wave of innovation and experimentation around sustainability standards of the past two decades needed to make way for a period of greater harmonisation, rationalisation and consolidation.[34]

ISSB's mandate is to become the global standard setter for sustainability disclosures for financial markets in the same way that its sister institution, the IASB, has (together with its predecessor institutions) established itself as the standard setter for accounting disclosure in most of the world over the past 40 years. Like IASB Accounting Standards, the ISSB Sustainability Disclosure Standards will focus first and foremost on the needs of investors and financial markets. They will apply a capital markets-centric definition of materiality. That said, it is expected that the multi-stakeholder consultative process that ISSB follows will result in standards that also meet the informational needs of stakeholder groups besides investors.

FIGURE 4.3 Organisation of the International Sustainability Standards Board

The ISSB established the Technical Readiness Working Group (TRWG), supported by the International Organization of Securities Commissions (IOSCO), to ensure that opportunities to build upon the knowledge and experience of existing standard setters and users of their standards are not overlooked. The TRWG began work even before the official announcement of the launch of the ISSB. It is composed of representatives from the Climate Disclosure Standards Board (CDSB), the IASB, the TCFD, the VRF (encompassing IIRC and SASB) and the WEF. Working from its members' existing content, the first task of the TRWG will be to present to the ISSB two unified prototypes for climate and more general ESG disclosure standards.

From the date of its announcement (again, at COP26), the IFRS Foundation and other supporters of the initiative have made clear that its first priority will be climate-related disclosure standards. This climate-first approach reflects the sense of urgency of governments, regulators and financial markets about the need for comparable and actionable information on greenhouse gas emissions, climate impact and climate resilience of companies. Although climate-related disclosure standards will come first, the IFRS Foundation has been clear that its intention is for ISSB standards to cover the full panoply of ESG topics, providing both thematic and industry-specific guidance, within the first few years of its existence.[35]

November 2021 also marked the announcement of further institutional rationalisation among sustainability standard setters. The VRF (formed by the merger of SASB and IIRC in June 2021) and the CDSB announced their intention to consolidate their operations and staff with those of the ISSB, folding themselves into the IFRS Foundation. Although every combination of institutions presents challenges and risks, the addition of the VRF and CDSB should provide ISSB with early institutional capacity to deliver on its ambitious agenda.

Emmanuel Faber, former CEO of Danone, the multinational food products company, was named ISSB chair in December 2021. Reflecting the institutional consolidation of standard setters under ISSB, Janine Guillot, previously CEO of the Value Reporting Foundation (formed after the combination of SASB and IIRC in 2021), took up the role of special advisor to the ISSB chair. In line with the goal of compatibility of standards and approach between IASB and ISSB, Sue Lloyd, previously vice-chair of IASB, took up the same position at ISSB on 1 March 2022.

Later in March 2022, the ISSB launched two Exposure Drafts for public consultation on sustainability disclosure standards—one relating to general sustainability-related financial information and the other more specifically focused on climate-related disclosures. As noted earlier, the ISSB is employing the TCFD framework as a core foundation in the development of its standards. This approach should lead to greater global consistency in sustainability reporting. However, the ISSB's ultimate success will hinge upon its implementation in practice, and this in turn will depend on ISSB standards being approved by regulators in individual jurisdictions.

6. COMMERCIAL ESG RATING AND SCORING SERVICES—UTILITY AND LIMITATIONS

In addition to providing access to the underlying data they collect, many, but not all, ESG data providers rate or score the performance of companies they cover. For commercial data service providers, aggregated and disaggregated scoring is an important part of the value proposition they offer their customers. Investors can incorporate the actual scores assigned by companies such as MSCI, Morningstar's Sustainalytics, FTSE, Bloomberg, S&P Trucost, Moody's Vigeo Eiris, Diligent, Glass Lewis and others as inputs in their investment decision-making process.[36] And, as we will discuss in the following two chapters, investors may more selectively apply the scoring methodologies of commercial providers and others—'tweaking' or customising them to comport with the investor's own views on what ESG factors and indicators are most relevant to its investment universe.

The methodologies of ESG rating providers vary along three dimensions:

1. The scope of the elements considered by the rater as relevant to ESG performance.
2. The indicators selected by the rater from which the elements of the score are calculated.
3. The means of aggregating the indicators (weightings) used to generate the ratings.

For example, Table 4.2 demonstrates how the data provider MSCI breaks down its ratings into individual subcomponents.

The variation among the ESG rating agencies along all three of these dimensions is significant, with different ratings providers using a different mix of elements, indicators and weighting techniques. And the degree of transparency of their methodologies

TABLE 4.2 Components of MSCI's ESG ratings

Three pillars	Ten themes	35 ESG key issues	
Environment	**Climate change**	Carbon emissions Product carbon footprint	Financing environmental impact Climate change vulnerability
	Natural capital	Water stress Biodiversity & land use	Raw material sourcing
	Pollution & waste	Toxic emissions & waste Packaging material & waste	Electronic waste
	Environmental opportunities	Opportunities in clean tech Opportunities in green building	Opportunities in renewable energy
Social	**Human capital**	Labour management Health and safety	Human capital development Supply chain labour standards
	Product liability	Product safety & quality Chemical safety Financial product safety	Privacy & data security Responsible investment Health & demographic risk
	Stakeholder opposition	Controversial sourcing Community relations	
	Social opportunities	Access to communications Access to finance	Access to health care Opportunities in nutrition & health
Governance	**Corporate governance** **Corporate behaviour**	Ownership & control Board Business ethics Tax transparency	Pay Accounting

Source: MSCI, MSCI ESG Ratings Methodology, November 2020

provided by ESG rating agencies varies.[37] Recent analysis of ESG ratings carried out by researchers at MIT's Sloan School of Management indicated that about half of the variation among ratings assigned by different providers was explained by indicator selection, with the rest explained about equally by differences in the scope of elements included and the weightings assigned.[38] Therefore, it is critical that, whenever an investor (or any other stakeholder) uses a commercial rating, it should recognised that it is implicitly adopting that particular provider's rationale or bias for the elements and indicators it includes and the weightings it applies to them.

So, it is of fundamental importance for investors to understand to the extent possible the intricacies of the methodologies of the ratings providers they use, and to consider their consistency with the investor's own views on what ESG issues are of greatest relevance to companies in its investment universe and what are the right indicators against which to measure performance.

Since 2016, Japan's Government Pension Investment Fund (GPIF) has published mappings of the ESG scores assigned by FTSE and MSCI to Japanese listed companies. The resulting scattergram presented in Figure 4.4 could be a textbook example of low statistical correlation.

FIGURE 4.4 Comparison of ESG evaluation by FTSE and MSCI

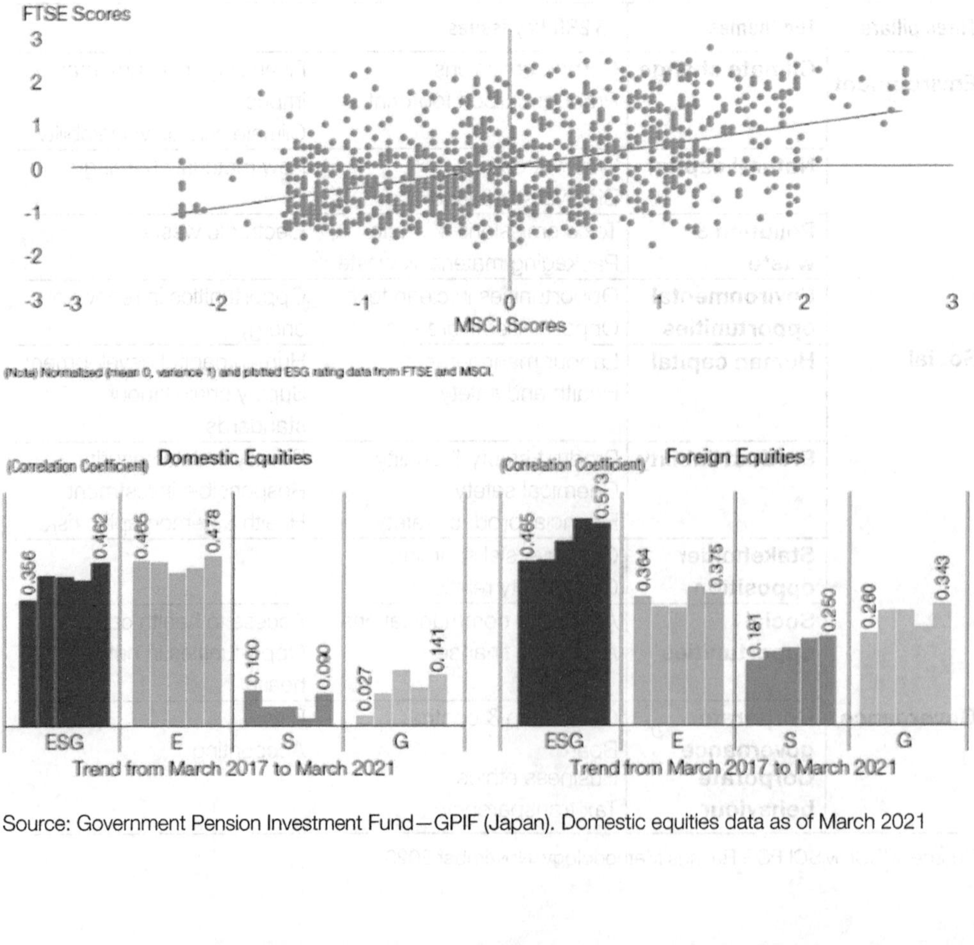

Source: Government Pension Investment Fund—GPIF (Japan). Domestic equities data as of March 2021

FIGURE 4.5 Correlations between the ESG scores of four major providers

	Sustainalytics	MSCI	RobecoSAM	BloombergESG
Sustainalytics	**1**	**0.53**	0.76	0.66
MSCI		**1**	0.48	0.47
RobecoSAM			1	0.68
BloombergESG				1

Source: State Street Global Advisors, ***The ESG Data Challenge***, March 2019. Cross Sectional Correlation for Constituents of the MSCI World Index, 30 June 2017

However, comparing correlations over time (from 2017 to 2021 in the GPIF figures) reveals a general trend towards greater consistency between the two providers. However it is interesting to observe that the greatest correlation relates to environmental factors, most likely because they are more objectively quantifiable. Possibly more interesting is that social factors clearly have the least correlation, suggesting more subjective—and less consistent—metrics among ESG ratings providers. Large asset owners, such as GPIF, continue to engage with commercial providers over the structure and composition of ESG ratings, as well as the indicators and metrics used in their construction. GPIF goes as far as to include in its own ESG report the topics it has addressed with the raters and the outcomes of such discussions.[39]

Low correlation of ESG scores is not unique to the Japanese market. State Street Global Advisors conducted a similar exercise comparing the scores assigned to the MSCI World Index by four providers, Sustainalytics, MSCI, RobecoSAM and Bloomberg ESG, in 2017. As shown in Figure 4.5, low correlations prevailed, from a high of 0.68 (RobecoSAM and Bloomberg) to a low of 0.47 (Bloomberg and MSCI).

Some observers have used the relatively low levels of correlation among the aggregate ESG scores of the major rating providers, illustrated in Figures 4.4 and 4.5, as evidence for the conclusion that the scoring of ESG performance of companies is a valueless exercise. But this overstates the case. Ratings that aggregate across the three individual pillars of ESG are probably the least useful scoring tool for investors. Discriminating users of ratings are likely to be more interested in comparing constituent scores and more focused on the scores assigned for elements that they believe are most germane to the companies in their investment universe. In the following chapter, we will discuss how ratings continue to be valued by investors as one, but by no means the only, important input of ESG integration methodologies tailored to their particular investment processes.

NOTES

1. Global Initiative for Sustainability Ratings was established in 2011 as a joint project of non-profit research and advocacy entities Ceres and Tellus.
2. Ogechukwo Ezeokoll, China Layne, Mier Statman and Oswaldo Urdapilleta, *Environmental, Social, and Governance (ESG) Investment Tools: A Review of the Current Field*, December 2017, prepared for the US Department of Labor, provides a concise scan of ESG data service providers.

3. *OECD Corporate Governance Factbook 2021*, Chapters 1–2: www.oecd.org/corporate/corporate-governance-factbook.htm
4. Ronald J. Gilson, Controlling Shareholders and Corporate Governance: Complicating the Comarative Taxonomy, April 2006, *Harvard Law Review*, vol 119, no 6, p. 1641.
5. Going further back in the annals of the history of corporations, the British East India Company, ostensibly a trading firm, built a private army and engaged in private diplomacy, slave trading and opium distribution for the better part of a century. The poor quality of long-distance communication in the eighteenth and early nineteenth centuries meant that it was decades before the British public and government were sufficiently informed about its activities to begin efforts to rein it in. William Dalrymple, *The Anarchy: The East India Company, Corporate Violence, and the Pillage of an Empire*, 2019, Bloomsbury.
6. For examples, see Snowkap (www.snowkap.com) and Metric (www.metric-esg.com).
7. Niceland Seafood: https://nicelandseafood.com/our-story/
8. Know the Chain: https://knowthechain.org
9. S&P Global, *How Can AI Help ESG Investing?* 25 February 2020: www.spglobal.com/en/research-insights/articles/how-can-ai-help-esg-investing
10. Truvalue Labs, *ESG Research in the Information Age*, 2019: https://insights.truvaluelabs.com/white-paper/esg- research-in-the-information-age. Truvalue Labs, a pioneer in AI-driven technology in the ESG space was acquired by FactSet, a global provider of integrated financial information, in October 2020.
11. Much of this section draws from OECD, Corporate Governance and the Management of ESG Risks, in *Business and Financial Outlook: Sustainable and Resilient Finance*, 2020: www.oecd.org/daf/oecd-business-and-finance- outlook-26172577.htm, to which co-author Mike Lubrano was a contributor.
12. International Sustainability Standards Board, ISSB: Frequently Asked Questions, February 2022, www.ifrs.org/groups/international-sustainability-standards-board/issb-frequently-asked-questions/
13. See SEC Standard instructions for filing forms under Securities Act of 1933, Securities Exchange Age of 1934 and Energy Policy and Conservation Act of 1975—Regulation S-K Subpart 229.104 (Mine safety disclosure): www. ecfr.gov/cgi-bin/text-idx?SID=fd3f92d14b821275a59c8aeecaabb6e9&mc=true&node=se17.3.229_1104&rgn=div8
14. The electronic reporting form that every Brazilian public company must file each year requires detailed disclosure of all material labour controversies (judicial, administrative or arbitration), along with any other potential labour-related contingencies. Comissão de Valores Mobiliários, Instruction No. 480, 9 December 2009: www.cvm.gov.br/export/sites/cvm/subportal_ingles/menu/investors/anexos/CVMInstruction480.pdf
15. In France, the famous Article 173 has been superseded by Article 29 of the Energy-Climate Law of November 2019. Among other things, Article 29 places greater emphasis on biodiversity, in addition to climate change, with regard to investor disclosure.
16. Alliance for Corporate Transparency Research Report, *An Analysis of the Sustainability Reports of 1000 Companies Pursuant to the EU Non-Financial Reporting Directive*, 2019.
17. For an analysis of the state of ESG reporting in Central, Eastern and Southern Europe, see Frank Bold, *Enforcement Activities, Summary Report EUKI Research 2020*: www.frankbold.org/sites/default/files/publikace/enforcement_activities_corporate_sustainability_reporting_summary_research_s.pdf; for the specific case of climate-related risk disclosures, see Carbon Tracker Initiative and PRI, *Flying Blind: The Glaring Absence of Climate Risks in Financial Reporting*, 2022: www.unpri.org/download?ac=14597
18. SASB, www.sasb.org/company-use/sasb-reporters/
19. Morrow Sodali, 2021 Institutional Investor Survey: https://morrowsodali.com/insights/institutional-investor-survey-2021
20. SASB, www.sasb.org/about/global-use/
21. SASB, *Connecting Businesses and Investors on the Financial Impacts of Sustainability*, 2020: www.sasb.org/wp-content/uploads/2019/02/About-SASB-Sheet-021219.pdf
22. International Integrated Reporting Council Framework, 2013: https://integratedreporting.org/wp-content/uploads/2013/12/13-12-08-THE-INTERNATIONAL-IR-FRAMEWORK-2-1.pdf
23. OECD, *Due Diligence Guidance for Responsible Business Conduct*, 2018: www.oecd.org/investment/due- diligence-guidance-for-responsible-business-conduct.htm
24. Morrow Sodali, 2021, op. cit.

25. Ibid.
26. David M. Silk, Sabastian V. Niles, and Carmen X. W. Lu, BlackRock nudges Companies Toward a Common Standard (SASB + TCFD), 18 January 2020, Harvard Law School Forum on Corporate Governance,: https://corpgov.law.harvard.edu/2020/01/18/blackrock-nudges-companies-toward-a-common-standard-sasb-tcfd/
27. Robert G. Eccles, *A Comparative Analysis of Three Proposals for Climate-Related Disclosures*, Forbes, 11 June 2022.
28. NASDAQ, ESG Reporting Guide 2.0: A Support Resource for Companies, May 2019: https://www.nasdaq.com/ESG- Guide
29. Ibid.
30. Japan Exchange Group, *Practical Handbook for ESG Disclosure*, 2020: www.jpx.co.jp/english/corporate/ sustainability/esg-investment/handbook/index.html#:~:text=The%20aim%20of%20the%20Handbook,with%20 investors%20and%20other%20stakeholders
31. Value Reporting Foundation, *Exploring Materiality*: https://materiality.sasb.org/
32. Robert G. Eccles, *Dynamic Materiality in the Time of COVID-19*, April 19, 2020, Forbes: www.forbes.com/sites/ bobeccles/2020/04/19/dynamic-materiality-in-the-time-of-covid-19/?sh=13193ba24f07
33. By 2019, the Better Alignment Project of the Corporate Reporting Dialogue, a group made up of major sponsors of reporting frameworks and standards, was launched to explore how framework and standard setters could work together to better support organisations in preparing ESG disclosures. On the topic of climate disclosure, the project issued *Driving Alignment in Climate-related Reporting*, which mapped the major standards and frameworks to the recommendations of the TCFD. The following year it published its *Statement of Intent to Work Together Towards Comprehensive Corporate Reporting* with the support of the World Economic Forum (WEF) and Deloitte. The statement committed the group to provide: (a) joint market guidance on how its frameworks and standards can be applied in a complementary and additive way; (b) a joint vision of how these elements could complement financial generally accepted accounting principles (Financial GAAP) and serve as a natural starting point for progress towards a more coherent, comprehensive corporate reporting system; and (c) a joint commitment to drive toward this goal through an ongoing programme of deeper collaboration between members and a stated willingness to engage closely with other interested stakeholders.
34. Following a 3-month consultation period, during which existing standard setters were generally supportive of the idea of a single global set of ESG reporting standards, the IFRS Foundation announced on 1 February 2021 the formation of a steering group to take the project forward. The establishment of a Sustainability Standards Board under the IFRS Foundation was endorsed later that month by IOSCO, which cited the existing collaboration among standard setters as having the potential to 'form the basis for a future common set of international standards for sustainability-related disclosures.'
35. ICGN supported the International Sustainability Standards Board concept and strongly urged the IFRS Foundation and ISSB supporters to build on existing standards and the work of existing organisations to make them complementary. ICGN, Comment letter on IFRS Foundation's Consultation Paper on Sustainability Reporting, 21 December 2021: www.icgn.org/sites/default/files/27.%20ICGN%20Letter%20to%20IFRS%20Foundation%E2%80%99s%20Consultation%20Paper%20on%20Sustainability%20Reporting_0.pdf. See also *ICGN Statement of Shared Climate Change Responsibilities to the United Nations Climate Change Conference of the Parties* (COP26): www.icgn.org/sites/default/files/23.%20ICGN%20Letter%20to%20President%20of%20COP26%2CStatement%20of%20Shared%20Climate%20Change%20Responsibilities%2C%20October%202021.pdf
36. For a comprehensive review of the ESG ratings landscape and some of the public policy and market regulation issues around the industry, see IOSCO, *Environmental, Social and Governance (ESG) Ratings and Data Products Providers—Final Report*, November 2021: www.iosco.org/library/pubdocs/pdf/IOSCOPD690.pdf
37. Opacity around their rating methodologies and other concerns have led some to call for regulation of ESG rating and data providers. See ibid and Securities and Exchange Board of India, *Consultation Paper on Environmental, Social and Governance (ESG) Rating Providers for Securities Markets*, 24 January 24 2022: www.sebi.gov.in/reports-and-statistics/reports/jan-2022/consultation-paper-on-environmental-social-and-governance-esg-rating-providers-for-securities-markets_55516.html

38. Florian Berg, Julian F Kölbel and Roberto Rigobon, *Aggregate Confusion: The Divergence of ESG Ratings*, 18 May 2020, Massachusetts Institute of Technology (MIT)—Sloan School of Management: https://papers.ssrn.com/sol3/ papers.cfm?abstract_id=3438533
39. Government Pensions Investment Fund (Japan), ESG Report 2020, pp 29–33: www.gpif.go.jp/en/investment/GPIF_ESGREPORT_FY2020.pdf

FURTHER READING

OECD, *Corporate Governance and the Management of ESG Risks*, in *Business and Financial Outlook: Sustainable and Resilient Finance*, 2020: www.oecd.org/daf/oecd-business-and-finance-outlook-26172577.htm

Florian Berg, Julian F Kölbel and Roberto Rigobon, *Aggregate Confusion: The Divergence of ESG Ratings*, 18 May 2020, Massachusetts Institute of Technology (MIT), Sloan School of Management: https://papers.ssrn.com/sol3/papers.cfm?abstract_id=3438533

Alliance for Corporate Transparency Research Report, *An Analysis of the Sustainability Reports of 1000 Companies Pursuant to the EU Non-Financial Reporting Directive*, 2019: https://allianceforcorporatetransparency.org/assets/2019_Research_Report%20_Alliance_for_Corporate_Transparency-7d9802a0c18c9f13017d686481bd2d6c6886fea6d9e9c7a5c3cfafea8a48b1c7.pdf

S&P Global Ratings, *Environmental, Social and Governance Evaluation Analytical Approach*, April 2019: www.spglobal.com/ratings/en/research/pdf-articles/190410-environmental-social-and-governance-evaluation-analytical-approach#:~:text=S%26P%20Global%20Ratings'%20environmental%2C%20social,financial%20impact%20on%20the%20entity

Kris Douma and George Dallas, *Investor Agenda for Corporate ESG Reporting*, October 2018, ICGN and PRI: www.icgn.org/investor-agenda-corporate-esg-reporting

Principles for Responsible Investment, *Shifting Perceptions: ESG, Credit Risk and Ratings, Part 1: The State of Play*, 2017: www.unpri.org/credit-ratings/esg-credit-risk-and-ratings-part-1-the-state-of-play/78.article

Chapter 5

ESG and investment decision-making: Designing an effective methodology

DOI: 10.4324/9781003307082-5

This chapter examines important considerations institutional investors need to take into account in incorporating ESG analysis into the investment decision-making process. It discusses the practical challenges of integrating ESG analysis in a way that is consistent with, and contributes to, the achievement of an asset manager's investment objectives. While the operational procedures that institutional investors follow to make investment decisions certainly share some core commonalities, every investor's process will differ in important ways from those of its peers. Factors including asset class, return objectives, risk appetite, investment style, time horizon, the expertise and experience of staff, resource constraints and the firm's investment beliefs account for these differences. Accordingly, there are no one-size-fits-all solutions. Each institutional investor needs to understand the available resources and possible approaches to considering ESG factors in investment decision-making and adopt inputs, analytical tools and outputs that fit with its unique investment process.

1. COMPONENTS OF INVESTMENT DECISION-MAKING

Before delving into ways to incorporate ESG data and analysis into investment decision-making, it is worth clarifying what we mean by investment decision-making. Many discussions of investor stewardship and ESG integration are framed as somehow 'bolting' ESG analysis on to 'traditional' investment decision processes. But perhaps it is more accurate to describe the approaches discussed in this book as ways that the ultimate investment decision-makers (be they portfolio managers or investment committees) take ESG factors into account when assigning valuations and deciding whether to invest in a security and, as part of that investment decision, fashion an appropriate approach to stewardship of the asset.

Employing this definition of the 'investment decision'—where ESG analysis and stewardship are part and parcel of the valuation and buy/sell/hold components of 'traditional' investment decision-making—has important implications for the responsibilities

FIGURE 5.1 What do we mean by investment decision-making?

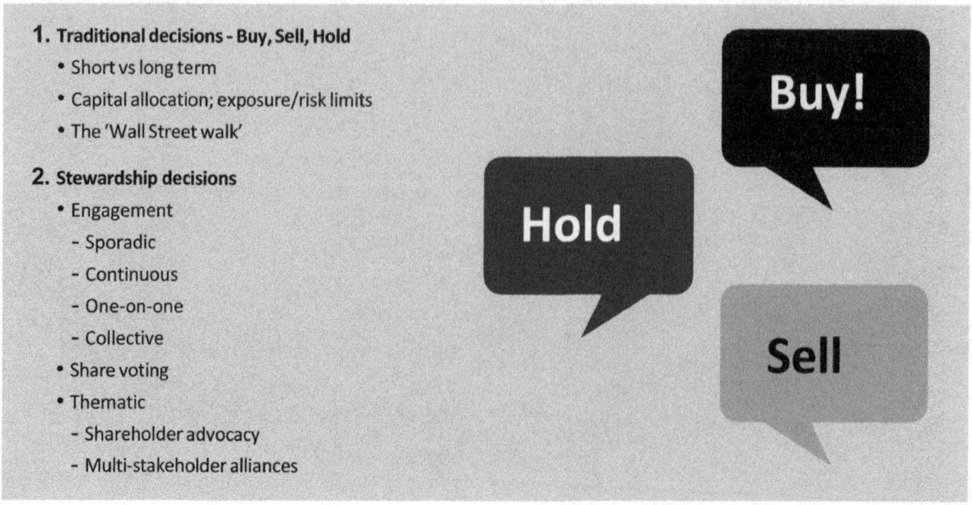
1. Traditional decisions - Buy, Sell, Hold
• Short vs long term
• Capital allocation; exposure/risk limits
• The 'Wall Street walk'
2. Stewardship decisions
• Engagement
- Sporadic
- Continuous
- One-on-one
- Collective
• Share voting
• Thematic
- Shareholder advocacy
- Multi-stakeholder alliances
Buy!
Hold
Sell

of portfolio managers, investment analysts and other investment decision-makers within asset owners and asset managers.

In reality, decisions around investing in securities go beyond simply determining at any point in time whether to buy, sell or hold a share, bond or other financial instrument. They also relate to determinations of valuation, or credit risk assessment. Just as with investment in other assets (think real estate, homes, cars, other business or personal assets), the holder of a financial asset also implicitly makes decisions about the amount and types of resources to allocate to understanding, preserving and even enhancing the asset's continued utility.

The importance of investor decision-making around understanding, preserving and enhancing asset value is especially the case when buy/sell is off the table (as is the case with index strategies, universal owners or illiquid assets). Of course, investors are not all the same. Just as how they go about determining valuations and making buy, sell and hold decisions (and the factual considerations and analysis behind them) varies depending on their strategies, investment beliefs and resources, so too do decisions around stewardship vary.

Placing stewardship firmly in an asset owner's or asset manager's definition of investment decision-making is more than just a semantic exercise. It locates the real responsibility for stewardship where it belongs—with those who are responsible for the asset's performance in the portfolio. Explicitly including stewardship decisions within the investor's definition of investment decision-making makes chief investment officers (CIOs), investment committees and portfolio managers accountable for the quality of stewardship planning and execution and aligns their incentives with stewardship's objectives.

Motivations

Institutional investors are a heterogeneous lot. Every asset owner's and asset manager's mix of skills and experiences, as well as the personal peculiarities of its leadership and staff, is unique. The motivations for incorporating ESG analysis into investment decision-making and implementing stewardship likewise vary, often dramatically, from institution to institution. What all this means is that there are almost as many approaches to implementing stewardship as there are institutional investors themselves. What is important for each investor is to craft a dynamic approach to stewardship that is consistent with its overall investment philosophy, decision-making processes and institutional capacity.

An Investor Responsibility Research Center (IRRC) and Sustainalytics 2017 publication lays out a useful typology of the motivations that drive investors to incorporate consideration of ESG issues into the investment process.[1] The six types of ESG investor identified in the publication and included in Table 5.1 are not intended to be mutually exclusive. Combinations are possible. In fact, there are probably few investors that fall neatly and exclusively into one category alone. Aspects of the six types recognised in the IRRC publication can be found in investment firms across different asset classes and investment objectives. Finally, there is probably no natural progression from one type to another.

TABLE 5.1 Six types of ESG investor

Type	Description
The Believer	ESG integration is clearly structured and consistent throughout the organisation
The Cautionary	Considers ESG factors to improve risk management focus on company-specific research rather than broad ESG trends
The Statistician	Uses statistical analysis to uncover correlations between historical ESG performance and historical financial performance to identify material ESG factors that are likely to generate alpha
The Discretionary	Considers ESG factors as a supplement to traditional financial analysis usually with a focus on idiosyncratic risk management
The Transition-focused	ESG factors are central research inputs. Concentrates on risks and opportunities associated with broad ESG-related economic shifts
The Fundamentalist	Integrates ESG thoroughly by considering both company-specific ESG factors as well as macro ESG trends

Source: *How Investors Integrate ESG: A Typology of Approaches*, 2017, IRRC Institute and Sustainalytics.

Understanding and articulating the motivations for integrating ESG into its investment process is an essential first step for an institutional investor to tailor a stewardship approach and a methodology that are likely to be effective over time. To have any value, an institutional investor's expressed motivations for ESG integration and stewardship must be consistent with, and hopefully reinforce, its overall value proposition, key market differentiators and competitive strengths.

For example, the stewardship approach of a fund manager with a strong focus on quantitative analysis will probably be more effective if its ESG analysis leverages the firm's technology for identifying correlations between company performance and material ESG indicators. Likewise, the success of the stewardship activities of an investor with a strong industry focus is likely to be greater when these efforts are built around the deep sectoral expertise of the firm's professionals. A clear statement of the investment firm's fundamental rationale for ESG integration provides its leadership and its staff (as well as its clients) with a touchstone for judging the consistency of stewardship policies and practices with the firm's ultimate objectives.

2. TAILORING AN ESG METHODOLOGY TO AN INVESTOR'S MOTIVATION

Any methodology for consideration of factors in a decision-making process is comprised of processes and practices that tie together inputs, analytical tools and outputs (analysis, actions) in a rational manner. The design and adaptation of an effective methodology require the leadership of an organisation to take careful account of the quality of available inputs, the nature of existing processes, and the strengths and limitations of internal and external resources. In the context of considering ESG factors in its overall investment process, an institutional investor should accordingly ensure that any methodology it adopts:

- Is consistent with the investor's motivations for ESG integration.
- Fits as seamlessly as possible within the overall investment process.
- Clearly assigns ownership and accountability within the investment team.
- Makes efficient use of resources (internal and external).
- Carries over and contributes to the effectiveness of monitoring, engagement, voting and reporting (discussed in Chapter 6).
- Is adaptable to new sources of information, learning and institutional experience.

Basic taxonomy of implementation methods

One useful way to help us think about the variety of approaches to ESG integration and stewardship is to organise them across a spectrum from least- to most-intensive focus on ESG risks and opportunities. The Sonen Impact Investing Spectrum© in Figure 5.2 presents a framework for some of the principal approaches and their key similarities and differences. The five most commonly cited ways of incorporating consideration of ESG factors into investment strategies and processes are: negative screening/exclusion, positive screening, ESG integration, thematic investing and impact investing. It is common to see these terms used in prospectuses and offering memoranda for products offered by investment managers. Just like the types of ESG investors discussed at the beginning of this chapter, these approaches are probably not mutually exclusive. Combinations are possible. But, unlike IRRC's and Sustainalytics' typology of ESG investors, there probably are some natural patterns of progression as stewardship gradually becomes more systematically integrated into an investor's decision processes, at least among the first four approaches (ie excluding impact investing).

FIGURE 5.2 Sonen Impact Investing Spectrum©

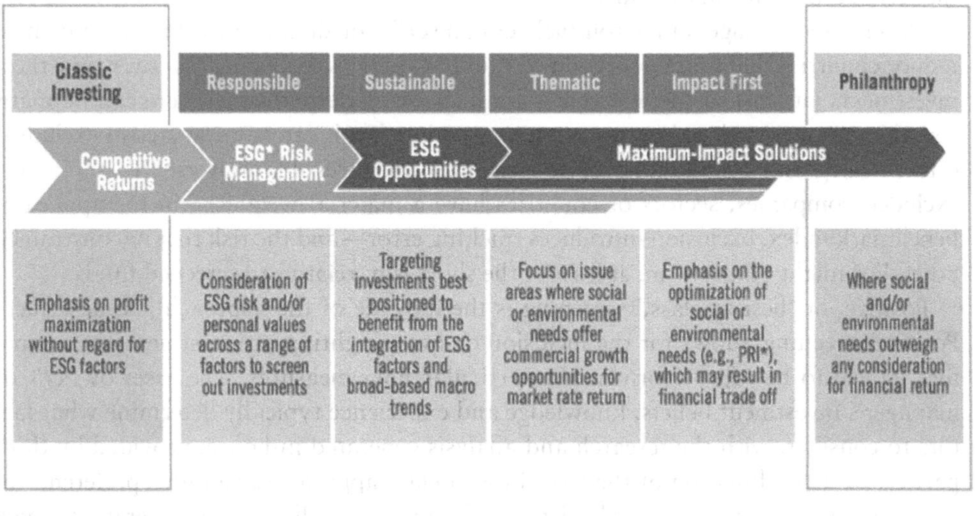

Source: Sonen Capital

Screening

The first two tactics, negative and positive screening, are the simplest to describe and perhaps can now be referred to as 'traditional' ESG integration approaches. Negative screening involves an investor limiting its exposure to, or entirely excluding from consideration, certain companies or categories of companies, sectors or markets because they are judged incompatible with the investor's mission or investment beliefs and/or are otherwise deemed unacceptable or controversial.

Most asset managers who invest monies for public pension funds practice some form of negative screening or exclusion. Exclusion of certain classes of assets or particular companies can be driven by legal mandates, requirements imposed by beneficiaries or the investor's own best judgement in exercise of its fiduciary duties.[2] The movement for divestment of university endowments and public pension funds from apartheid South Africa, which began in the 1970s, was one of the first highly visible examples of negative screening.

Some national and sub-national pension funds have for decades excluded companies in the tobacco industry from their portfolios[3] or provided their beneficiaries the option of investing in funds that exclude tobacco. Similarly, asset owners may also require managers to exclude investments in companies that produce certain types of weapons (such as cluster munitions) or in sectors and countries that have poor human rights, environmental and/or bribery and corruption records.[4] More recently, high-profile asset owners, including the California State Teachers' Retirement System (CalSTRS), have mandated that their managers exclude investment in companies with material thermal coal operations from their investible universe.[5] In a similar vein, the Cambridge University Endowment Fund has published a case study of its internal debate on whether or not to divest from—or engage with—fossil fuel companies.[6]

Of course, asset managers may apply screens on a voluntary basis as an integral part of executing their investment thesis. For example, governance-focused investors may by policy limit or completely exclude investments in companies that issue non-voting shares, in the conviction that these misalign incentives and reduce accountability of management, leaving such companies unlikely to be operated in the long-term best interests of minority shareholders.

Other asset managers may routinely circumscribe or discard investments in companies or countries that score poorly on certain ESG indices, believing that over time these investments (at least in the aggregate) are likely to underperform. There can be many sound investment rationales for negative screening, but it can come at a cost: excluding certain categories or specific securities reduces the investible universe. To the extent excluded companies, sectors or countries have a material weighting in the applicable benchmark index, exclusion introduces tracking error—and the risk that unconstrained portfolios might outperform, at least in the short run, relative to screened funds.

Positive, or 'best-in-class,' screening is the flip side of the approach just described. Positive screening allows for the inclusion or overweighting of investments in companies judged to be top performers on particular ESG measures. The asset owner's or manager's investment beliefs, knowledge and experience typically determine what factors to consider, with the research and analysis generated in-house, provided by third parties, or a combination of the two. Best-in-class approaches can give preference to companies that are regarded as leaders in addressing specific ESG considerations, such as climate change risk, based on the theory that they will be best placed to exploit the business opportunities of CO_2 emission mitigation and remain competitive and profitable in the long term. Just as in the case of negative screening, positive screening can introduce tracking risk. To the extent that positive screens rely on external ESG information providers or raters, they can skew a portfolio to large caps, as smaller companies are less covered (especially in emerging markets) and may be systematically under-scored. The availability of ESG data and the quality of ESG scores are correlated with disclosure—larger companies tend to have better disclosure because they have more resources to allocate to ESG reporting.

ESG integration

Full ESG integration can be described as the hard-wiring of the assessment of ESG factors throughout the investment and portfolio management process. ESG-integrating investors consider every company's performance along with material ESG dimensions and financial metrics when making investment decisions. Portfolio management can include the investor engaging with the company with the goal of improving its ESG performance, aiming ultimately to contribute to its long-term sustainable profitability and investor returns. Conceived in this fashion, ESG integration is therefore a long-term strategy to manage downside risk and/or exploit competitive advantages of sustainable enterprises.

Full ESG integration is challenging. It generally requires considerably more resources than negative or positive screening. Determining the weight that specific ESG factors should carry in investment decisions is an art rather than a science. It can be difficult to explain to clients and potential clients, with precision, how its application affects portfolio construction, investee company behaviour and, ultimately, performance. Finally, ESG integration may expose an investor to reputational risks should it prove to have misestimated a portfolio company's prospective ESG performance.

Thematic investing

An investor's conviction (supported by its experience and expertise) in one or more sustainability themes can also serve as the cornerstone of its approach to the incorporation of ESG factors into investment decision-making and stewardship. Thematic ESG investors target companies and sectors that have the potential to capitalise on emerging environmental and/or social developments and opportunities. Examples of thematic ESG approaches include investing in companies or sectors in clean energy, sustainable agriculture, water conservation, education, health care, access to finance (fintech) or other sectors that support the SDGs. However, it is worth underlining that, while the success of such companies may well promote positive environmental and/or social outcomes, unless trading off benefits to third parties is explicitly part of its investment mandate from beneficiaries, the asset manager's fiduciary obligation and investment goal still remain to maximise risk-adjusted returns and sustainable value creation for beneficiaries.

There are often very significant challenges to thematic ESG investing. Predicting global environmental and social mega-trends is a risky endeavour. Thematic investors must allocate significant financial and personnel resources to keeping up with the science and social developments that link to ESG factors. Companies that focus on addressing emerging environmental and social needs are very often early-stage enterprises with untested technologies and limited track records. There may be few listed companies in the space to provide reference points for valuations. Certain environmental and social themes may come into fashion in ways that approximate fads, subjecting companies in attendant sectors to bubbles and busts, with investors suffering high volatility. For example, the prices of shares of companies involved in emerging energy technologies have proven highly volatile in recent years.[7]

Impact investing

Impact or 'double bottom line' investors seek in the first instance for their investments to achieve defined, positive environmental or societal outcomes. They invest in companies with the express goal of creating a measurable positive environmental and/or social impact, while realising some level of financial return. The sectors that impact investors focus on can be similar to those that interest thematic ESG investors. Impact investor clients are often mission-driven entities, such as foundations and certain family offices. European impact investment managers such as responsAbility and Triodos have long attracted a significant number of retail investors.

FIGURE 5.3 Operating principles for impact management endorsed in 2019 by a set of public and private sector institutional investors and since then signed on to by more than 150 others

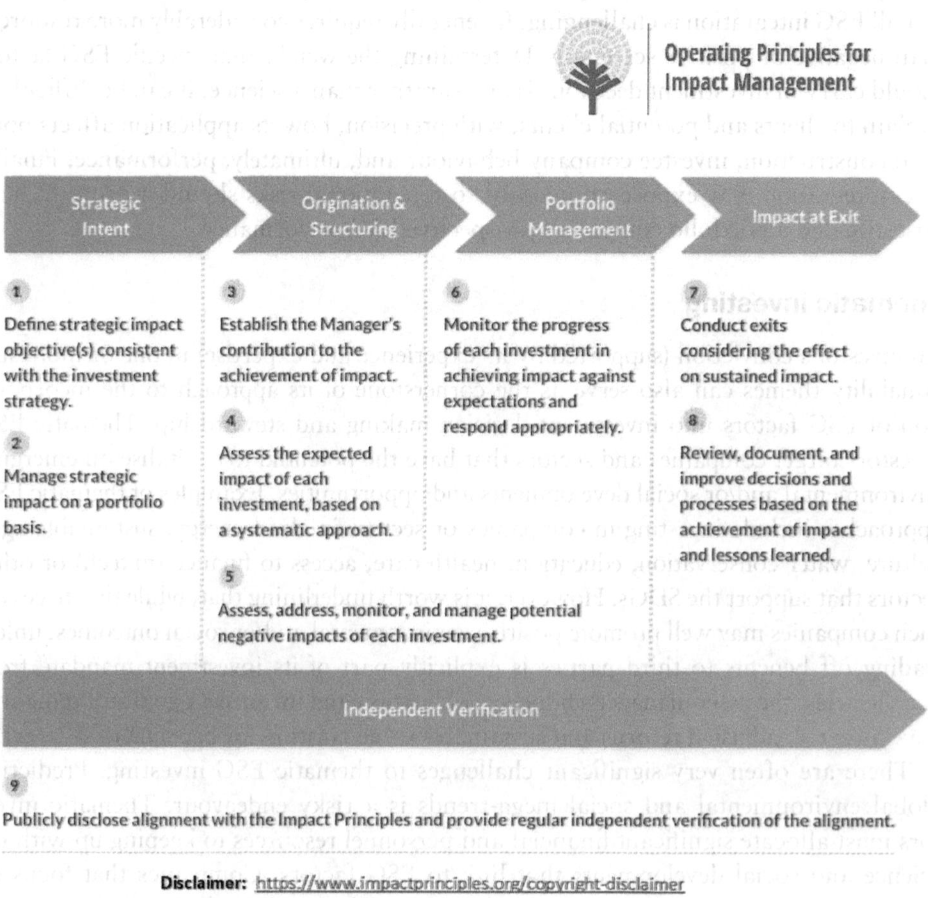

Source: *Operating Principles for Impact Management*, 2019

More recently, more mainstream European, North American and global fund managers have tapped into the growing segment of their clients (particularly Millennials) who want their savings to achieve more than simply financial returns. Moreover, new types of company structures have emerged to make it easier for companies to blend social and financial objectives in ways that are potentially attractive to impact investors. Legislation in some US states, in the UK and in many other jurisdictions now permit the establishment of benefit corporations—sometimes known as 'B Corps.'. The charters of B Corps explicitly empower directors and managers to balance profits for shareholders against positive social outcomes.[8]

Defining 'impact investment' is a work in progress. A central challenge is how to articulate the expected impact *ex ante* and measure it *ex post*. The *Operating Principles for Impact Management* have made an important contribution by stressing the importance of clarity of strategic intent, identification of sensible metrics, continuous monitoring and independent assurance in impact investing.[9]

In essence, efforts such as the *Operating Principles for Impact Management*, illustrated in Figure 5.3, seek to provide asset owners and beneficiaries with a framework for understanding the objectives, metrics and oversight of the impact of their investments that is as robust as the framework around financial return. Their goal is a clear and common understanding about an investment's non-financial goals, the strategy for achieving them, the risks and trade-offs that may be involved, and how such impacts will be measured, assured (audited) and reported. Although progress in all these dimensions has greatly accelerated in recent years, impact investment is still playing catch-up with the much longer-established framework for defining, measuring and reporting financial objectives, risks and results.[10]

3. ANALYTICAL TOOLS: MAKING SENSE OF THE DATA/GUIDING THE PROCESS

A methodology for translating data into decisions requires establishing a logically consistent and replicable framework for analysis. Analytical tools around ESG serve at least two purposes for institutional investors—they translate data into rational bases for decisions and they provide the groundwork for managing the process of monitoring, engaging, voting and reporting discussed in Chapter 6.

So how can information on a company's sustainability policies, practices and performance actually be applied in the course of company analysis? Most methodologies developed for use by institutional investors incorporate one or more of the following types of analytical tools:

1. Scoring (commercially available or proprietary).
2. Benchmarking (against peers, against third-party standards, against proprietary standards or a combination).
3. Red flags or best practice identification.
4. Progression matrices.

Deciding which type, or combination of types, of ESG analytical tools work best with their strategy and investment process is an iterative process for most investors. As new data sources become available, an investor's views on what ESG factors matter most for its investment universe and investment style will likely evolve. To the extent that sustainability analysis becomes gradually more hard-wired to its overall investment process, the types of analytical tools an investor finds of greatest utility can be expected to change.

Scoring

Scoring tools are straightforward in principle. Data are collected from one or more sources, and some sort of relative weighting is applied to each of the various data indicators to generate an absolute or relative score. A particular score's value for decision-making depends on how well it reflects the actual quality of the underlying environmental, social and/or corporate governance practices it purports to measure. While statistical analysis can help, practical limitations and subjective judgements are unavoidable when deciding what factors are material, what indicators are representative and what relative weight to assign to each indicator.

Data sets are likely to be most complete for items required to be reported in accordance with regulatory requirements, including, in the case of corporate governance indicators, national and international codes of best practice. The graphic in Figure 5.4 illustrates how one analytics company, Aktis Intelligence, organised data along the lines of the Basel Committee's *Corporate Governance Principles for Banks* so that they could be used to generate absolute and relative corporate governance scores for individual banks.

ESG scoring by its nature suffers from contextual limitations. Two companies that generate the same data will receive the same raw score, regardless of whether other, unmeasured or unmeasurable, factors would lead an informed investor to judge one company's ESG practices better than the other's.

The complexities and practical limitations of aggregating ESG indicators to generate an overall ESG score for companies were discussed in Chapter 4. But even a company's score in just of one of the three main pillars (or a particular element within E, S or G), may not

FIGURE 5.4 Scoring tool example

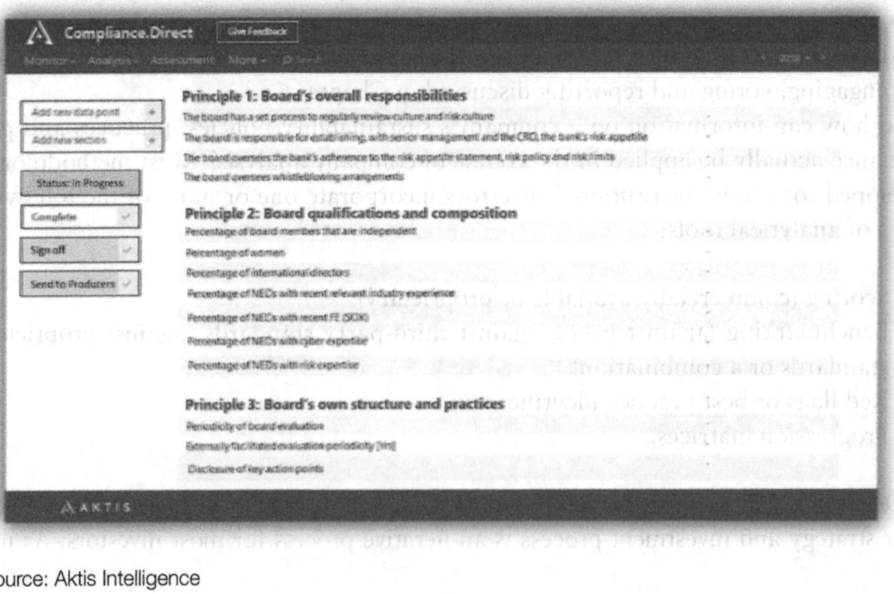

Source: Aktis Intelligence

be indicative of the level of risks presented or how well the company is likely to handle particular challenges that may arise. For example, two companies might receive the same governance score, but with one company scoring higher on shareholder rights and the other scoring higher on board quality. The outcome of a conflict between the interests of controlling and minority shareholders is probably more likely to be positive for minority shareholders of the former company, whereas challenges that require thoughtful adjustments to strategic direction may be better handled by the company with the stronger board.

Investors may rely on commercial providers for the ESG scores they use in investment decision-making. Or they may choose their own indicators and develop their own scoring methodologies using data provided by third parties or collected internally. Hybrid approaches are also possible, with commercial providers increasingly offering their clients the ability to 'tweak' the off-the-shelf scoring methodologies to reflect the client's own judgements about which ESG indicators are most relevant and what weightings are appropriate, given the investor's particular investment universe. In recognition of the interplay between various indicators, sophisticated scoring systems apply conditional weightings to some or all indicators, varying a particular indicator's weighting depending on other ESG characteristics reflected in the company's data.

The quantitative character of ESG ratings allows scores to be applied in a more-or-less mechanical fashion in negative screening, best-in-class and ESG integration strategies. An investor may set minimum criteria that screen out or underweight exposure to poorly scoring companies. An investor with a best-in-class strategy might only invest in companies whose ESG scores are in the higher deciles, or scale maximum exposures based on each company's scoring.

An investor may also directly incorporate ESG scoring into its valuation models. For example, such an investor's valuation models may adjust its estimate of a company's weighted average cost of capital (WACC) based on its relative governance score, if it believes there is evidence that governance risk impacts the cost of equity. Similarly, an investor might revise estimates of future costs of production based on anticipated efficiency gains or losses the company might experience as a result of labour practices.

Benchmarking

Benchmarking tools seek to provide a meaningful indication of how well or poorly a company's policies, practices and/or performance compare with those of peers or relevant standards. Internal or externally generated ESG scores and/or raw data can be used as points of comparison when benchmarking against peers. Benchmarking against standards (eg corporate governance code recommendations, CO_2 emissions targets, adoption of reporting frameworks), by its nature, relies mostly on raw data comparisons.

Construction of peer groups and selection of relevant standards unavoidably inject a degree of subjectivity into any benchmarking exercise. Should the peer group include all companies in the industry, or only those that rely on the same technologies or produce the same range of industry products? Should international peers be included in the set? Against whose set of best practice recommendations should the company's governance practices be measured—the national securities regulator, the local shareholder association or international best practices? Or against the practices of a competitor? In the case study on Volkswagen in Chapter 8, we see in Figure 8.4 an example of how the company benchmarked its ESG performance against its peers in 2014.

TABLE 5.2 Sample benchmarking tool

Name	Country	Mkt cap (US$ millions)	Most recent Bloomberg ESG disclosure score	E score	S score	G score	GRI report
Colgate-Palmolive Co	United States	$60,161	66.12	78.29	38.60	66.07	**Y**
Natura Cosmeticos SA	Brazil	$3,509	57.85	57.36	63.16	53.57	**Y**
L'Oreal	France	$103,153	57.44	53.49	59.65	64.29	**Y**
Fancl Corp	Japan	$971	52.48	54.26	54.39	46.43	**N**
Kao Corp	Japan	$23,635	49.17	42.64	56.14	57.14	**Y**
Unilever NV	United Kingdom	$125,339	42.15	35.66	38.60	60.71	**N**
Pola Orbis Holdings Inc	Japan	$5,163	40.08	34.11	36.84	57.14	**Y**
Procter & Gamble Co	United States	$222,695	39.67	39.53	22.81	60.71	**Y**
Mandom Group	Japan	$1,084	35.12	26.36	38.60	57.14	**Y**
Estee Lauder Companies	United States	$29,139	34.30	27.13	28.07	57.14	**Y**
Godrej Consumer Products Ltd	India	$7,697	26.45	9.30	43.86	48.21	**N**
Marico Ltd	India	$4,828	25.62	11.63	35.09	48.21	**N**
Dabur India Ltd	India	$7,160	25.21	13.95	28.07	48.21	**N**
Average			42.43	37.21	41.84	55.08	
Median			40.08	35.66	38.60	57.14	

Policies, certificates or standard	Marico Ltd	Dabur India Ltd	Colgate Palmolive Co	Mandom Corp	Natura Cosmeticos Sa	Fancl Corp	Pola Orbis Holdings Ltd	L'Oreal	Procter & Gamble Co/The	Unilever Nv-Cva	Godrej Consumer Products Ltd	Kao Corp	Estee Lauder Companies Cl A
Human rights policy	**N**	**Y**	**Y**	**Y**	**Y**	**Y**	**N**	**Y**	**Y**	**Y**	**Y**	**Y**	**Y**
Health & safety policy	**Y**	**Y**	**Y**	**Y**	**Y**	**Y**	**Y**	**Y**	**Y**	**Y**	**Y**	**Y**	**Y**
Supply chain/sourcing policy	**N**	**N**	**Y**	**Y**	**Y**	**Y**	**Y**	**Y**	**Y**	**Y**	**Y**	**Y**	**Y**
Emissions reduction initiatives	**Y**	**Y**	**Y**	**Y**	**Y**	**Y**	**Y**	**Y**	**Y**	**Y**	**N**	**Y**	**Y**
Water policy	**Y**	**Y**	**Y**	**Y**	**Y**	**N**	**N**	**Y**	**Y**	**Y**	**N**	**Y**	**Y**
Energy efficiency policy	**Y**	**Y**	**Y**	**Y**	**Y**	**Y**	**Y**	**Y**	**Y**	**Y**	**Y**	**Y**	**Y**
Environmental supply chain policy	**N**	**N**	**Y**	**Y**	**Y**	**Y**	**Y**	**Y**	**Y**	**Y**	**Y**	**Y**	**Y**
Sustainable packaging	**N**	**Y**	**Y**	**Y**	**Y**	**Y**	**Y**	**Y**	**Y**	**Y**	**N**	**Y**	**Y**
UN Global Compact	**N**	**N**	**N**	**Y**	**Y**	**Y**	**N**	**Y**	**N**	**Y**	**N**	**Y**	**N**
CDP questionnaire responder	**N**	**N**	**Y**	**Y**	**Y**	**N**	**N**	**Y**	**Y**	**Y**	**Y**	**Y**	**Y**

Despite its inherent subjectivity, benchmarking is undeniably a valuable tool. Benchmarking can help identify priorities for due diligence by highlighting sustainability topics where the company seems either to be leading or lagging. Company executives are almost always obsessed with what their competitors are doing; identifying for them where a company's ESG efforts appear to differ from those of its competitors can be an effective point of departure for a broader conversation with management around a company's approach to sustainability. Similarly, benchmarking exercises, such as the example provided in Table 5.2, can make an important contribution to the course of investor-company engagement. They demonstrate the investor's understanding of other companies' sustainability policies, practices and performance, highlight the practical possibilities for improvement and establish with specificity investor expectations.

Red flags or best practice identification

Benchmarking is similarly useful for identifying outliers and companies with characteristics that the investor has identified as especially problematic (red flags) or associated with good performance (best practices). Aktis Intelligence generated the graphic in Figure 5.5 by sifting through the governance data of banks to identify governance characteristics that its clients deemed problematic (red flags), of potential concern and requiring further investigation (yellow flags) and best practices (green flags). Red flag tools are typically employed in the early stages of an investment process to weed out companies whose ESG characteristics make them unlikely candidates for investment and thereby to channel investment analysis resources (especially human resources) towards more promising prospects. In this context, red flags may act as a sort of 'gatekeeper.'

FIGURE 5.5 Example red flags tool

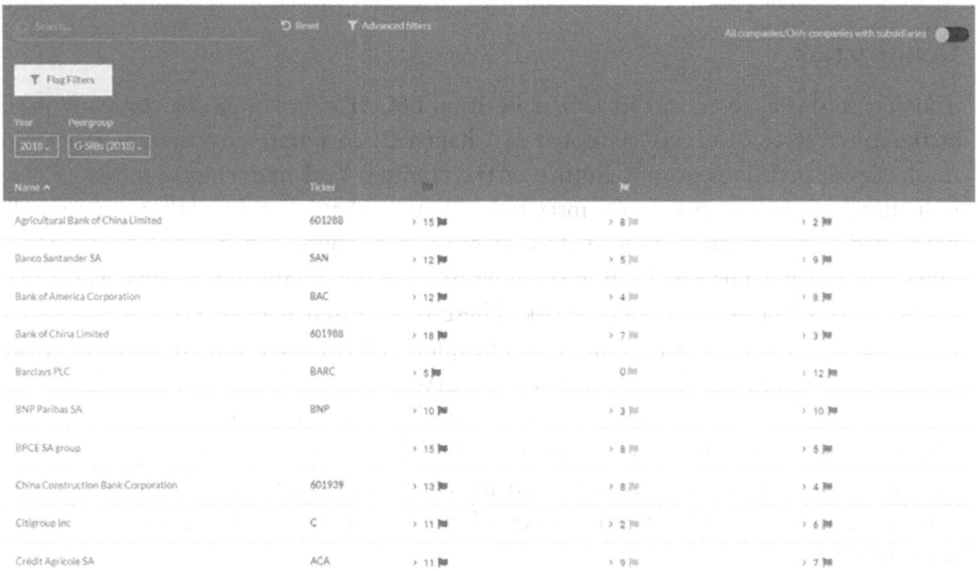

Source: Aktis Intelligence

Progression matrices

The International Finance Corporation (IFC) introduced the progression matrix as the centrepiece of its methodology for analysing the corporate governance of investee companies in the early 2000s.[11] Since then, this approach has been adopted by most other development finance institutions.[12] Similar tools have also been employed by managers of private equity and concentrated public equity portfolios. Analysts locate a target company's current policies and practices (be they corporate governance, environmental or social) with reference to a tabular display of typical policies and practices ordered from the most basic (or non-existent) to best practices. Since 2018, the set of IFC's progression matrices (one for each of six different kinds of companies—listed, family-owned or founder-owned, financial institutions, state-owned enterprises, funds, and small and medium-sized enterprises) integrates environmental and social issues consistent with the IFC's *Policy on Environmental and Social Sustainability*.[13]

The progression matrix approach is of particular utility to investors, such as development finance institutions, other impact investors and active ownership fund managers, who seek improvements in the ESG performance of investee companies, either because such improvements are part of their mission or because they believe such improvements will contribute to investment returns. Identifying where a company's ESG performance practices fit along the various dimensions included in the matrix focuses internal and external discussion around the next typical steps for improvements. Instead of an aggregate score, a progression matrix generates a sort of frontier line that shows where practices are relatively stronger or weaker (progressively stronger practices typically running from left to right). Progression matrices can also serve as particularly valuable tools for internal discussions, during both the pre-investment and post-investment stages, by facilitating quick reference to particular topics or practices that team members may believe deserve particular attention.

Country risk

Thus far in this chapter, our focus has been on ESG risk factors in the company itself, at the micro level. However, as noted in Chapter 2, corporate governance, aspects of the business environment and culture at the country level importantly influence how individual companies operate. Country risk is a factor that investors with internationally diversified portfolios are accustomed to assessing. But country risk has traditionally been looked at somewhat narrowly, in the context of economic/financial risk (such as through a sovereign credit rating) or political risk. These are certainly relevant considerations that can affect a country's access to and cost of capital and can have similar spillover effects to individual companies domiciled in the country—the so-called 'sovereign ceiling.'

In addition to the traditional economic and political dimensions, it is also possible to compare countries in an ESG context. There exist a number of indicators in the public domain or from commercial providers that distinguish ESG risks across countries, and it is relatively easy to develop basic country ESG scoring tools from such indicators.

Table 5.3 is an illustrative example of a country ESG index of indicators compiled in October 2020. It examines 16 prominent countries, in developed and emerging

FIGURE 5.6 Sample progression matrix

Basic Practices: Understanding the need to professionalize the Company	**Intermediate Practices:** Steps Toward Best Practices	**Good International Practices:** Implementation of Good Practices	**Leadership**
A. Commitment to Corporate Governance			
1. The basic formalitiesof corporate governance are in place including: a. Board of directors b. Annual shareholders' meeting c. Shareholders and shareowners identified and recorded	1. Written policies established addressing key elements in family-firm governance a. Succession planning b. family-member share ownership and family-member employment 2. Board memberor high-level company executive charged with improving corporate governance practices	1. Corporate governance policycovers the role of board vis-a-vismanagement 2. The company has a written Code of Ethics, approved by the board that is included in employee onboarding/training	1. Company fully complies or explains any deviations from all appliable provisions of voluntary code of best practices of the country 2. Written policiesthat address, at a minimum, compliance with E&Slaw and regulation
B. Structure and Functioning of the board of directors			
1. Board of directors established and meets periodically	1. Board meetings held according to a regular schedule, agenda prepared in advance, minutes prepared and approved 2. Non-family members appointed to the Boardand core competency (skill mix) review of board conducted 3. Advisory board of independent professionals established and consulted on a regular basis	1. Board members meet quarterly andis charged with approving strategy and objectively overseeing management 2. Board composition (competencies/skillmix) adequate to oversight duties 3. Audit committee of management and owners nominated tothe board 4. Directors independentof management and owners nominated to the board 5. Annual evaluation conducted 6. Period board training conducted	1. Role of chair and CEOseparate 2. Audit committee membership 100% independent 3. Specialized committees address special topics, as needed (eg nominations, compensation, technology/ cybersecurity, ESG/ sustainability, risk management, etc) 4. Formal performance evaluation of management conducted annually 5. Board ensures that management systems in place to identify andmanage E&S risks andimpacts 6. Board trained on industry E&S risk issues, which are a periodic agenda item

Source: International Finance Corporation

TABLE 5.3 Comparing ESG risks and financial risks at the country level

Country	ESG composite score	Rule of law	Corruption	Regulatory quality	Yale Environmental Protection Index	Human Development Index	Freedom House Index	S&P Sovereign Credit rating	
		2019	2019	2019	2019	2019	2020	2020 Q3	
Australia	86.69	93.27	77.00	98.56	74.9	93.8	82.6	AAA	Australia
United Kingdom	85.78	91.35	77.00	93.75	81.3	92	79.3	AAA	Canada
Germany	85.51	92.31	80.00	96.15	77.2	93.9	73.5	AAA	Germany
Canada	84.80	94.71	77.00	95.67	71	92.2	78.2	AA+	United States
Japan	81.96	90.38	73.00	88.46	75.1	91.5	73.3	AA	France
United States	80.96	89.90	69.00	88.94	69.3	92	76.6	AA	Korea Rep.
France	79.63	89.42	69.00	90.87	80	82.5	66	AA	United Kingdom
Korea, Rep.	76.39	86.06	59.00	82.21	66.5	90.6	74	A+	China
Spain	76.15	82.69	62.00	81.73	74.3	89.3	66.9	A+	Japan
Italy	69.09	61.54	53.00	76.92	71	88.3	63.8	A	Spain
South Africa	54.82	50.96	44.00	61.54	43.1	70.5	58.8	BBB	Italy
Turkey	54.35	44.71	39.00	54.81	42.6	80.6	64.4	BBB-	India
Brazil	51.95	47.60	35.00	48.08	51.2	76.1	53.7	BBB-	Russian Federation
China	50.26	45.19	41.00	42.79	37.3	75.8	59.5	BB-	Brazil
India	48.46	52.40	41.00	48.56	27.6	64.7	56.5	BB-	South Africa
Russian Federation	47.16	25.00	28.00	36.06	50.5	82.4	61	B+	Turkey

Notes: Data collected as of October 2020.

Rule of Law: World Bank governance indicator. Perceptions of the extent to which agents have confidence in and abide by the rules of society, and in particular the quality of contract enforcement, property rights, the police and the courts, as well as the likelihood of crime and violence.

TI Corruption Index: the Transparency International Corruption Perceptions Index ranks 180 countries and territories by their perceived levels of public sector corruption, according to experts and business people.

Regulatory Quality: World Bank governance indicator. Regulatory Quality captures perceptions of the ability of the government to formulate and implement sound policies and regulations that permit and promote private-sector development.

Environmental Performance Index: the Yale Environmental Protection Index (EPI) provides a data-driven summary of the state of sustainability around the world. Using 32 performance indicators across 11 issue categories, the EPI ranks 180 countries on environmental health and ecosystem vitality.

Heritage Foundation Index of Economic Freedom: the Heritage Foundation's Index of Economic Freedom presents the state of human freedom in the world based on a broad measure that encompasses personal, civil and economic freedom.

Human Development Index: the UNDP's Human Development Index is a summary measure of average achievement in key dimensions of human development: living a long and healthy life, being knowledgeable and having a decent standard of living.

Credit rating: Standard & Poor's sovereign ratings are opinions about credit risk, reflecting financial strength and management at the country level. They can express a forward-looking opinion about the capacity and willingness of an entity to meet its financial commitments as they come due. The credit ratings used in the table are S&P's foreign currency credit ratings.

markets, along a range of diverse indicators, each of which has been normalised on a 100-point scale:

- *Governance*:
  - Corruption: Transparency International Corruption Perception Index.[14]
  - Rule of Law: World Bank Rule of Law Indicator.[15]
  - Regulatory Quality: World Bank Regulatory Indicator.[16]
- *Environmental*:
  - Environmental quality: Yale University Environmental Protection Index.[17]
- *Social*:
  - Index of Economic Freedom, the Heritage Foundation.[18]
  - United Nations Development Program's Human Development Index.[19]

All the indicators in this example are carefully constructed and compiled by credible researchers. Yet, however appealing it may be to have these broad concepts quantified into a single number, it must be recognised that metrics of this nature are very ambitious, and inevitably subjective to some degree. They should be taken with a grain or two of salt.

There is also the question of which variables to choose and how these are weighted to arrive at a composite score, or whether an ESG composite score is likely to be a meaningful input for investment decision-making. This illustrative model features five indicators—three 'Gs', one 'E' and one 'S.' It also weights each of the factors individually, so that, in this case, the governance dimensions strongly influence the overall composite score.

Country ESG risk tools of this nature can include ESG indicators different from those used in this example, resulting in different scores and relative rankings. There are other respected indices and indicators, in the public domain or commercially available, that investors could choose from if they wish to focus on different issues/topics. For example, one could add to this stew the World Bank's 'Gini coefficient,' which is a measure of income inequality.[20] That would mean our illustrative index was more influenced by 'S' factors.

So, while bearing in mind the subjectivity in these indicators and the subjective allocation of equal weighting across these five factors, the results of this crude index for the most part seem to make intuitive sense. It is interesting to note that there is a broad correlation between these individual ESG indicators by country, and that developed countries score more highly than emerging or frontier economies.

Tools like this can serve to heighten investor awareness of ESG risks at the macro (country) level, similar to 'red flags' for individual companies. Scores of this nature (aggregated or by pillar) could be applied to adjust capital cost modelling in valuation—and potentially asset allocation across countries. They can also affect portfolio construction. For example, the asset manager BlackRock announced in October 2020 a sovereign bond Exchange Traded Fund (ETF); among other countries, German sovereign bonds were underweighted, given the country's relative reliance on coal as an energy source.[21]

In Table 5.3, we have added on the right a separate comparison—a sovereign credit rating from Standard & Poor's. A sovereign credit rating is an assessment of the overall level of financial risk at the country level and an indicator of the country's financial management; it is not focused on ESG factors per se, unless specific ESG factors might be regarded as material in the country's own credit assessment. Here too, we see a broad correlation of credit ratings and ESG factors. But there are some differences.

For example, Russia, India and China rank in the bottom three of this 16-country group in terms of their composite ESG scores. But their investment grade credit ratings are higher than other emerging market countries, particularly in the case of AA-rated China, largely reflecting stronger external financial positions. An interesting comparison is Japan, whose A+ credit rating is one notch lower than China's, and yet its ESG profile is much higher. This is the type of mismatch that an ESG-focused sovereign bond investor might consider in the context of assessing the relative value of Chinese and Japanese sovereign bonds.

4. PUTTING THE PIECES TOGETHER: ESG INPUTS, ANALYTICAL TOOLS AND OUTPUTS

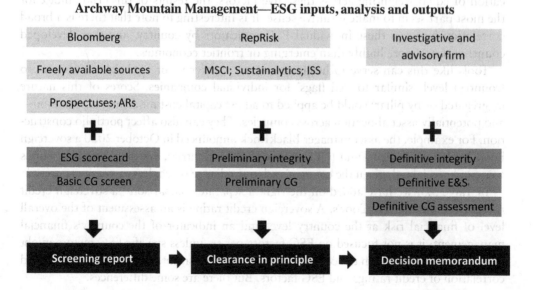

It is dangerous to describe any investment process as 'typical.' This reason alone accounts for why a book like this can only begin to introduce some of the practical issues involved in incorporating ESG and stewardship into how investors actually think about and make investment decisions. But it is probably safe to say that three-stage investment processes are common, at least in the actively managed equity space, and therefore can serve as a useful starting point for illustrating the 'pre-investment' stage of the decision-making process. The graphic in Figure 5.7 lays out the external inputs, the analytical tools and the decision-making outputs of a fictional, but hopefully illustrative, asset manager—Archway Mountain Management—that runs reasonably diversified and actively managed portfolios of listed equity securities for a set of pension fund investors and other asset owners. For simplicity, we use a single market example, which does not address the country risk considerations that were discussed earlier. It illustrates the sorts of informational and analytical inputs around ESG factors that might be integrated into a three-stage investment process.

FIGURE 5.7 Sample ESG methodology diagram

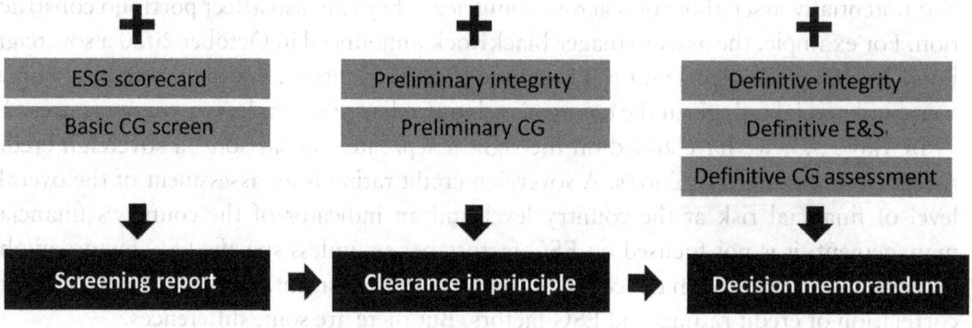

Archway Mountain's investment process can be described as organised around three sub-processes or stages, each of which is intended to arrive at a better-informed level of understanding of the proposed investment and a greater level of conviction (for or against) around investing in the subject security. The actual decision-maker at each stage may be an individual portfolio manager or some sort of investment committee (which may include stewardship or ESG professionals).

Each stage in such a process involves a number of financial and non-financial informational and analytical inputs. Only ESG inputs are included in the graphic—financial information and analytics might, of course, include historical performance data projections, market and competition data and analysis, and business and valuation models (including relative value models for creditors). The end product of each stage of the investment process is a document that summarises the results of such analysis—in our illustration, a 'screening report,' a 'clearance in principle' report and a final 'decision memorandum.' Each of these also records the determination by the decision-maker (again, a portfolio manager or some sort of investment committee) as to whether or not to advance to the next stage. In the case of a final 'decision memorandum,' this would include the fundamental drivers for the investment decision (including valuation), along with expected performance, exposure limits and, importantly, considerations for monitoring and other actions for preserving and enhancing the value of the investment once it becomes part of the portfolio (including stewardship activities).

Every enterprise has limited resources. Asset owners and asset managers are no exception. Designing an investment process that explicitly takes into account ESG factors requires some tough decisions about what informational and analytical resources to devote to each stage of the investment process. As discussed in Chapter 3, a particular institutional investor's motivation for ESG integration and its considered approach to stewardship ultimately drive the purposes for which ESG information and analysis are considered in the investment process. Whatever the approach, to ensure efficiency and effectiveness, institutional investors need to consider exogenous and endogenous factors when determining what ESG inputs and what sorts of analysis of such inputs are likely to achieve its goals in each stage of the investment process.

Exogenous factors

- What ESG information sources for the asset class are available and at what cost?
- How accurate and comparable are such information sources?
- How consistent are the underlying assumptions and philosophy of particular external analytics (such as ratings and scorings) with the firm's own investment beliefs?
- How important are particular sources to other investors?

Endogenous factors

- How much and what types of ESG information can be practically absorbed by the investment team and decision-makers at each stage of the process?
- How much can and should the firm rely on outside expert advice, and how much and what kind of expertise should it develop in-house?
- What synergies can the firm generate for the collection and analysis of ESG and non-ESG data and analysis?

Like most strategic decisions, the decisions derived from the answers to these questions need to be consistent with the investor's investment style, risk appetite, investment beliefs and human and other resource limitations. Importantly, adapting an asset owner's or manager's investment process to incorporate ESG data and analysis to achieve its investment objectives cannot be a static exercise. Sources of ESG information and analytics are constantly evolving, and new information portals and tools continuously come online. Moreover, the relative importance that investors, markets and others ascribe to various ESG factors will certainly shift over time.

An investor's processes for integrating ESG factors into investment decision-making and stewardship also need to evolve apace with the (hopefully!) growing sophistication of its own personnel. Asset owners and managers can and should expect their analysts and portfolio managers (and those in the industry at large) to develop experience and expertise in areas of ESG analysis that they may currently consider novel. This may require specialised internal or external support. Indeed, institutional investors' professional development and training programmes should anticipate and seek to accelerate this process.

Implicitly or explicitly, ESG specialists often play the role of disseminators of ESG knowledge and expertise within the investment firm. Institutional investors should facilitate the mainstreaming of capacity to absorb and analyse the sorts of ESG information that non-specialist investment analysts can most efficiently assess themselves, allowing specialists to focus on emerging topics, trends and technologies in the field, and to identify ESG data and develop analytical tools that allow investment decisions to make good use of the data.

Inputs

The boxes in Figure 5.7 are intended to illustrate the sorts of ESG information and analysis provided by external sources that an investor like Archway Mountain might take into consideration at each of the stages of a three-stage investment process. As one would expect, these tend to increase in level of sophistication and cost if and when a proposed investment advances through the decision-making process (left to right in the graphic). Again, just for illustration, the initial ESG informational inputs that Archway Mountain relies on are from basic and relatively inexpensive sources: the firm's Bloomberg subscription, perhaps sector and industry E&S information available from NGOs, and ESG information provided in the prospective investee's public disclosures.

An investor like Archway Mountain may consider dozens of investments each year that never advance beyond the first stage of the investment process for one reason or another. It might, as reflected in this illustration, refrain from spending significant financial or even staff resources at this stage, beyond collecting basic data and screening for any ESG red flags. However, should the candidate advance to the clearance in principle stage, paying for the sorts of inputs that external data and analytics companies such as RepRisk, MSCI, Morningstar's Sustainalytics or ISS provide may make more sense.

ESG information can be collected from a variety of sources besides public reporting and data service providers. Specialised investors may rely on their own proprietary databases that draw information from a range of public and non-public networks and sources. And, again just for illustration, once an investment prospect enters the final stage of consideration, an investor like Archway Mountain might hire outside investigative and advisory firms to help it better understand and evaluate the company's ESG challenges and performance.

The inputs included in the Archway Mountain example are by no stretch comprehensive. Clearly, for passive investment strategies, particularly involving large numbers of individual holdings, individual company analysis will be much less substantial, and often minimal at best. Such investors may find it more practical and economically efficient to develop analytical tools that apply across entire markets, sectors and sub-sectors, along with red flag tools, to identify companies that might ultimately be targets for engagement.

Analytical tools

Of course, it is not just the information you collect, but how effectively you understand and analyse it that determines how valuable it is in the decision process. The boxes in the graphic in Figure 5.7, and Table 5.4 provide some examples of analytical tools that an investor might develop internally to make sense of ESG data and contribute to its proper evaluation in the course of the investment process. As in the case of external inputs, the sophistication and cost of applying an investor's ESG analytical tools can be expected to increase as a prospective investment advances through the investment process.

As, in the example, the first stage of the investment process is in the nature of a screening, Archway Mountain employs two main tools to analyse and present the basic data available at that stage: an ESG scorecard; and a basic CG (corporate governance) screen. Such tools would be expected to be as automated as possible, perhaps in the nature of an Excel spreadsheet that provides some basis for comparison of the available ESG data on the investment with a basic peer group and/or against market or country averages.

There is no single way for investors to weight individual ESG variables on company scorecards or other screens. As discussed in Chapter 4, ESG rating providers such as MSCI or Morningstar's Sustainalytics provide holistic company ESG ratings based on their own selection and weighting of company data. But investors can develop proprietary ESG screens themselves. If we think of individual ESG indicators, at least for the

TABLE 5.4 Sample analytical tools

Internal analysis	Description
ESG scorecard	Proprietary weighting of Bloomberg and publicly available information
Basic CG screen	Review of high-level CG structures and practices to identify red flags
Preliminary integrity check	Prepared from news, publicly available information, internal contacts (eg other investors)
Preliminary CG assessment	Completion of CG questionnaire from public sources; identification of key risks and opportunities
Definitive integrity assessment	Includes results of investigative advisory firm reports and communications with all firm contacts with potential knowledge of the target company
Definitive ES assessment	Application of propriety tool to evaluate transparency and reported performance against mandatory and aspirational standards for the industry (SASB, GRI, IIRC); identification of opportunities and entry points for engagement
Definitive CG assessment	Benchmarking against national and international best practices and peers; identification of CG risks; and opportunities and entry points for engagement

moment, as pizza ingredients, investors can 'make their own pizza,' customising their screens by choosing the individual indicators and assigning them proprietary weightings.

The CG screen might likewise serve to benchmark the company's governance practices against local corporate governance code recommendations or the corporate governance criteria that Archway Mountain has decided, based on its own experience, are most important in the classes of companies in which it invests. Again, assuming the case of an active investor that considers and rejects many investments, the analytical tools at the first stage in the process would be characterized by their economy and simplicity and would serve mostly to indicate possible red flags and give decision-makers a general idea of how the company in question might stack up against its peers.

The observant will notice that the analytical tools employed in the clearance in principle stage of Archway Mountain's investment process include a preliminary integrity check and a preliminary CG assessment, but no preliminary E&S assessment. This is to illustrate that different investors might give preference to detailed analysis of some ESG issues at differing stages of the investment process. In this example, the senior management of Archway Mountain may believe that reputation for integrity and corporate governance practices are the most important factors in evaluating investments in the market in which it invests. Or, it may feel the Archway Mountain investment team (including its stewardship professionals) is better equipped professionally to evaluate sponsor integrity[22] and corporate governance risks than it is to assess E&S risks at the clearance in principle stage. In such cases, Archway Mountain might rationally allocate greater internal and external resources at the clearance in principle stage to sponsor integrity and CG analysis than to E&S assessment. An investor in the same market with a different assessment of the importance of particular ESG factors (or different human resources strengths and weaknesses) might prioritise in a different fashion (make the pizza differently), and this would be reflected in the type of analytics it undertakes at distinct stages of its investment process.

Outputs

The content and format of the sorts of reports that serve as the principal outputs of each stage of the investment process vary dramatically from one institutional investor to another. For some investors, the outputs of each stage of the investment process record all the material information and analysis that went into the investment decision to proceed with the prospective investment. In such cases, the reports tend to be long, detailed and organised according to a reasonably rigid and uniform format or electronic template.

Other investors favour more concise records that cite only the most important background on the prospect, the main factors and concerns raised by the team, and the basic rationale for the ultimate decision. Of course, whatever their content and organisation, it is increasingly common for all inputs, tools and outputs to be completed and accessed through an electronic document management platform.

Whatever the outputs of a particular stage look like, the role that consideration of ESG factors played in the decision needs to be recorded in a manner commensurate with the firm's commitment to their inclusion in the investment process. The sustainability portion of an early stage screening report might include little more than a basic

FIGURE 5.8 Sample ESG content of screening report

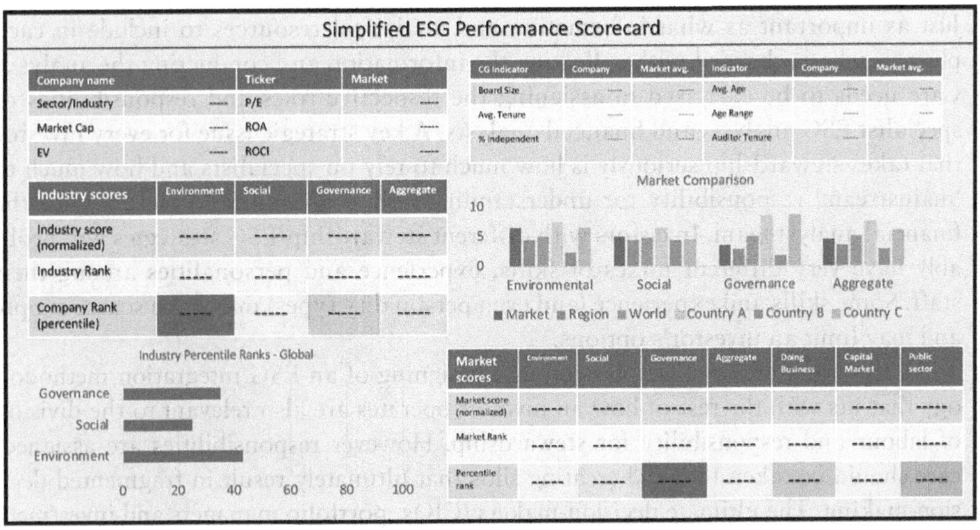

scorecard generated almost exclusively from raw data or scores gathered from ESG data providers, as in Figure 5.8, with a paragraph or two on the more important ESG issues facing companies in the particular industry. Clearance in principle might require a comprehensive identification of the sustainability risks and value drivers identified by the investment team (see Figure 5.9), along with an indication of what additional information would need to be collected and analysed or other conditions met before final decision.

The sustainability content of the definitive decision memorandum would be expected to nail down the team's judgement on how all material ESG factors identified during due diligence should impact valuation, along with an estimate of the amount and type of resources likely to be required to execute stewardship (including, if anticipated, an engagement plan—see Figure 6.4 in Chapter 6).

FIGURE 5.9 Matrix of outputs of an E&S-focused investor

Material issue identified	Risk/ opportunity	Acute/ progressive	Near, medium or long term	Channels of financial impact	Commentary on systems in place and disclosure	Assessment

Who does what?

Just as important as what information and analytical resources to include in each phase is who is charged with collecting the information and conducting the analysis. Care needs to be exercised in assigning the respective roles and responsibilities of specialist ESG analysts and financial analysts. A key strategic issue for every investor that takes stewardship seriously is how much to rely on specialists and how much to 'mainstream' responsibility for understanding and analysing ESG factors with the financial analyst team. Investors with different stewardship/ESG strategies will probably have very different mixes of skills, experience and personalities among their staff. Some skills and experience (and even personality types) may be in scarce supply and may limit an investor's options.

All the usual factors that play into the designing of an ESG integration methodology that fits with the rest of how an investor operates are also relevant to the division of labour and responsibility for stewardship. However responsibilities are assigned, care should be taken to avoid creating silos that ultimately result in fragmented decision-making. The ultimate decision-makers (CIOs, portfolio managers and investment committees) should not become divorced from responsibility for ensuring that the ESG inputs and analysis figure in decisions as contemplated in the firm's strategy and policies.

Keeping up

As emphasised earlier, integrating ESG data and analytics into any investment process is not a 'one and done' exercise. The dynamic nature of the topics it encompasses, along with continuing advances in the availability of information and analytical technology around ESG, requires that investors constantly re-examine their practices to ensure they are fit for purpose. An investor's governance structure and practices should ensure and facilitate the periodic review of how adequately and effectively the firm collects and analyses ESG information in its investment process.

One useful way to structure such self-re-examination is through the periodic completion of a table such as the one provided in Figure 5.10. Mapping the participants, inputs (formal and informal), analytical tools and outputs to each stage of the investment process and evaluating the contribution each makes to the decision-making process can help investment teams think through whether alternative combinations might be more effective.

The strengths and weaknesses of the contributions of the participants (staff and outsiders), inputs, tools and outputs involved in the consideration of ESG factors in the investment process should be assessed along several dimensions:

- *For participants:*
  - *Co-ordination*: is the work of team members on ESG and on more purely financial analysis well co-ordinated? Do ESG specialists and non-specialists share information well? How can duplication of effort be avoided?

FIGURE 5.10 Investment process self-assessment

	Stage 1	Strength/ weaknesses	Stage 2	Strength/ weaknesses	Stage 3	Strength/ weaknesses
Participants						
Formal inputs						
Informal inputs						
Analytical tools						
Outputs						

- *Inclusion*: are the right people in the investment process receiving the information/analysis at the right time? Do they sometimes say 'I wish I had known that earlier, it would have saved a lot of unnecessary effort!'?
- *Access*: do all team members have sufficient access to senior staff to ensure that the analysis they conduct is properly transmitted to and understood by the ultimate decision-makers?

- *For inputs and analytical tools*:
  - *Accuracy*: how confident are you that the information/analysis is correct?
  - *Completeness*: is this all the information/analysis you need for this stage?
  - *Clarity*: is the format of the information/analysis easily understood by the various users?
  - *Efficiency*: is the information/analysis conveyed/considered in a concise manner and at the optimal stage/s in the investment process for it to be actionable?
- *For outputs*:
  - *Proportionality*: consistent with the discussion above, do the outputs reflect the actual application of the firm's approach to ESG incorporation in the process and the weight that ESG factor consideration had in the ultimate decision?

NOTES

1. IRRC Institute and Sustainalytics, *How Investors Integrate ESG: A Typology of Approaches*, April 2017: https:// connect.sustainalytics.com/how-investors-integrate-esg-a-typology-of-approaches
2. For a discussion of some of the challenges of implementing negative screening, see ICGN Viewpoint, *Investment Exclusions: Some Technical Considerations*, February 2018: www.icgn.org/investment-exclusions-some-technical-considerations
3. Responsible Investor, *Tide May Be Turning for Tobacco as CalPERS Reveals Its 2001 Divestment Is Finally Making Money*, 30 November 2020: www.responsible-investor.com/articles/tide-may-be-turning-for-tobacco-as-calpers- reveals-its-2001-divestment-is-finally-making-it-money

4. In 2007, a Dutch current affairs programme, *Zembla*, broadcasted a report revealing that several Dutch pension funds were invested in US companies that manufactured cluster munitions. The programme went on to outline the horrors that cluster munitions inflict on innocent civilians in conflict zones. This had the immediate effect of pressuring investors, in the Netherlands and many other jurisdictions, to systematically exclude cluster munitions manufacturers from investment portfolios. It remains a common exclusion practice globally.
5. California State Teachers' Retirement System, *CalSTRS Takes Action to Divest of All Non-US Thermal Coal Holdings: Action Follows Prior Divestment of US Thermal Coal Holdings*, 17 June 2017, press release: www.calstrs.com/ news-release/calstrs-takes-action-divest-all-non-us-thermal-coal-holdings
6. David Chambers, Elroy Dimson and Ellen Quigley, To Divest or to Engage? A Case Study of Investor Responses to Climate Activism, 2020, *The Journal of Investing*, Special ESG Issue: https://joi.pm-research.com/content/29/2/10. abstract
7. *Financial Times*, Shares of Lithium Producers Rattled by Gloomy Forecast, 26 February 2018: www.ft.com/ content/4faf029a-1ae7-11e8-aaca-4574d7dabfb6
8. Suntae Kim, Matthew J. Karlesky, Christopher G. Myers and Todd Schifeling, Why Companies Are Becoming B Corporations, 12 June 2016, *Harvard Business Review*: https://hbr.org/2016/06/why-companies-are-becoming-b- corporations
9. Operating Principles for Impact Management: www.impactprinciples.org/
10. Investors will need to play a role in revision of impact indicators and metrics as learning progresses. In particular, channels for investors to provide feedback to fund managers (such as limited partnership advisory committees—LPACs) may take on renewed importance in the current stage of evolution of impact investing. Metrics, and even, ultimately, non-financial objectives themselves, may shift over the life of an impact investment fund. What were considered the right indicators or metrics when a fund is established might prove later to be inapt, obsolete or perverse outcomes. LPACs and similar investor fora can serve a validation and legitimation function in such cases of 'moving the goalposts.'
11. Co-author Mike Lubrano served as manager of IFC's Corporate Governance Unit from 2000 to 2007 and oversaw the development of its progression matrix approach to corporate governance analysis.
12. Corporate Governance Development Framework: http://cgdevelopmentframework.com/
13. International Finance Corporation, *Corporate Governance Tools*: www.ifc.org/wps/wcm/connect/topics_ext_ content/ifc_external_corporate_site/ifc+cg/investment+services/corpo rate+governance+tools
14. Transparency International Corruption Perception Index, 2019: www.transparency.org/en/cpi#
15. World Bank, *Worldwide Governance Indicators*, 2019: https://info.worldbank.org/governance/wgi/Home/Reports
16. Ibid.
17. Yale University Environmental Protection Index, 2020: https://epi.yale.edu
18. The Heritage Foundation, *Index of Economic Freedom*: www.heritage.org/index/about
19. United Nations Development Program's Human Development Index: http://hdr.undp.org/en/content/human- development-index-hdi
20. World Bank Gini Index, 2018: https://data.worldbank.org/indicator/SI.POV.GINI
21. Steve Johnson, BlackRock ETF Thrusts Climate Change into Political Sphere, 6 October 2020, *Financial Times*: www.ft.com/content/112e536a-91db-426a-aef6-3106f0717972
22. For these purposes, sponsor integrity has to do with the controlling shareholders' and management's reputation for veracity, compliance with laws and honest business practices, and living up to commitments to business counterparties and stakeholders.

FURTHER READING

OECD, *Integrating ESG Factors in the Investment Decision-Making Process of Institutional Investors*, in *Business and Financial Outlook: Sustainable and Resilient Finance*, 2020: www.oecd.org/daf/oecd-business-and-finance-outlook-26172577.htm

ICGN Viewpoint, *Investment Exclusions: Some Technical Considerations*, February 2018: www.icgn.org/investment-exclusions-some-technical-considerations

IRRC Institute and Sustainalytics, *How Investors Integrate ESG: A Typology of Approaches*, April 2017: http://marketing.sustainalytics.com/acton/attachment/5105/f-0945/1/-/-/-/-/Typology%20of%20ESG%20Integration-Final-Apri2017.pdf?_ga=2.91886428.777715877.1599876269-1091782402.1599876269

Principles for Responsible Investment, *Integrated Analysis: How Investors Are Addressing Environmental, Social and Governance Factors in Fundamental Equity Valuation*, 2013: www.unpri.org/download?ac=312

Chapter 6

Effective stewardship in practice: Monitoring, engaging, voting and reporting

DOI: 10.4324/9781003307082-6

This chapter addresses the practical issues related to the stewardship building blocks of monitoring, engaging, voting (for equity investors) and reporting. In addition to listed equities, we also consider other asset classes—in particular, creditors. An institutional investor's post-investment stewardship activities should not be divorced from its methodology for incorporating ESG factors into its pre-investment due diligence and decision-making process. Rather, an investor's policies and practices around monitoring the ESG performance of companies, engaging with company management on sustainability issues, and share voting should be natural extensions of its comprehensive ESG methodology.

1. STEWARDSHIP, MONITORING AND ENGAGEMENT

As stressed in the previous chapter, investment decision-making encompasses more than just buy/sell/hold calls. Effective stewardship requires that the investment process take into consideration how the investor will measure, monitor and manage the sustainability risks and opportunities of investee companies once they are in the portfolio, and, in the case of an equity investor, how it should exercise its voting rights. A robust ESG methodology also seeks to identify early and often emergent issues that may become the subject of value-adding dialogue between the investor and the company, and what strategies and resources may be required to successfully carry out such engagement.

Of course, every investor's ability to conduct the kinds of stewardship activities discussed in this chapter is limited by at least two factors: foresight and resources. The possible engagement items that an investor identifies during the pre-investment phase of decision-making may be overtaken by events after the company is in the portfolio. Investors can predict what sustainability factors will be most important to a company over time with no greater precision than they can predict its financial performance. This underlines the importance of not just monitoring those sustainability factors identified in the pre-investment phase, but also paying careful attention to newly evident risks and opportunities that may merit further analysis. There will always be surprises—unexpected (at least by the investor) events at a particular company or in particular sectors or industries—that bring into focus previously ignored or underestimated sustainability risks or opportunities.

The principle of economy applies to the activities discussed in this chapter as it applies to everything institutional investors do. Even institutions with the very largest stewardship teams have to spread those teams across aggregate portfolios of companies that can number in the multiple thousands, and so they must have a thoughtful process for focusing stewardship resources on those engagement targets and issues where value can best be added or preserved for client beneficiaries. For an overall programme of monitoring and engagement to be effective, priorities must be set and periodically re-evaluated, with resources marshalled to those activities likely to achieve the greatest ultimate return. This inexact science involves allocating scarce resources among (potentially unlimited) engagement opportunities and crafting engagement strategies and individual interactions with target companies that make use of available internal and external resources and tools in ways that are most likely to achieve desired outcomes.

FIGURE 6.1 GSP 3: monitoring and assessing investee companies

ICGN Global Stewardship Principle 3:
Monitoring and assessing investee companies.

"Investors should exercise diligence in monitoring companies held in investment portfolios and in assessing new companies for investment"

1. Monitor the portfolio, targeting efforts appropriately
2. Apply thoughtful risk analysis across a full range of indicators in the monitoring process
3. Remain conscious of the context of the individual company and apply intelligent judgement
4. Identify priority companies for more detailed focus
5. Have a clear approach to whether and when the investor is willing to become an insider
6. Review monitoring approach, including its effectiveness, periodically

Just as importantly, investors must remain abreast of technological innovations and keep their eyes open for potential new tactics that promise to make their monitoring and engagement activities more efficient and effective. These latter can include collaboration with other investors (including creditors) and non-investor stakeholders, escalation and engagement across asset classes.

Continuous monitoring and assessment of all factors material to the long-term success of investee companies are the focus of ICGN *Global Stewardship Principle 3* presented in Chapter 1.[1] The fiduciary duties and stewardship obligations of institutional investors require, in ICGN's view, that their portfolio supervision policies and practices include 'thoughtful risk analysis across a full range of indicators,' incorporating analysis of ESG and sustainability indicators. The purpose of regular monitoring of sustainability risk factors of investee companies is twofold. First, it allows for testing and reconsideration over time of the initial investment thesis behind inclusion of the company in the portfolio. Second, but just as important, it prepares the investor to refine its priorities for engagement as circumstances change and to react to engagement opportunities in a timely fashion.

ICGN *Global Stewardship Principle 3* incorporates the principle of economy. It recognises the importance of continuous monitoring and assessment of investee companies to allocating, and re-allocating, analytical and engagement resources between investee companies. It also recognises the importance of monitoring the monitoring process itself. As noted earlier, we are in the early to middle stages of understanding how sustainability issues affect long-term company performance. The relative value of the various indicators used to measure and track ESG performance remains a topic of continuing research and intense debate. New indicators can be expected to come into focus over time. And a particular institutional investor's view of what information is most important to include as part of its portfolio supervision process can and should evolve with experience.

The ICGN GSP acknowledge the potential regulatory risks that can arise from the more intensive forms of monitoring and engagement. Institutional investors are subject to insider trading laws and regulations in most jurisdictions. If a company provides an institutional investor with material non-public information in the course of investor–company dialogue, the investor may become subject to trading restrictions and potential civil and criminal liability if such restrictions are not followed.

Accordingly, every institutional investor in public securities should establish a clear approach to whether and when the investor is willing to become an insider. Every investor should have a policy for when discussions with a company may result in the receipt of material non-public information and the placing of the company on the investor's 'restricted trading list.'

The investment styles of some institutional investors may be incompatible with trading restrictions. Other investors may, under certain circumstances, be willing to place a company on their restricted trading list if they believe the value of temporarily becoming an insider, in terms of increasing the likelihood of engagement success, is commensurate with the risks inherent in not being able to trade for a period of time.

The policies established by such investors need to be reasonably granular, setting forth the internal standards and approval procedures for initiating communications with a company that might result in receipt of material non-public information. They should also include a robust framework for ensuring compliance with legal requirements around confidentiality and record keeping. Staff need to be provided clear guidance and periodic compliance training. Finally, as a matter of risk management, policies and practices around receipt of material non-public information should include planning out the steps for the earliest practical public disclosure of the information by the company and the lifting of the restrictions.

2. PLANNING AND IMPLEMENTING ENGAGEMENT

Assigning responsibilities

Responsibility for the conduct of particular aspects of an engagement may be assigned to the asset owner, the asset manager or contracted parties. But this does not imply that fiduciary duty itself may be 'outsourced.' Fiduciary duties can never be delegated by the fiduciary. In the course of carrying out their duties of loyalty and care to beneficiaries, fiduciaries may hire service providers to perform certain functions required to carry out those duties, but the fiduciary remains responsible to the beneficiary for their proper execution.

Applying this principle to the case of asset owners means that asset owners may hire asset managers and others to execute stewardship activities, but, as a legal matter, this never relieves the asset owner of its fiduciary duties to beneficiaries with respect to such activities. Likewise, an asset manager may contract for the provision of services in connection with an engagement, but its duty to its beneficiaries (asset owners) remains absolute. In practice, this means that, under the fiduciary duty of care, the asset owner or asset manager needs to ensure that any assignment of responsibility for such activities is reasonable (ie that the person or entity hired to carry out the activities is competent to do so effectively). To establish a reasonable level of confidence requires, at a minimum, clarity with respect to the assignment of responsibilities (in the mandate or other document), due diligence by the asset owner or manager of the service provider's capacity and track record of providing the services, and a system for accurate and timely reporting of the execution and results of the activities the service provider undertakes for the asset owner.

Institutions with concentrated long-term portfolios (particularly those in illiquid markets such as securities of smaller companies or emerging markets) will find that, in the main, engagement fits most naturally as part of the work of their internal fund management teams. At the opposite extreme, predominantly passive asset owners and managers with limited active fund management typically need to build specialised internal engagement teams or contract with specialist resources to deliver engagement. Most investment houses are somewhere between these extremes and employ a combination of internal capacity as well as externally contracted specialist resources, and put the combination to work to deliver engagement.[2] This philosophy and this approach need to be considered carefully and probably developed over time so that they are tailored to suit the investor's style and asset class.

Grounding engagement priorities in investment considerations

ICGN *Global Stewardship Principle 4* embraces engagement (including collaboration among investors in company dialogue) as integral to stewardship. As in the case of the other elements of stewardship addressed in the GSP, Principle 4 reflects ICGN members' conviction that engagement should be firmly grounded in fiduciary duty and investment objectives, 'with the aim of enhancing value on behalf of beneficiaries.' Accordingly, the principle and the sub-principles under it emphasise engagement's strategic character and the need for clear policies and practices around prioritisation,

FIGURE 6.2 GSP 4: engaging companies and investor collaboration

ICGN Global Stewardship Principle 4:
Engaging companies and investor collaboration

"Investors should engage with investee companies with the aim of preserving or enhancing value on behalf of beneficiaries and should be prepared to collaborate with other investors to communicate areas of concern"

1. Operate strategically to identify and target engagement efforts
2. Establish clear engagement policies
3. Ensure internal team views are consistent and efforts are integrated
4. Consider the use of all available tools to escalate as necessary
5. Be prepared to collaborate with others to deliver effective engagement
6. Review engagement approach, including its effectiveness, periodically

resource allocation (including personnel), tactics (including escalation) and evaluation of effectiveness.

An engagement is a proactive dialogue with an investee company for a specific purpose. It should not be an on-again, off-again unfocused interaction, but rather a purposeful series of communications. It therefore requires the institutional investor to follow a systematic approach, with a specific plan for each engagement and a clearly focused agenda for each interaction with the company. To be consistent with investor fiduciary duties, institutional investors' engagement priorities must be grounded in well-articulated investment considerations.

An institutional investor can prioritise allocation of engagement resources in one of three ways: (1) identifying potentially addressable sustainability issues on a company-by-company basis, either in the course of investment due diligence or post-investment portfolio company monitoring (bottom–up); (2) establishing themes that it considers a priority and identifying for which companies in the portfolio such themes are most salient (top–down); or (3) some combination of (1) and (2). Every investor's process for setting engagement priorities needs to be flexible enough to adjust the particular ESG issues around which it engages individual companies. Sustainability themes may also shift in priority across the portfolio, as new information, novel issues, improved techniques, greater understanding and the lessons of institutional experience merit their reconsideration.

ASSET CLASS

Asset class is an important driver of the content, strategy and tactics of an institutional investor's overall engagement programme as well as its interventions with individual companies. Engagement is incorrectly assumed by some to be an activity solely of investors in public equities. In principle and in practice, there are compelling reasons why investors in other asset classes, in the exercise of their stewardship obligations, should engage with investee companies. Even without equity investors' power to vote shares, fixed income investors' contractual rights, market influence and potential impact on cost of capital give them a voice that companies ignore at their peril. Where their issues converge and their interests are aligned, investors in debt and investors in equity can combine their efforts to achieve mutually beneficial engagement outcomes. (See below for a discussion of the role of the creditor and scope for collective engagement between creditors and equity investors.)

Private equity investors, including private equity funds that take only minority positions, can, of course, exercise significant influence over company behaviour, including sustainability policies and practices. Private equity funds typically negotiate for certain governance rights in company charters and/or shareholder agreements. Taking things one step up the investment chain, investors in private equity funds (limited partners) can themselves influence the shape and content of the engagement activities of the private equity fund managers (general partners) they contract.

In 2011, ICGN published its *Model Contractual Terms between Asset Owners and Asset Managers* with the goal of providing asset owners with a practical tool to ensure that their contracts with all asset managers, including private equity general partners, reflect their expectations around 'effectively integrating relevant environmental, social and governance factors into investment decision-making and ongoing management.' In 2022, ICGN, in partnership with the UN-supported Global Investors for Sustainable Development (GISD), launched a revised version, the *ICGN/GISD Model Mandate*. The updated version of the *Model Mandate* places particular emphasis on incorporating sustainability and the 17 Sustainable Development Goals into the contract terms of asset management agreements between asset owners and their asset managers.[3]

In addition to private equity, asset classes such as infrastructure finance and real estate also warrant consideration from a stewardship perspective, and ESG factors can be very relevant in these cases, but we do not explore these additional asset classes in this book.

Engagement for creditors

Among the various asset classes, other than listed equity, that come under the stewardship umbrella, we would like to highlight in particular creditors—which can include bondholders, holders of other debt securities, lenders or counterparties. Debt is part of the permanent capital of most company capital structures—even though individual debt obligations themselves are serviced and then reissued or retired. It is important to note that many institutional investors may have debt and equity holdings in the same company, often managed by different investment teams in the same investment firm.

Sustainable and healthy companies should seek to maintain constructive long-term relations with both creditors and shareholders to ensure cost-effective access to both debt and equity capital. In turn, boards should ensure that company governance and capital allocation mechanisms reflect a fair and appropriate balancing of shareholder and creditor interests.

Both creditors and shareholders want to provide capital to companies that are well governed, even though they may differ in what elements of governance are most important to them. As noted in a 2019 ICGN *Viewpoint*, common areas of interest between shareholders and creditors include:

- Clarity on financial policy and capital allocation.
- Competent risk management (and risk oversight by boards), including of ESG risks.
- Strong boards to provide independent oversight and constructive challenge of management.
- Robust accounting and audit policies and practices—both for financial information and ESG disclosures.
- Remuneration structures that provide appropriate management incentives.[4]

FIGURE 6.3 Overlapping interests between shareholders and creditors

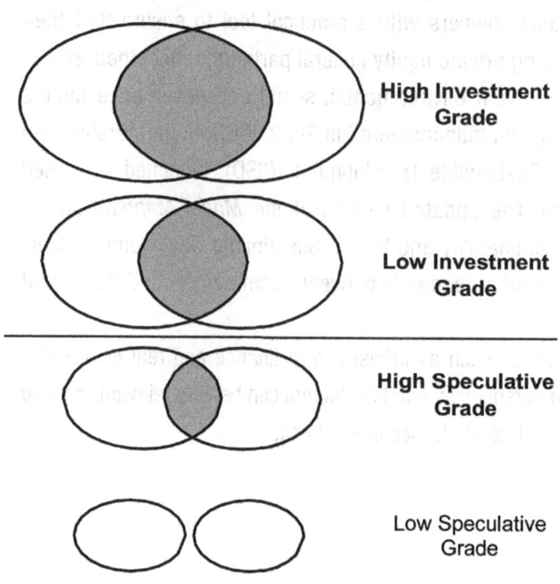

While debt and equity may be different asset classes, there is only one company. This requires the company's management and board to focus on their fiduciary duty to the long-term sustainability of the company itself. But it also requires management and the board to understand and balance the potentially competing interests of equity holders for the generation of returns and the concerns of the more risk-averse creditor for the company to maintain an appropriate credit risk profile.

The degree to which shareholder and creditor preferences overlap—or conflict with one another—is fundamentally linked to the company's own financial strength and credit quality. When a company's financial position is strong ('investment grade' in credit rating terms), the interests of shareholders and creditors may overlap significantly. But, as the company's financial position deteriorates from a solid going-concern status to a 'junk bond' speculative grade status, or to something approaching bankruptcy, these overlaps diminish, if not disappear. Figure 6.3 seeks to demonstrate the dynamic nature of how creditor and shareholder interests may vary with the financial strength of the company.

We do not offer an exhaustive treatment of how to engage from a creditor's perspective. However, greater attention on creditors is likely to build, if for no other reason than that the size of the global public debt market (over US$100 trillion) is larger than the public equity market (roughly US$95 trillion). The creditor perspective may bring a more holistic and more unified approach to engagement, particularly for investment firms with both debt and equity holdings in the same company. As the diagram in Figure 6.3 suggests, there are significant overlaps between creditors and shareholders when the company has a strong going-concern status. Particularly in these areas of overlap, there is scope for collaborative engagement.

We do not consider here engagement by investors in non-corporate fixed-income instruments such as sovereign bonds or other public-sector debt issues. That is both an ambitious and more complex matter than engaging with corporate entities. The political agenda of a government is unlikely to be easily swayed by a possibly differing agenda of institutional investors around ESG-related issues such as climate change or human rights. So, there are limits, at least in the near term, as to what sovereign bondholders might expect to achieve in terms of ESG engagement with national and sub-national governments (apart from not buying the bonds on ESG grounds in the first place). However, as noted in the discussion of country risk factors in Chapter 5, the relative ESG risks of individual countries can be identified and compared. If nothing else, ESG factors might play a greater role in credit risk assessment, cost of capital and relative value analysis by managers of sovereign bond portfolios.

Strategy, tactics and tools

A disciplined process for achieving the desired outcome of an engagement requires clarity around the issues to be addressed, the strategy for influencing company behaviour, the likelihood of achieving the desired changes and the potential benefits of success to the investor. The methodologies and tools discussed in Chapter 5 can set the stage for designing and then launching each engagement. One useful way of articulating the goals, strategy and tactics of a proposed engagement is through engagement matrices such as the ones presented in Figure 6.4 (for a CG-focused investor) and Figure 6.5 (for a more E&S-focused investor).

An engagement matrix or any other tool designed to summarise and guide an institutional investor's engagement activities with a company must inevitably be a living document that is updated throughout the lifetime of the investment. The engagement matrix provided in Figure 6.4 is one example of how an investor with a corporate governance-focused methodology for assessing ESG risk and opportunity in potential investee companies and a unique set of engagement priorities and resources might outline its engagements with a company (in this case, focused company-by-company and reasonably extensive). The first column organises the various ESG issues identified by the investment team during due diligence or in the course of monitoring subsequent to the investment in the company's securities. Reflecting the investor's corporate governance focus, E&S issues are addressed principally through a governance lens—in the example, through advocacy for improved E&S disclosures.

FIGURE 6.4 Matrix of engagement topics, strategy and tactics of a CG-focused investor

Engagement topic (examples)	Desired action	Why not addressed yet	Champions, resistors & alignment	Engagement strategy	Probability of success (high, medium, low)	Upside estimate (%)
Disclosures —operational						
Disclosures —E&S						
Board composition						
Contingent liabilities						
Non-core business						

A specific strategy for engaging company management on each issue is then laid out in the rest of the columns. In an effort to identify the best possible points of entry for engagement, the table in Figure 6.4 includes a column that lists the potential actors within the company that might be sympathetic (as well as potentially resistant) to the investor's proposals. The reasons for the attitudes of such company insiders are further fleshed out in the column on alignment of interests. The right-hand columns of the matrix provide estimates of the likelihood of success of engagement for each topic and the expected upside in such event.

An investor whose approach is more focused on E&S issues might encapsulate its engagements with companies in the form of a matrix like the one presented in Figure 6.5. For each issue of concern identified during investment due diligence, the investment team identifies an internally or externally generated score and one or more applicable standards it believes the company should match, but does not. The score and standards, together with the company's ranking vis-à-vis peers around each topic serve as a basis for both assessing the relative priority of engagement efforts and as potential elements of the strategy for convincing the company to make the requested changes in policies and practices. As in the case of the matrix presented in Figure 6.6, the last column provides the investment team's assessment of the possible value-addition from a successful engagement on each particular topic.

As noted above, engagements frequently originate in the application of a particular ESG theme to an investor's prospective or existing portfolio of investee companies. For example, a technology that received little attention in the past (say, microplastics pollution) may suddenly reveal itself to be a major environmental concern and therefore a threat to the sustainability of companies whose production processes include it.

An investor that believes it should reduce the risk this technology poses to the long-term performance of its portfolio companies would seek to engage with investee companies that utilise it, press for reduction in their dependence on the technology and

FIGURE 6.5 Matrix of engagement topics, strategy and tactics of an E&S-focused investor

Engagement topic (examples)	Objectives	Internal or external score	Applicable standards	Ranking v peers	Engagement strategy	Upside estimate
Toxic emissions						
Energy efficiency						
Carbon emissions						
Health & safety						
Community relations						
Labour conditions						

continuously monitor progress towards its replacement with newer, more environmentally friendly technologies.

Figure 6.6 lays out how an investor pursuing one or more sustainability themes across its portfolio might organise its strategy to spur investee companies to address them. For each company, the investor lays out the relative performance of that company on the issue against a benchmark. (For the microplastics case, it might be a measure of the amount of microplastic released per unit of production.) Explanations for both over- and underperformance might be provided directly by the company, by regulators or by NGOs or arrived at by the investor's own internal or external experts. Based on these and other considerations, the investor maps out its strategy for engagement, specifying what particular entry points might be most promising and estimating the potential benefit to the portfolio of success (which might include brand enhancement).

The matrixes presented in Figures 6.4, 6.5 and 6.6 are included in this book merely as illustrations. They are in no sense comprehensive of the kinds of tools investors use to prioritise, structure and articulate engagements with companies. One can imagine myriad formats for engagement tools, varying in form and substance depending on each investor's investment style, asset class, size and complexity of portfolio, market characteristics and extent of analytical and engagement resources and experience. For example, all three matrices presented in Figures 6.4, 6.5 and 6.6 reflect an investor with an apparent 'go it alone' engagement strategy.

An investor whose strategy relies more on collective engagements might focus on identifying collaborators for influencing companies—either among similarly situated investors or even non-financial stakeholders. Likewise, an investor with a more time-bound engagement approach might include deadlines that trigger a change of tactics (including escalation) if results do not materialise. It is worth emphasising that, in whatever way an investor chooses to frame, articulate and internally communicate its engagement strategy, the approach should not be static. It should be open to continuous reassessment and consideration of new facts, technologies and priorities as they become evident, as well as the fruits of learning that come out of the engagement experience itself.

FIGURE 6.6 Thematic screening approach

Company	Performance v benchmark	Explanations for over or under-performance	Entry point/strategy	Upside (%)

3. CHANNELS OF ENGAGEMENT AND ESCALATION

The set of communications between an investor and a company that comprise an engagement can range from a simple exchange of letters or emails to repeated and intensive face-to-face discussions with senior management and/or board members that take place over an extended period of time. When an investor pursues a multi-issue engagement with a company, different elements of the engagement may involve different communications channels. To be truly strategic, an investor's engagement plan for a company needs to consider the communications channels likely to be available to it, and to determine at each point in time what channels are most likely to advance the objectives of its engagement agenda. An engagement plan should also contemplate reconsidering the tactics of the engagement and escalating up the company's chain of command, should engagement through the initial channels prove less than fruitful.

A recent academic study of the stewardship practices of the UK asset manager Standard Life Investments (SLI, now Aberdeen Standard) provides a practical example of co-ordinated linkage of engagement with investment decision making. The firm employs a 'watch list' system to portfolio companies to identify concerns that target companies for more intensive engagement. The study concluded that SLI's engagement with portfolio firms had a significant influence on trading decisions and that monitoring and engagement by the asset manager contributed to an informational advantage, which in turn generated alpha.[5]

A comprehensive explication of all the channels of communication that investors employ in engagements would be a book unto itself. What follows is merely an introduction to some of the more important ways that investors engage with companies and their personnel, with some ideas about when these are likely to be of particular utility.

Written outreach

A written communication sent by an investor to a company laying out its questions or concerns about an issue of sustainability is perhaps the most basic and common form of engagement. This tactic might involve sending the company the investor's own governance or stewardship policies as a reference. It is often employed by an investor that has decided that a particular issue is relevant to a number of companies across its portfolio and wants to 'send a signal' that it, and presumably other similarly sentient investors, are aware of its potential importance. In its simplest form, written outreach may be directed to the company officer in charge of responding to shareholder communications. This would typically be the chief of investor relations or in certain cases other personnel identified by the company to respond to inquiries on particular topics, such as remuneration, climate change or labour relations.

Such communications explain the issue of concern and typically request the company to acknowledge receipt of the communication and provide some sort of response about what the company is doing, or plans to do, to address the concern. Letter writing campaigns across a portfolio by an investor may involve follow-up communications whose content may vary depending on the initial response. By themselves, letter-writing campaigns are rarely expected to accomplish earth-shattering results. But they do serve to sensitise companies to investor concerns and can set the stage for more personal and intense engagement methods.

'Standard' channels—investor relations and analyst calls

Investor relations departments are usually investors' and securities analysts' main point of contact in a company. Senior management look to investor relations to 'direct' traffic—by handing routine requests themselves and notifying others within the company of requests that are out of the ordinary. Investment professionals often have existing constructive relations with the staff of investor relations departments. These relationships can sometimes be leveraged to help an investor reach those within the company with influence over the topic or topics that are the subject of the engagement. Working through investor relations has advantages and limitations. Investor relations officers are trained to be responsive. They will generally respond to requests in some fashion. However, they can also serve as buffers between investors and senior management, insulating the real decision-makers in the company from direct dialogue with investors.

Listed companies in most markets conduct some form of regular outreach to the investment community. They may hold quarterly calls with analysts and investors to present operational and financial results and/or hold 'investor days' on an annual basis to update the market on more strategic and long-term developments. Investor conferences can also provide opportunities for investors to meet one-to-one with senior management and investor relations personnel.

All these fora generally allow for participants to ask questions and request information. So they present opportunities for investors to engage with company leadership on issues of concern to them. One advantage of such fora is their public nature. Information that a company divulges in quarterly earnings calls and in the public portion of investor conferences can usually be treated by investors as public and therefore do not raise insider trading or compliance issues. These fora also provide an investor with the opportunity to involve other investors in the dialogue with the company by alerting them to the issues the investor wants the company to address.

Engagement with specialists

Companies in industries that are the subject of particular environmental and social scrutiny not infrequently charge specialised personnel with responding to public enquiries about such topics (for example, climate change). When these exist, such specialists can be important interlocutors in investor–company engagements. Because of their special expertise, they can be expected to understand the issues raised by the investor. They should also be more aware of trends and developments in the area that is the subject of the engagement and, hence, more persuadable when solid evidence backs up the investor's position. Of course, specialists are rarely final decision-makers. But they can nonetheless be important internal allies, vouching for the relevance of technical investor requests that the senior executives may not be able to fully appreciate or respond to themselves.

Engagements with c-suite and boards

Gaining access to executive management (the 'c-suite') and board members to discuss the topics of an investor–company engagement is a fundamental challenge for most investors. Only the largest investors, or the largest shareholders in an individual company, can expect to receive a positive response to a request to meet with the CEO, CFO or chair or other members of the board. The best strategies for escalating discussions to this level vary dramatically depending on the nature of the investment, the size and type of investor, the particular issue involved, the attitudes of company leadership and market practices.

Executives and board members in some markets are much more accustomed to meeting with shareholders than their counterparts in others. For example, in the UK, it is a fairly common practice for shareholders to meet with a range of board members, including the chair and chairs of key committees such as remuneration, nomination and audit. In Germany, however, there is still strong cultural resistance in many quarters to allowing shareholders to engage directly with the Supervisory Board—despite the new German corporate governance code's call for the chair of the Supervisory Board to be available to meet with investors to discuss a narrowly defined set of issues.[6]

The potential for misuse of inside information is a legitimate concern for the c-suite and board members in all markets. However, insider trading rules are also too frequently used as a convenient pretext for reluctant executives to avoid taking the time to meet with shareholders. Company leadership should never share material non-public information with an investor without compliance controls that ensure such information would be kept confidential and not used for any party's unfair advantage. But in no market is it illegal for management or board members to meet with shareholders to hear their concerns.

Public campaigns

The types of engagement channels just discussed can be classified as essentially private (or semi-private in the case of the public portions of investor conferences) and generally not openly confrontational. More public, and typically more confrontational, methods of communicating an investor's concerns around a company's sustainability policies, practices and performance and ultimately of achieving desired engagement outcomes include:

1. *Public campaigns of a general nature*: where one or more shareholders publicise their concerns around a particular issue to generate market and public pressure for a response. Such campaigns may explicitly identify companies considered 'offenders' or may leave this to the market's and public's own determination. An example of a public campaign of a general nature includes the regular statements of individual investors and investor associations such as ICGN, the US Council of Institutional Investors (CII) and the Asian Corporate Governance Association against the practice of non-voting or multiple-voting shares.[7] In the specific area of climate risk, Climate Action 100+ is an investor-led initiative, founded in 2017, the focus of which is to achieve commitments from investee companies to cut emissions, improve governance and strengthen climate-related financial disclosures. It encourages investor engagement with companies on these themes.[8]
2. *Shareholder resolutions and other exercises of shareholder rights*: where investors act through the general meeting of shareholders to direct management and the board to undertake prescribed actions. Subject to local law and regulations, one or

more investors may introduce for discussion and approval of shareholders a resolution of the general meeting of shareholders directing company management to take actions that are responsive to the objectives of the engagement.

Climate change has been a particular focus of shareholder resolutions. Climate Action 100+ alerts investors to shareholder resolutions related to climate issues at individual company AGMs. The shareholder voice has been heard through this use of the voting process. For example, at Chevron's 2020 AGM, the majority of shareholders approved a resolution that aligns Chevron's lobbying activities with the Paris Agreement. As another example, shareholders of UK-based Barclays proposed in May 2020 a special resolution for the bank to set an ambition to be a net zero bank by 2050, and to set and report on a strategy for its financial services to align with the goals of the Paris Agreement. This resolution was recommended by the board and won 99.93% support (however, another, further-reaching shareholder resolution on climate was not recommended by the board and did not win a majority).[9]

Similarly, shareholders may try to influence the outcomes of director elections to replace those seen as resistant to the steps they want to see the company take. These efforts may be undertaken with respect to a single company or as a concerted effort across many companies identified as presenting the same issue. Perhaps the highest profile example of investors replacing recalcitrant board members in recent years is Engine No. 1's 2021 campaign to put more climate-conscious directors on ExxonMobil's board. Engine No. 1 is a relatively small activist investor, but, with the support of giants including BlackRock, Vanguard and State Street (who collectively held 20% of ExxonMobil's shares), it succeeded in replacing three directors with nominees it proposed.[10]

As initiatives of this nature are almost always seen by management as a hostile act, the company can be expected to expend significant legal resources to prevent a shareholder resolution from presentation at the shareholders meeting. Accordingly, the process of getting a shareholder's resolution on the agenda of a shareholders meeting is generally complex and expensive. Collective efforts, through formal associations or ad hoc groups of similarly minded investors, can reduce the burden on each investor.

3. *Litigation*: legally compelling the board or management to act in a way consistent with shareholders rights. Lawsuits brought by shareholders against the management and board of a company most frequently involve alleged violations of shareholder rights. The rights infringed can range from procedural rights (eg over refusal to table a proposed shareholder resolution) to substantive claims (eg for damages caused through self-dealing or violations of fiduciary duty). The remedies requested can involve changes to a company's governance structure as well as financial compensation to investors. As in the case of shareholder resolutions, the local legal framework and the efficiency of the judicial system determine the practicality (and cost) of this route.
4. *Participation in derivative and class action suits*: joining in actions initiated by others on behalf of shareholders. In several important jurisdictions (most notably the US), the legal framework provides for derivative lawsuits (brought by shareholders on behalf of the company against directors and/or management) and securities

class actions (brought by shareholders as a class against the company and its officers). The idea of bringing a derivative suit may originate with a specific investor or with a law firm that specialises in plaintiff-side securities and company litigation. In either case, the prospective lawsuit is then commonly 'shopped' to institutional investor shareholders in the target company, with the goal of getting them to sign on as co-lead plaintiffs in the eventual suit. (In the US, judges ultimately decide who may lead the litigation on behalf of the class, and the number and size of co-lead plaintiffs are important factors.[11])

Even when such suits are pursued on a contingent fee basis requiring no direct financial outlays by the plaintiffs, joining a derivative or class action suit as a co-lead plaintiff implies the expenditure of modest managerial resources and can carry with it potential reputational risks. Institutional investors should develop formal policies for when they will consider becoming named plaintiffs in class actions. In any case, all institutional investors in markets that have substantial securities class actions should have in place systems for tracking when they are potential beneficiaries of class action suits and filing the appropriate claim forms to ensure they receive their share of eventual judgments and settlements.

Collective engagements

When two or more investors' analyses coincide and their interests and objectives are aligned, working together to engage with a company can have distinct advantages. Involving more investors in the dialogue with a company increases the pressure on the company to take their concerns seriously. It accords greater credence to such investors' assertions that what they are requesting is in the interests of and supported by the market and investor base generally. Collectivising engagement can present efficiencies, allowing the investors (and potentially other stakeholders) to divide their efforts and share the costs. The earlier example of Engine No. 1's initiative to elect climate-sensitive directors to the ExxonMobil board is a good example of a successful collective engagement using shareholders' voting rights to bring about change.

Collective engagement also presents potential efficiencies for companies. Sub-principle 4.6 of ICGN's GSP encourages investors to collaborate on stewardship and engagement. ICGN reiterated this view more recently in its March 2019 letter to Japan's Council of Experts on that country's corporate governance and stewardship codes. It urged the Japanese authorities to clarify to the fullest extent possible that are no regulatory obstacles to collective engagements on ESG issues that do not involve agreements to vote shares in concert.[12]

However, investors should carefully evaluate potential risks before committing to working together on an engagement. Certain kinds of collective action by shareholders may trigger the requirements of 'acting in concert' regulations in some jurisdictions. Acting in concert rules, intended mainly to increase the transparency of efforts to obtain control of a company, may impose requirements on investors that are impractical or costly to comply with.

Co-ordination between investors involves costs and presents significant potential for getting signals crossed. The risks are compounded when non-investor stakeholders (such as NGOs) are included. Non-financial stakeholders have sets of interests that are quite distinct from, and often not as transparent as, those of investors. Investors may find non-financial stakeholders' capacities, incentives and behaviours to be less predictable than those of shareholders and debtholders. Accordingly, collective engagements need to be especially carefully planned, executed and co-ordinated. Before committing to work together, investors should vet their partners carefully, favouring more familiar and trusted institutions. In many cases, it may make sense to agree a formal memorandum of understanding to ensure that all the collaborators are clear on objectives, expected contributions, consultations and decision-making.

Collective engagements can be conducted through pre-existing shareholder groupings or organised on an ad hoc basis. The Netherlands' Eumedion, Italy's Assogestioni and the Brazilian Association of Capital Markets Investors (AMEC), among other investor associations, periodically initiate engagements with companies on behalf of their members. Other associations, including the CII, frequently organise sign-on letters on thematic issues and periodically set up meetings between members and regulators and standard setters, but leave it to members themselves to organise and conduct collective engagements with individual companies on an ad hoc basis. The Engine No. 1 example cited earlier involved an ad hoc effort initiated by a small activist whose ultimate influence was multiplied after it convinced a number of much larger shareholders to join its effort to make ExxonMobil's board more climate conscious and to reduce its carbon footprint.

International collective engagements can be a particularly challenging undertaking—but they can also be effective. International and domestic investors' interests may not always be completely aligned, with international investors frequently more prepared than local investors to abandon a company or even the whole market. International investors also often do not have the same understanding of local conditions and market dynamics as local investors. They naturally do not have the degree of experience with local folkways that local investors have and so are less expert in the subtleties of effective communication in the local business culture.

At the same time, especially in small markets, international investors may represent the bulk of discretionary investment in the market and, hence, have significant potential influence over the supply of capital for companies.[13] Perhaps not surprisingly, research seems to indicate that international engagements are most successful when local and international investors both play leading roles and carefully co-ordinate their efforts.[14]

4. TOOLS FOR MAKING THE CASE

To maximise the chances of success, investors' engagement communications with companies should be clear, concise, consistent and to the point. They should leave little doubt about the reasons for the investors' concerns, what the 'ask' is, and why it is both feasible and reasonable. And investors should strive to articulate their positions, present their evidence and define their 'asks' in language that the company's decision-makers can quickly absorb and understand.

Engagements ordinarily involve the preparation by investors of formal memoranda and/or slide decks intended to bring the company's management and board around to the investor's idea of what changes should be considered regarding a company's ESG policies and practices. As such, they need to make as clear a case as possible that it is in the company's long-term interest to take the steps the investor is urging it to consider. The toolkit an investor employs to make its case can include the same sorts of tools that are employed in pre-investment analysis, especially scoring, benchmarking and accepted progression matrices.

As noted in Chapter 5, company leadership is typically very sensitive to the behaviour of peers, including competitors in both the product and capital markets. Poor scores, especially in comparison with domestic peers, are likely to get their attention. Executives of companies with international ambitions generally also react to negative comparisons against global companies in the same industry. (Who hasn't heard a company bill itself as the 'Proctor and Gamble or Unilever of country X'?) Accordingly, arguments by an investor that can be supported by clear evidence that a company's peers have adopted the policies or practices it is advocating, or are clearly moving in that direction, are likely to have significant persuasive value. As more than one observer has noted without too much exaggeration, CEOs may be more likely to emulate what their peers are doing, even if it is demonstrably bad for the company, than they are to adopt practices their peers have so far not enacted, even if they are demonstrably good for the company!

A key element of successful engagement is understanding the interests of one's interlocutor. While, in theory, a corporation is an organism with its own legal personality and interests, in reality it is made up of a collection of sub-units, including formal functional divisions, informal groups and individuals. Each of these sub-units has its own set of interests and incentives. This is reflected in the inclusion in the table in Figure 6.4 of a column for identifying 'champions' and 'resistors' and assessing their incentive alignment with respect to individual engagement objectives. The wise investor engaging a company learns as much as it can about the various sub-units in the company and their respective interests in developing and adapting its strategy to determine whom to engage on which issues and what arguments (and threats) to direct to whom.

Typically, in engagement with a senior executive or board member, the engaging investor has little more than an hour or so to make its case. While the investor may have the chance to explore a series of issues, typically one or two of those issues will be the primary concerns and so will form the main focus for the meeting (though they may not always occupy most of the time). But, as well as pressing its positions, the investor should be seeking to understand the individual sitting across the table and also gain some insight into the working of the board or, in the case of a non-board-level executive, the constraints that he or she faces in seeking to deliver their role.

Often, engagement is about reading between the lines of what is said and seeing how the engager can best assist the right decisions to be taken, how they can best clear the path to allow the change that they believe is necessary to happen. It is never appropriate or fruitful for engagers to pretend to micro-manage the company, and it is wise to remember that key decisions will always have to be taken behind the closed doors of the boardroom and c-suite. An engager never takes the decision for the company; it rather helps to set the context for the board's decision-making. The role is therefore to persuade, not to instruct—the tone of engagement really matters to its ultimate effectiveness.

5. TRACKING ENGAGEMENT ACTIVITIES AND OUTCOMES

As stewardship and engagement are strategic processes, it is essential that the progress and outcome of activities carried out pursuant to them be recorded and regularly assessed. Stewardship and engagement activities with a company or around a theme typically involve employees across an institutional investor's operational units. No single individual or even department is likely to be involved in every bit of analysis or communication with a particular company. Institutional learning and memory are essential to the kind of regular re-examination of stewardship and engagement approaches, strategy and tactics that long-term effectiveness demands. Obviously, the larger and more complex an investment team and/or portfolio, the greater the importance of tracking engagement activities and outcomes.

We are not aware of any comprehensive surveys, but we suspect that most investors use internally developed systems to track engagement-related activities. These can be fully integrated with the portfolio tracking databases and spreadsheets or stand-alone. Whatever solution is used, it is crucial that an investor's tracking system be accurate and complete and that it provide a basis for tracking actions to outcomes.

Accuracy and completeness are essential for measuring the amount of resources expended by engagement and by type of engagement and ensuring that the finite set of resources is being allocated to priority activities. And determining which sorts of engagements should be prioritised requires knowing, to the extent possible, what actions contribute to positive and negative results. Of course, all investment and engagement outcomes result from a multitude of factors, and so ascribing stewardship activities to results is more an art than an exact science. But it is necessary to seek to understand this relationship.

6. BUILDING EFFECTIVE ENGAGEMENT TEAMS

The great diversity among asset classes, investment styles, stewardship approaches, investment beliefs and human resources among investors limits how much a book such as this can prescribe what kind of professional and interpersonal skills are required to successfully execute engagements with companies. Some strategies or specific engagements may place a premium on specialised environmental, social or governance expertise. Others may rely more on the work of generalists or sustainability-savvy investment analysts.

Table 6.1 compares some of the typical (but by no means universal) characteristics of three types of stewardship strategies—thematic, risk and opportunity, and risk-focused. It postulates that thematic investors commonly place a premium on staff with strong understanding of the link between the particular theme and investment fundamentals and solid communications skills so as to be able to explain to target companies the business case for implementing the thematic changes that are the subject of engagements. Risk-focused integrators need staff with strong ESG technical skills to conduct in-depth risk analysis that translates into valuations and portfolio composition decisions. Risk and opportunity-focused investors tend to seek long-term relations of trust with companies (especially for the exploitation of opportunities). Individuals with high scores on measures of emotional intelligence may serve well in the kind of

TABLE 6.1 Executing different stewardship/ESG strategies requires different and often scarce skill sets

	Thematic activists	Risk and opportunity ESG integrators	Risk-focused ESG integrators
Target companies	Flawed business models; poor management	Solid businesses; some receptivity to investors & change (champions); inexperience with investor expectations	Results of screening; static assessment—selection prospects not based on engagement/ likelihood of change
Objectives/ strategy	Changes reasonably quickly recognised by market	Mix of large & small, immediate & long-term changes that take time for market to value	Overall portfolio performance (alpha)
Tools/tactics	Public campaigns, shareholder votes, legal action	Private persuasion; alignment of interests; trust-building; exercise of corporate rights	Mostly internal analytics
Skills/personality/ emotional intelligence	Public communication skills & experience	Emotional intelligence; interpersonal skills; ability to make the business case	Technical; analytical
Holding periods	Short–medium term; until market recognises changes	Longer term	Infinity

engagements these firms undertake, whereas investors focused principally on identifying and measuring risk may find that technical risk-identification skills are their highest priority when hiring and assigning staff.

7. SHARE VOTING: OBJECTIVES AND EXECUTION

Voting is a crucial baseline element of stewardship activities for equity investors, something that needs to be applied across investment portfolios with intelligence and care. Some of the intelligence to be applied needs to be around deciding how many resources should be applied to voting decision-making and at which investee companies (if any) the voting decisions can be outsourced to service providers, whether proxy advisors or others. These decisions are likely to be driven by the investment style and approach and, thus, by the breadth of the investment portfolio, including its geographical spread and diversity.

The complexity of the voting chain and of voting processes is such that all stewardship staff need a basic understanding of how their legal rights of ownership are seen from the perspective of the investee corporation, not least because this frames broader stewardship rights beyond voting. Given that votes are a client asset like any other, and

FIGURE 6.7 ICGN Model disclosures on voting

1. Set out clear voting policies and coverage
2. Delineate the process of decision-making
3. Detail any use of third-party services
4. Describe process of communication of decision with companies
5. Reveal circumstances when physical attendance at meetings is appropriate
6. Address whether the investor seeks confirmation its votes have been received
7. Clarify the approach to the impact of stocklending on voting
8. Identify the approach to client and public disclosure of voting decisions
9. Revise voting policy and approach periodically

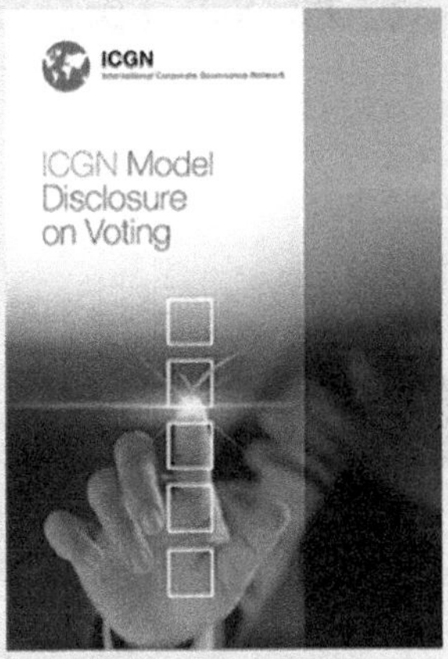

should be valued by a fiduciary as such, care needs to be taken to ensure that a successful vote has been placed and the risk of votes being lost minimised.

The voting chain

The systems by which voting decisions are made and transmitted from the shareholder to the company differ importantly from market to market. And the processes for cross-border exercise of voting rights adds an extra layer. But practically all systems exhibit a high degree of complexity, with unfortunately attendant degrees of cost and risk of failure.[15]

Description and analysis of the various systems for transmitting and recording shareholder votes are beyond the scope of this book. Figure 6.8, which diagrams in simplified form the voting decision and transmission process of Amundi Asset Management, is presented solely to illustrate the basic roles of the major players in most markets.

As Figure 6.8 cannot convey in full, the voting process involves the participation of a lot more than just investors, companies and their personnel. Proxy advisors such as ISS, Glass Lewis and ECGS provide Amundi with research and analysis of the items to be voted on at each shareholder meeting. Informed by such outside advice and its own analysis, and sometimes also after conversations with company management, Amundi makes voting decisions through a process that involves the participation of its portfolio managers and analysts and its corporate governance voting committee.

In the case of electronic voting, instructions are sent through the Broadridge and ISS systems,[16] which in turn pass on the instructions to Amundi's sub-custodians in each market. In the case of physical proxy cards, these are conveyed directly to the sub-custodians. Custodians and sub-custodians are critical to share voting because, in most markets, they are actually the shareholder of record on the companies' share registry. Accordingly, notices of meetings, agendas and proxy cards/ballots (electronic or otherwise) are transmitted through them, and only they can legally vote the shares.

FIGURE 6.8 Simplified voting chain of an asset manager

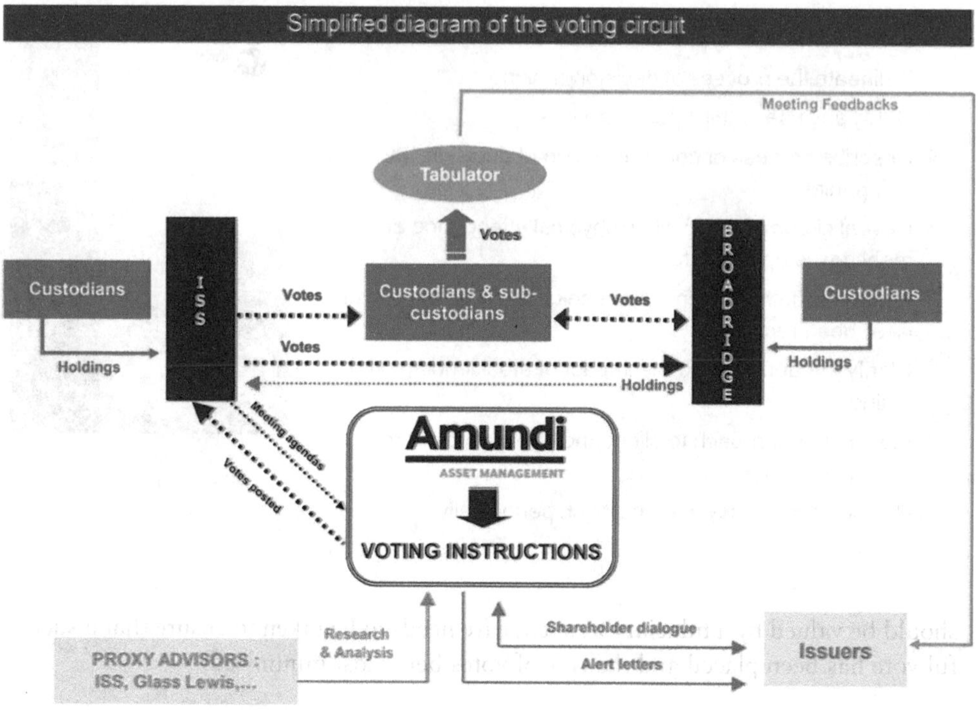

Source: Amundi Asset Management

Figure 6.8 provides a useful outline of most steps involved in the voting process, but leaves out the path that notices of meetings and their agenda follow from the company to the shareholder. It likewise omits the chain of legal powers of attorney that are still required to be executed and periodically updated in many markets (and the extra level of complication involved in notarising and consularising powers of attorney for cross-border voting). Obviously, even minor glitches in execution of all the stages of the voting process can lead to failures of votes to be validly cast and recorded. Nonetheless, voting rights are an asset, and, as a result, investment managers are obliged as fiduciaries to preserve their value for their ultimate beneficiaries.

Share voting policies

Every institutional investor in equity securities should have a clearly articulated share voting policy to explain to beneficiaries and the market how it carries out its fiduciary duty to maximise the value of the voting rights that the shares it holds confer. Such a policy should cover at least the following:

1. *General approach*: what are the key objectives the investor pursues in voting shares? The general approach statement should be fully consistent with and reinforce the investor's fundamental investment strategy. For example, in the case of an 'active ownership' fund manager that seeks to influence the ESG policies and practices of investee companies, the policy should explain how share voting is carried

out in tandem with engagement to reinforce the messages of the engagement and help achieve their objectives.

2. *Prioritisation and decision-making process*: how does the investor allocate responsibility to decide on how to vote at shareholder meetings? Does the process differ depending on the nature of the position or the issue to be voted on? Is voting on small positions or routine agenda items handled through the application of general policies by a proxy advisor? What sorts of voting decisions (which companies, what issues) are subject to more careful internal review? How is consistency ensured?
3. *Communication with companies*: when does the investor reach out to company management to influence the agenda for shareholder meetings or to express views on agenda items expected to be included in the agenda?
4. *Use of proxy advisors and other outside resources*: what outside resources and opinions does the investor take into consideration in deciding how to vote? Why were these inputs selected? How much does the ultimate decision depend on such inputs?
5. *Major policies*: what are the investor's positions on the most important corporate governance and other issues that can be potentially influenced by shareholder votes? These vary by jurisdiction, but typically include board composition (independent directors), chair/CEO separation, remuneration of officers and directors, auditor selection and rotation, shareholder resolutions and delegations to the board of authority to issue new capital. In some markets, such as a Germany, there may also be an opportunity for the shareholder to vote on discharging management and supervisory board members from liability. Such votes are typically regarded as symbolic in nature, but can be used by investors to express disapproval with individual board members or the board in aggregate.
6. *Co-ordination with other shareholders*: does the investor consult other shareholders in the process of deciding how to vote shares? Is it routine to consult with the authors of shareholder resolutions? Does the investor work with other shareholders (through shareholder associations or otherwise) to co-ordinate voting for minority shareholder-nominated directors in jurisdictions where this is a practice?
7. *Securities lending*: what are the investor's policies regarding securities lending, particularly over periods that include an AGM or shareholders meeting? (See below.)
8. *Post-meeting follow-up*: how does the investor ensure that the messages it intends to convey through its votes at shareholders meetings is received and understood by boards and management? For example, are votes against board and management recommendations routinely followed up with written or verbal communications to the company to explain the investor's rationale for opposition?

The actual content of institutional investors' share voting policies varies significantly depending on the usual factors—investment styles and objectives, types of equity securities held, size and complexity of portfolio, size of positions, jurisdiction/s and others. But consistency with the particular investor's approach to stewardship should be common to all policies. Beneficiaries and the market should understand from every share voting policy how the exercise of voting rights by the investor helps protect and enhance the value of the assets it manages on behalf of its beneficiaries, and how the approach to share voting complements and reinforces the goals of the investor's other stewardship activities.

Securities lending

Securities lending contributes importantly to the liquidity and efficiency of options and securities markets. Revenue from lending securities can also be a significant source of income for institutional investors (and by extension their beneficiaries and clients). However, the lending of equity securities creates the potential for an institutional investor to be deprived of the power to vote if shares it holds are 'lent out' on the date of record for a shareholders meeting.[17] Securities lending also poses operational and execution risks that can potentially harm investors.

ICGN's *Guidance on Securities Lending*, revised in 2016, recognises the important function that securities lending serves, particular in equity markets.[18] At the same time, it affirms the importance of clear and transparent policies grounded in an informed understanding and assessment of the risks presented by the lending out of shares in portfolio companies. Asset owners should require their managers to clearly state what factors will determine under what circumstances shares will, and will not, be permitted to be lent out. How will the manager ensure that the shares are in its name when they need to be for it to vote on issues of importance to shareholders? What are the systems in place to ensure compliance with the policy by both the manager's own staff and the various agents typically involved in the securities lending process?

Just as importantly, the ICGN *Guidance* underlines the importance of transparency around the economics of securities lending. Beneficiaries and clients of asset managers are entitled to full transparency with respect to how the fees generated by securities lending are shared among the asset manager, its beneficiaries and the agents typically entrusted to arrange and execute the transactions. Beneficiaries should likewise be provided a full accounting of the impact of the securities lending programme on overall returns. Full transparency around the economics, and also around the potential operational and execution risks, allows asset owners and beneficiaries to come to their own informed conclusions about the relative costs and benefits, and reasonableness, of a manager's securities lending policies.

Proxy advisors

Most large institutional equity investors rely, to at least some extent, on research provided by proxy advisors in deciding how to vote their shares in portfolio companies. Most, but not all, proxy advisors also provide explicit voting recommendations. Many institutional investors authorise a proxy advisor itself to send voting instructions for some or all portfolio companies in accordance with the application by the advisor of a set of agreed guidelines. The guidelines applied by an advisor on behalf of a client investor can be those recommended (and usually revised annually) by the proxy advisor itself, the investor's own criteria or a version of the advisor's guidelines, amended to reflect differences between the advisor's and the investor's views on particular issues.

Other investors, especially those with concentrated portfolios, make all voting decisions and execute their proxies and voting instructions themselves. But even investors who do not rely on proxy advisors to apply their voting policies and send their voting instructions typically review the research and recommendations of one or more proxy advisors in the course of deciding how to vote.

Proxy advisors perform an important function in equity markets by providing their customers with a transparent and efficient means of applying agreed principles (guidelines) to individual voting decisions. They can also provide a critical technology platform to deliver shareholder meeting ballots to investor desktops, facilitating the transmission of voting decisions in a timely manner.

Given the high number of companies in the portfolios of large institutional investors, and the concentration of shareholder meetings during particular periods in time (eg early second quarter in most Northern Hemisphere markets), proxy advisors are probably indispensable to effective share voting. However, the corporate community in some markets (especially those such as the US where shareholding is atomised, but also largely institutional) has brought increasing pressure on governments and regulators to reduce the influence of proxy advisors. Corporates allege that proxy advisors sometimes make recommendations based on factual inaccuracies and do not provide company management with sufficient opportunity to provide input into the process, despite the fact that proxy advisors' recommendations, taken as a whole, are overwhelmingly in favour of management positions.

Such efforts have, not surprisingly, been broadly opposed by shareholder organizations. The CII has long fought calls by the corporate community for the US Securities and Exchange Commission (SEC) to bring proxy advisors under its regulatory umbrella and vehemently objected to amendments to the proxy solicitation rules issued in July 2020 that would have required advisors to notify companies in advance of vote recommendations and provide clients 'an efficient and timely means of becoming aware of any written responses by [companies] to proxy voting advice.'[19] In the view of CII and its institutional investor members, such requirements are redundant and 'could result in delays in distribution of proxy advice, driving up costs for investors, impairing the independence of proxy advice and causing uncertainty for institutional investors.'[20] ICGN has also weighed in to the SEC on this issue, conveying similar views from the overseas investment community.[21] Following the change of administration in Washington, the SEC reversed course in November 2021, proposing amendments to the 2020 rule that would eliminate the requirements for proxy advisors to give companies prior notice of their recommendations and to make available to investors the companies' responses.[22]

In the view of many institutional investors, the corporate community, at least in the US, has presented a false narrative about proxy advisors, painting them as more influential than they actually are. As noted in Chapter 1, institutional investors may assign certain practical functions, such as applying voting policies to individual company shareholder ballots, but they may not delegate their fiduciary duties to beneficiaries (including stewardship duties). It is accordingly up to institutional investors to decide whether the services they receive from proxy advisors are fit for purpose and, whenever they believe they are not adequate, to seek other means, alternatively or in combination, to help them decide how to effectively exercise their voting rights.

Most investment managers retain some degree of voting decision-making in-house. Deciding which shares of which companies can be properly voted through 'automated means,' such as application of general or tailored guidelines by a proxy advisor, and which voting decisions should be made on a more case-by-case basis is for

FIGURE 6.9 Example of an internal voting decision process

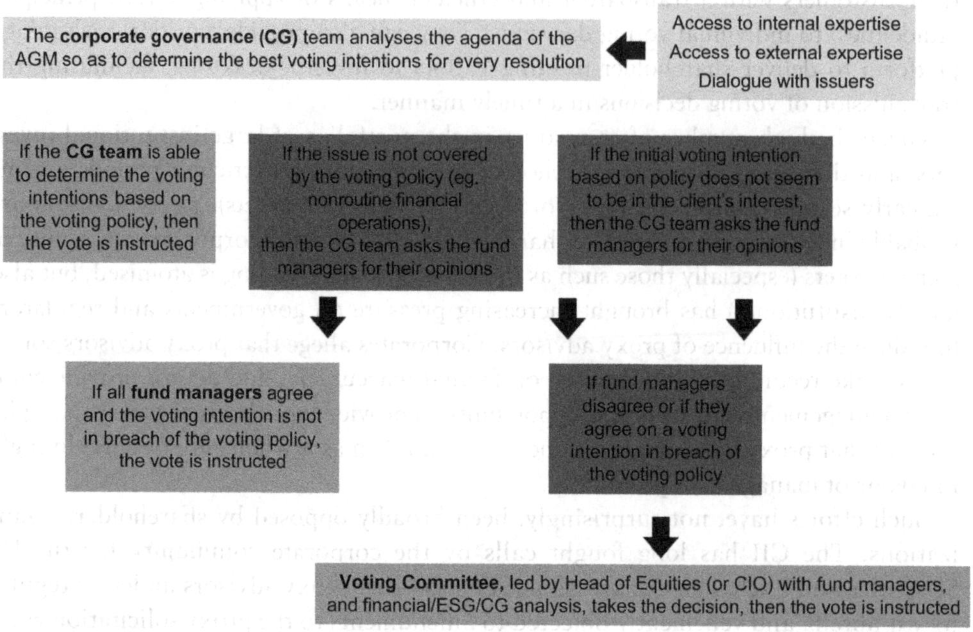

each institutional investor to decide based on its own investment style and stewardship strategy and its own balancing of the costs and benefits. Active company engagements, whether company-specific or thematic, require careful consideration of how voting decisions are made to ensure that shares are voted (and signals sent) in a manner consistent with engagement objectives.

Figure 6.9 provides an illustration of how one asset manager makes voting decisions. The manager's specialist corporate governance team initiates the process by analysing information about the upcoming vote from internal and external sources, including, if appropriate, contact with the company. If the item to be voted fits neatly within the investor's pre-established voting guidelines, the corporate governance team can send the instructions up the voting chain.

However, if the voting guidelines do not cover the item to be voted on, or if application of the guidelines appears to the corporate governance team to not be in beneficiaries' interests, the investment team (fund managers) are brought into the process. The illustrated process even includes a voting committee to make final decisions in cases where there are disagreements among the corporate governance and investment teams on how to vote. Examples might include complicated shareholder proposals or the approval of important capital transactions.

Again, Figure 6.9 is provided simply for illustration. There are probably dozens of different ways that institutional investors can structure their share voting process. However the process is structured, it must be designed to result in decisions that are consistent with the firm's investment objectives and that reinforce its stewardship and engagement goals.

8. STEWARDSHIP REPORTING

As discussed in Chapter 1, institutional investors are fiduciaries accountable for acting exclusively in the best interests of beneficiaries. A fundamental component of accountability is transparency. A fiduciary must provide its beneficiaries the information necessary for the latter to make an informed judgement about how well the beneficiary is carrying out its duties. Recognising this, ICGN *Global Stewardship Principle* 7 states that 'investors should publicly disclose their stewardship policies and activities and report to beneficiaries or clients on how they have been implemented so as to be fully accountable for the effective delivery of their duties.' Signatories of the Principles for Responsible Investment (PRI) similarly commit to 'report on [their] activities and progress towards implementing the Principles.'

ICGN's GSP make a subtle distinction between the audiences for stewardship disclosure. An institutional investor's disclosure of its stewardship policies and the kinds of activities in which it engages in execution of such policies should extend beyond its beneficiaries to the broader public. Observers beyond an asset owner or asset manager's clients should be able to understand the institution's approach and commitment to stewardship.

Public disclosure serves the important purpose of putting markets, companies and others on notice of the growing commitment to stewardship and the direction in which investors are heading in implementing stewardship in their investment processes and engagement with companies. The first supporting comment to Principle 7 underlines the importance of sending clear signals to the market about an investor's commitment to stewardship by recommending that investors should signify this commitment by becoming a signatory to a relevant national code (if one exists in the investor's jurisdiction).

Meaningful public disclosure around an investor's stewardship policies and activities needs to be more than a general statement of its stewardship philosophy, objectives and commitment. The discussion of the investor's stewardship and engagement polices should explain their rationale and prioritisation. An investor should lay out how it goes about setting its stewardship strategy for individual asset classes and particular

FIGURE 6.10 ICGN *Global Stewardship Disclosure Guidance*

investments and describe the sorts of resources and processes that go into executing the strategy, including escalation, collaboration with other parties and outsourcing. Such public disclosure should endeavour to explain how these stewardship 'inputs' are expected to translate into achievement of the objectives or 'outputs' of the investor's stewardship activities.[23]

ICGN's *Global Stewardship Disclosure Guidance series*,[24] in particular the ICGN *Model Disclosures on Monitoring, Voting and Engaging*, are intended to help investors work out the content and format of their stewardship for both the public and their beneficiaries and clients. As noted above, becoming a signatory of a national code can be a powerful signal of commitment to stewardship. National stewardship codes can also provide investors with a framework for public disclosure of their stewardship policies and practices.

As noted in point 7.2 of ICGN's *Global Stewardship Principles*, investors can describe their stewardship policies and practices with reference to a national stewardship code in a 'comply or explain' context and provide meaningful explanations regarding aspects of the stewardship code that the investor does not comply with. Signatories of the PRI must report on their responsible investment activities on an annual basis and in accordance with a standard, detailed questionnaire. The portion of each signatory's responses that are published in the Public Transparency Report can also provide points of reference for an investor's overall public stewardship disclosures.

Competition, compliance and strategic concerns impose certain limits on the amount and quality of information that investors publicly disclose. Protection of an investor's intellectual property (including proprietary tools and processes around stewardship) and the need to treat non-public information in accordance with national law and regulation justify and sometimes require that not all details of an investor's stewardship activities be publicly known. Some engagement strategies involve conversations with individual companies or groups that need to be treated as confidential if they are to be effective.

But investors can and should provide their beneficiaries and clients with more detailed and granular stewardship disclosure than they provide to the public. According to point 7.6 of ICGN's *Global Stewardship Principles*, investors should provide regular and appropriate reports to clients, which may be more detailed than public disclosure, regarding stewardship activities and performance. Such reports should include their major stewardship priorities and forward-looking engagement strategy.

While efforts such as ICGN's *Global Stewardship Disclosure Guidance* and national stewardship codes are helping to shape investor disclosure practices and beneficiary expectations, it is clear that stewardship reporting remains a work in progress. Two particular topics—the role of independent assurance and disclosure of engagement results—are the focus of considerable current debate and merit discussion here.

Independent review and confirmation of investors' stewardship processes and activities are at an even more incipient stage than is assurance of company ESG disclosures (discussed in Chapter 7). The threshold questions are: what aspects of stewardship are amenable to meaningful audit and assurance, and whose benefit would such assurance serve? As discussed below, in most cases it is hard to affirm with any certainty that particular engagement efforts are in and of themselves responsible for particular outcomes. Provision of assurance around stewardship and engagement outcomes is unlikely to be possible in the near term, if ever. However, review of an investor's actual stewardship activities against its stated policies and procedures should, in principle, be feasible.

Qualified independent assurance providers should be able to develop ways to review whether practices and procedures are consistent with stated policies and whether staff are in fact actually carrying out such practices and procedures. Akin to a compliance audit, such a review could provide investors with some degree of assurance that an investor's stated stewardship policies and practices are more than self-serving window dressing. The review process itself, which would by its nature directly involve senior management and hopefully the board, could also serve to focus the investor's senior leadership attention on whether its stewardship approach is fit for purpose.

It is clear that, to comply with their fiduciary duties and adequately report to their beneficiaries, investors must keep careful track of their stewardship activities, including voting records, collaboration with other actors in collective thematic efforts, and individual and collective engagements with companies. Large investors increasingly maintain a database that allows them to measure the types and amount of resources allocated to stewardship activities. Aggregate data drawn from such databases provide input into stewardship reporting to the public, beneficiaries and clients. But investors are currently divided on whether it is possible or appropriate to measure and report the success of stewardship and engagement separately from investment performance itself.

Some investors conduct periodic reviews of engagement with the goal of measuring outcomes against their stated *ex ante* objectives. For example, AVIVA Investors (UK) state that, where engagement

> is undertaken for specific purposes, the effectiveness of such engagements will be measured against the objectives set at the outset. We maintain a database to record our voting and engagement with companies which allows us to review the effectiveness of our work.[25]

Others do not attempt to measure the effectiveness of engagement on its own, but rather regard it as best reflected in overall investment performance. Investors in this camp generally believe that directly linking cause and effect in stewardship is inherently speculative, as many other influences (including pressure from other actors, competition and management's own initiative) also play a part in whether stewardship and engagement objectives materialise. For example, Allianz Global Investors

> sees engagement as a way to reduce investment risk, help improve corporate performance and better assure long-term business prospects of investee companies. Consequently, while we keep records of our engagements and positive stewardship outcomes, we do not seek to measure success of our engagements separately from our investment performance.[26]

Whether one approach ultimately prevails, and which one it will be, would seem to depend on whether proponents of outcome measurement and disclosure can ever develop credible methods of tracing their stewardship activities to specific results and whether they and their beneficiaries and clients judge that such outcome tracing is worth the cost.

NOTES

1. ICGN *Global Stewardship Principles*, 2016: www.icgn.org/sites/default/files/ICGNGlobalStewardshipPrinciples.pdf
2. Some investment firms, such as Hermes and BMO Global Management, offer 'overlay' services, in which they provide engagement and/or voting services across agreed client portfolios—even if the specific corporate holdings are managed by other asset managers.
3. ICGN–GISD Alliance Model Mandate, June 2022: www.icgn.org/sites/default/files/2022-06/ICGN%20GISD%20Model%20Mandate%202022.pdf
4. ICGN Viewpoint, *What Is the Role of the Creditor in Corporate Governance and Stewardship?* September 2019: www.icgn.org/what-role-creditor-corporate-governance-and-investor-stewardship
5. Marco Becht, Julian R. Franks and Hannes F. Wagner, *Corporate Governance through Voice and Exit*, 1 October 2019, European Corporate Governance Institute—Finance Working Paper No 633/2019, Available at SSRN: https://ssrn.com/abstract=3456626 or http://dx.doi.org/10.2139/ssrn.3456626
6. See Klaus J. Hopt, *The Dialogue between the Chairman of the Board and Investors: The Practice in the UK, the Netherlands and Germany and the Future of the German Corporate Governance Code under the New Chairman*, 2017, ECGI—Law Working Paper No 365/2017: https://papers.ssrn.com/sol3/papers.cfm?abstract_id=3030693
7. For example, see ICGN's 2020 letter to the Hill Review with regard to listings and dual class shares: www.icgn.org/sites/default/files/26.%20ICGN%20Letter%20to%20UK%20Hill%20-%20Call%20for%20 Evidence%20–%20UK%20Listings%20Review.pdf
8. Climate Action 100+: www.climateaction100.org
9. Simmons & Simmons, *More Hot News: Climate Related Shareholder Resolutions*, 22 January 2021: www. simmons-simmons.com/en/publications/ckk8k0rnl1hik0918wl0w6qwr/more-hot-news-climate-related-shareholder-resolutions
10. *New York Times*, Exxon's Board Defeat Signals the Rise of Social-Good Activists: www.nytimes.com/2021/06/09/business/exxon-mobil-engine-no1-activist.html
11. Kessler, Topaz, Meltzer & Check, *A Primer on Shareholder Litigation*: www.ktmc.com/files/522_Primer.pdf. For a useful primer on global securities litigation see Pensions and Lifetime Savings Association, *Global Securities Litigation Made Simple Guide*, September 2022: https://www.plsa.co.uk/Securities-Litigation-Made-Simple
12. ICGN, *Statement to the Council of Experts for the Follow-up of Japan's Stewardship Code and Japan's Corporate Governance Code*, 9 March 2019: www.icgn.org/sites/default/files/4_FSA%20Statement%20to%20the%20 Council_5Mar19_0.pdf
13. Given the internationalisation of institutional investment, the 'overseas' (ie non-domestic) investor base is often substantial, if not the dominant investor base. For example, the overseas investor base is over 50% in the UK and Germany, and around 35% in the very large markets of the US and Japan.
14. Elroy Dimson, Oğuzhan Karakaş and Xi Li, *Co-ordinated Engagements*, European Corporate Governance Institute (ECGI)—Finance Working Paper No 721/2021, January 2021: https://ssrn.com/abstract=3209072; Craig Doidge et al, *Collective Action and Governance Activism*, 30 August 2017: https://papers.ssrn.com/sol3/papers.cfm?abstract_ id=2635662
15. Their ricketiness and dependence on manual processes would seem to make systems for share voting good candidates for application of encrypted distributed general ledger technologies such as blockchain. See Mark Fenwick and Erik P. M. Vermeulen, *Technology and Corporate Governance: Blockchain, Crypto, and Artificial Intelligence*, November 2018, ECGI: https://papers.ssrn.com/sol3/papers.cfm?abstract_id=3263222. Unfortunately, in part owing to resistance from entrenched participants, such modern technological solutions have yet to materialise.
16. Corporate services companies, such as Broadridge Financial Solutions, facilitate the prompt delivery (usually electronically) of company communications to shareholders. They direct proxy statements, annual reports and other communications to shareholders and handle the collection of completed proxies and share voting instructions for transmittal back to those authorised to vote the shares (usually sub-custodians). Some, but not all, proxy advisors bundle their share voting research and recommendations services with similar company–shareholder communications and voting execution services.
17. Securities 'loans' are actually sales—title to the shares rests with the securities 'borrower' until the 'loan'/sale is reversed.

18. ICGN, *Guidance on Securities Lending*, 2016: http://icgn.flpbks.com/icgn_securities-lending_2015/files/extfile/ DownloadURL.pdf
19. US Securities and Exchange Commission, *SEC Adopts Rule Amendments to Provide Investors Using Proxy Voting Advice More Transparent, Accurate and Complete Information: SEC Issues Supplemental Guidance Concerning Proxy Voting Responsibilities of Investment Advisers*, 22 July 2020, Press Release: www.sec.gov/news/press-release/2020-161
20. Council of Institutional Investors, *Leading Investor Group Dismayed by SEC Proxy Advice Rule*, 22 July 2020, Press Release: www.cii.org/july22_sec_proxy_advice_rules
21. See ICGN letter to the US Securities and Exchange Commission, 21 November 2019: www.icgn.org/sites/default/files/19.%20SEC%20Proxy%20Advisor%20Interpretation%20and%20Guidance.pdf
22. US Securities and Exchange Commission, SEC Release No 34-93595, 17 November 2021: www.sec.gov/rules/proposed/2021/34-93595.pdf
23. These are criteria that guide ICGN's annual stewardship disclosure awards.
24. These disclosure documents are available to ICGN members at www.icgn.org
25. AVIVA Investors, *Stewardship and Responsible Investment Policy*, January 2017. Principle 4, p. 13: www.avivainvestors.com/en-us/about/responsible-investment/
26. Allianz Global Investors, *Stewardship Statement*, p. 8: www.allianzgi.com/-/media/allianzgi/globalagi/our-firm/ ouresgapproach/allianzgi-stewardship-statement-sept-2020.pdf

FURTHER READING

ICGN–GISD Alliance Model Mandate, June 2022: www.icgn.org/sites/default/files/2022-06/ICGN%20GISD%20Model%20Mandate%202022.pdf

David Chambers, Elroy Dimson and Ellen Quigley, To Divest or to Engage? A Case Study of Investor Responses to Climate Activism, 2020, *The Journal of Investing*, Special ESG Issue: https://joi.pm-research.com/content/29/2/10.abstract

UK Financial Conduct Authority, *Building a Regulatory Framework for Effective Stewardship*, January 2019: www.fca.org.uk/publications/feedback-statements/fs19-7-building-regulatory-framework-effective-stewardship

ICGN, *Model Disclosure Templates on Conflicts of Interest, Monitoring, Voting and Engagement*, 2018: www.icgn.org/policy/guidance/icgn-model-disclosure-templates

Tamas Barko, Martijn Cremers and Luc Renneboog, *Shareholder Engagement on Environmental, Social, and Governance Performance*, September 2018, CentER Discussion Paper Series No 2017-040; European Corporate Governance Institute (ECGI)—Finance Working Paper No 509/2017; TILEC Discussion Paper No DP 2017-021: https://papers.ssrn.com/sol3/papers.cfm?abstract_id=2977219

Elroy Dimson, Oğuzhan Karakaş and Xi Li, *Co-ordinated Engagement*, 1 July 2018: https://ssrn.com/abstract=3209072

Klaus J. Hopt, *The Dialogue between the Chairman of the Board and Investors: The Practice in the UK, the Netherlands and Germany and the Future of the German Corporate Governance Code Under the New Chairman*, 2017, ECGI—Law Working Paper No. 365/2017: https://papers.ssrn.com/sol3/papers.cfm?abstract_id=3030693

Craig Doidge et al, *Collective Action and Governance Activism*, 30 August 2017: https://papers.ssrn.com/sol3/papers.cfm?abstract_id=2635662

Chapter 7

Company perspective: Sustainability governance and reporting

DOI: 10.4324/9781003307082-7

Thus far, our book has focused on investor stewardship and on both why—and how—to integrate ESG factors into the investment process. But we believe it is important to address the company perspective in terms of both the governance of sustainability and how material sustainability issues are best reported and assured. However, the investor angle remains, as we present investor expectations of and aspirations for how sustainable companies might best approach sustainability governance and integrated reporting. This includes consideration of the role of audit and assurance in both financial and non-financial performance reporting.

1. THE GOVERNANCE OF SUSTAINABILITY

The ICGN *Global Governance Principles* (GGP) are not explicitly focused on the governance of sustainability as distinct from corporate governance more generally. But central to this book is the importance of sustainability, which, in a corporate context, we define as operating within acceptable social, ethical and environmental norms—both to generate long-term value and contribute positively (or at least neutrally) in a social context. The growing focus on company purpose, stakeholder relations and ESG factors means that these sustainability considerations should be built into the main board activities covered in the GGP.

The motivations for a company to govern sustainability issues may vary. For some companies, the motive may be fundamentally one of 'greenwashing'—wishing to paint a positive public image, whether or not that image is justified. Such an approach can be superficial, and deceitful in the extreme. Boards should take heed that, in an era where society's trust of business is low, negative publicity for questionable business practices can quickly escalate through the intense, and sometimes relentless, scrutiny of conventional or social media. Unanticipated reputational crises can be easily triggered, and companies with limited forms of control mechanisms relating to ESG factors may find themselves vulnerable to significant financial, operational and reputational damage.

Our focus is on companies that take sustainability seriously, and not as window dressing. But, in these cases, there can also be differing—but more legitimate—perspectives on sustainability and the purpose of the company, as was discussed in Chapter 2 in the section on shareholders and stakeholders. Some companies may focus on the traditional purpose of generating sustainable value for shareholders and are sufficiently 'enlightened' to recognise that ESG and other sustainability factors are an essential component of long-term value generation. Other companies, such as B Corporations,[1] may build sustainability and social impact into their direct mission and purpose. Seeking a positive social impact is certainly laudable, but, for many ESG-focused investors, the baseline emphasis or minimum common denominator is not having a negative impact—as in the Hippocratic oath to 'do no harm.' Whether a company is seeking to do good or at least not do harm will require similar thought processes and awareness of key sustainability issues, by both executive managers and company boards.

Global frameworks and legislation: is Europe setting the pace?

There is no one right way for companies to develop an approach to the governance of sustainability. But companies can be supported by public guidance, such as the OECD

Guidelines for Multinational Enterprise,[2] that establish a framework for responsible business conduct. The UN *Sustainable Development Goals* (SDGs) also present companies and investors with a range of sustainability issues where private sector involvement is important and required.

Regulatory frameworks, particularly in Europe, have incorporated sustainability elements into law and regulation. As an example of company law linking to sustainability, section 172 of the UK Companies Act (2006) effectively hardwires sustainability into director duties, requiring directors to show appropriate regard for company stakeholders including employees, suppliers and customers, typically from a long-term perspective. It also speaks to the more general impact on communities and the environment and the need to maintain high standards of business conduct. These are all important to sustainable performance and long-term value creation.

Through its Sustainable Finance agenda, the European Union (EU) has long been an active protagonist in its promotion of sustainability in finance and corporate governance. It is demonstrating global leadership by prioritising the sustainability agenda through a range of initiatives that frame sustainability from the EU perspective and impose obligations, mostly relating to disclosure, on both companies and investors. While the EU's agenda encompasses ESG in a broad context, it places much emphasis on climate change and related natural capital and environmental issues.

The EU focus is clearly on businesses and investors domiciled in the EU, but its impact is global, particularly given that many non-EU companies and institutional investors have European operations that need to meet EU requirements. Moreover, the EU's proactivity in promoting sustainability in many ways has established it as a global benchmark—even though there are criticisms of the EU's agenda, particularly with regard to potential changes in company law. Nevertheless, for executives and boards globally that are focusing on enhancing the governance of sustainability in their companies, the EU Sustainable Finance initiative provides an important framework in terms of what sustainability means and how it should be reported, both by companies and investors.

A complete discussion and analysis of the EU Sustainable Finance agenda is beyond the scope of this book, but we provide short descriptions of some of the key EU sustainability initiatives below:

- *Non-Financial Reporting Directive* (NFRD): enacted in 2014, this is the EU's first key initiative on corporate reporting of ESG/sustainability performance and required large companies to publish information on: environmental matters, social matters and treatment of employees, respect for human rights, anti-corruption and bribery, and diversity on company boards (in terms of age, gender, and educational and professional background).[3]
- *Corporate Sustainability Reporting Directive* (CSRD): this proposal was published in 2021 to amend reporting requirements under the NFRD. The CSRD extends the scope of the NFRD to all large companies and all companies listed on regulated markets (except listed micro-enterprises); requires the audit (assurance) of reported information; introduces more detailed reporting requirements and a requirement to report according to mandatory EU sustainability reporting standards; and requires companies to digitally 'tag' the reported information, so

it is machine readable and can be accessed through a single point. The intent is to give sustainability reporting a similar standard of quality, consistency and assurance that is found in financial reporting. This initiative will lead to development of EU-wide sustainability reporting standards.[4]

- *Sustainable Finance Disclosure Regulation* (SFDR): as a sort of counterpoint to the CSRD, the SFDR is a disclosure regime introduced in 2021 that applies specifically to institutional investors, and in particular asset management firms providing investment services to pension funds and other beneficiaries. It lays down sustainability disclosure obligations for financial products with regard to the integration of sustainability considerations in investment product creation, investment decision-making and investor stewardship. With a discipline supported by the EU Taxonomy Regulation (see below), the SFDR is intended in part to protect and inform end investor beneficiaries and to prevent 'greenwashing' by investors in terms of how they make, define and market investment products.[5] With regards to investment funds that are listed in Article 8 and Article 9 of the SFDR as having an ESG focus, Article 8 refers to funds that employ ESG criteria in their investment process, but mainly as a means for better fund performance, not to create a social impact. Investment funds under the scope of Article 9 have an explicit goal of positive social and environmental impact that ranks alongside investment returns.
- *Taxonomy Regulation*: the EU Taxonomy Regulation was enacted in 2020 as a classification system establishing a list of six environmentally sustainable economic activities that can be linked to sustainable investment as a guide for companies, investors and policymakers. The Taxonomy Regulation establishes a framework of six sustainable environmental objectives: climate change mitigation, climate change adaptation, the sustainable use and protection of water and marine resources, the transition to a circular economy, pollution prevention and control, and the protection and restoration of biodiversity and ecosystems. More generally, beyond environmental issues, there is also the requirement that companies respect basic human rights and labour standards and 'do no significant harm.' It provides a foundation and discipline for the CSRD and SFDR in terms of defining sustainable activity and seeking to avoid 'greenwashing' by both companies and investors. From accounting year 2021 onwards, EU listed companies are required to disclose their expected taxonomy eligibility and taxonomy non-eligibility activities within revenue, capital expenditure and operating expenditure (comprising a restrictive list of certain operating expenses) contributing to climate adaptation and mitigation.

  In a subsequent development, the EU Taxonomy Climate Delegated Act, agreed in April 2021, defines the technical screening criteria for economic activities that can make a substantial contribution to climate change mitigation and climate change adaptation.[6] To build upon the existing taxonomy, which focuses on environmental issues, a similarly intended social taxonomy is also in the works.[7]
- *Sustainable Corporate Governance initiative*: on top of these initiatives, which focus primarily on disclosure obligations, the EU is also exploring legislative ways to hardwire sustainability practices into the governance of European companies.

In 2020, the EU undertook a review of company law and corporate governance, conducted by the consultancy EY, seeking to enable companies to focus more on long-term sustainable value creation and to better align the interests of companies, their shareholders, managers, stakeholders and society.[8] Building from the EY study, the EU launched a public consultation in late 2020–early 2021 exploring a range of reform proposals, including the redefinition of directors' duties and legal prescriptions relating to issues of human rights and social and environmental due diligence, including supply chain oversight.

However, the quality and legitimacy of the underlying EY study supporting these proposals was roundly, and savagely, critiqued by academic commentators.[9] For example, several Harvard scholars identified the following flaws, including inappropriate conflation of sustainability with time horizons, flawed evidence, biased use of research literature and ill-considered reform proposals.[10] ICGN expressed similar caution in its comment letter to the EU. While sharing the goal of more sustainable corporate governance practices, ICGN was not supportive of legislative changes in director's duties, expressing the view that some of the EU's proposed prescriptions might be better suited to a comply or explain-based corporate governance code than to hard law regulation at the EU level.[11]

No doubt influenced by this pushback, this EU initiative morphed in 2022 into a proposal for a new corporate sustainability due diligence directive that was less far-reaching in redefining the fiduciary responsibilities and duties of directors.[12] Nevertheless the EU proposal sets out a corporate due diligence duty to identify, prevent, bring to an end, mitigate and account for adverse human rights and environmental impacts in the company's own operations, its subsidiaries and their value chains. It builds on the UN's *Guiding Principles on Business and Human Rights* and the OECD *Guidelines for Multinational Enterprises*[13] and responsible business conduct, and is in line with internationally recognised human rights and labour standards.

It is worth noting that Article 25 of the EU's 2022 proposed Directive on corporate sustainability due diligence contains a requirement for directors to 'take into account the consequences of their decisions for sustainability matters, including, where applicable, human rights, climate change and environmental consequences.'[14] This language closely resembles duties outlined in section 172 of the UK Companies Act of 2006 for directors to 'have regard for' stakeholder considerations.

In practice, the new proposal will require the companies within its scope to:

- Integrate due diligence into policies.
- Identify actual or potential adverse human rights and environmental impacts.
- Prevent or mitigate potential impacts.
- Bring to an end or minimise actual impacts.
- Establish and maintain a complaints procedure.
- Monitor the effectiveness of the due diligence policy and measures.
- Publicly communicate on due diligence.[15]

Our focus here on Europe in terms of the governance of sustainability and sustainable finance is because this package of initiatives is more comprehensive in content and scope than in any other jurisdiction globally. Although it clearly sets the agenda in Europe, the EU's sustainability framework is also influencing the global debate—including in the United States, where the SEC recently proposed rule changes that would require registrants to include certain climate-related disclosures in their registration statements and periodic reports, including information about climate-related risks that are reasonably likely to have a material impact on their business, results of operations, or financial condition, and certain climate-related financial statement metrics in a note to their audited financial statements.[16] Company executives, board directors and investors globally with an interest in sustainable corporate governance should be aware of and monitor the dynamics of the European sustainability agenda and how this agenda might complement —or possibly face challenge from—other global initiatives such as the development of the International Sustainability Standards Board.

Board governance

As a matter of fiduciary, duty sustainability issues should feature as a regular part of board discussion and debate—not as a topic detached from the company's core business operations, but rather integrated into board deliberations on planning, strategy, operations and controls.[17] While different forms of corporate social responsibility/sustainability committees exist within some corporate boards, there is no requirement to establish a standalone committee as long as the board as a whole is able to monitor and oversee its material sustainability risks effectively.

However, it is important to ensure that sustainability does not slip through the cracks, and that social expectations and impacts are monitored by the board with rigour to help it better understand potential risks or vulnerabilities. As will be discussed below in the section on integrated reporting, corporate boards need to build greater appreciation of the different pools of capital that companies have, beyond the basic financial accounting capital. The IIRC's integrated reporting model features six forms of capital,[18] whereas ICGN's GGP draw from a similar, but less granular, multi-capital framework, focusing on three basic forms of capital: financial capital, natural capital and human capital.

Boards can and should build and enhance their understanding of and sensitivity to these forms of capital and how these link sustainability factors through direct engagement with shareholders and relevant stakeholder groups. It is increasingly relevant for nomination committees to seek board directors with expertise in sustainability practices that are important for the industry in which the company operates. All board members should be 'fluent' in discussing and evaluating those ESG factors that are material to the company and its key stakeholders.

Boards should also ensure that appropriate codes of conduct are in place in the company addressing legal, compliance and ethical behaviour standards. In part depending on the company's sector and geography, boards also may wish to consider adding non-executive directors with established understanding of key ethical risks in the company's sector—to help provide guidance and sensitise other board members to relevant corporate social responsibility (CSR) issues the company may face.

CSR V SUSTAINABILITY/RESPONSIBLE INVESTING V ESG INVESTING

The terms 'corporate social responsibility,' 'sustainability' and 'ESG' are frequently used interchangeably in ways that can be both sloppy and confusing. And, of course, there is no globally accepted arbiter to determine what each term should mean. But, as commonly employed, the three expressions have some subtle, but important, differences in scope and emphasis when used in reference to a company's operations.

CSR is probably the oldest and broadest of these three terms. It is typically used to refer to all the activities of a company that contribute to public welfare. CSR can encompass not just what steps a company takes to maximise the value it creates for stakeholders and minimise the damage its activities may inflict on society and the environment, but also other contributions to society that might fall under the rubric of 'corporate citizenship.' These can include philanthropic initiatives, such as promoting civic engagement among employees, running blood donor drives on its facilities and donating to local and national charities. Employed in this sense, CSR covers both how a company makes its money (its core operations) and how it uses some of the money it makes (including discretionary spending to benefit society and burnish its reputation).

In contrast, sustainability and ESG refer more narrowly to the impacts of a company's core operational activities—how it makes its money. Of the two, sustainability is the broader term, with ESG focusing more narrowly on the three key, externally monitorable pillars of environmental and social impact and the firm's governance. As such, discussions around a company's ESG performance are more likely to make reference to specific measurements or comparisons against benchmarks and key performance metrics and progress towards aspirational standards.

In similar fashion, the terms 'responsible investing,' 'socially responsible investing,' 'ESG investing' and 'sustainable financing and investing' are often used interchangeably to refer to investment styles that are sensitive to environmental, ethical and social issues. The first two expressions, responsible investing (RI) and socially responsible investing (SRI), were used initially to refer to particular investors' policies to exclude from their portfolios industries or companies whose activities were deemed sufficiently deleterious to the public that investing in them would be 'irresponsible.' Boycotting companies that did business in apartheid South Africa and excluding investments in the tobacco or thermal coal industries or in particular companies that employ child labour would qualify as RI and SRI.

ESG investing and sustainable finance and investing generally refer to more proactive incorporation of ESG and sustainability factors in investment selection and stewardship. ESG investing relies more on comprehensively incorporating consideration of ESG factors and metrics in the investment decision-making process. Sustainable finance also encompasses specialised financial instruments (such as 'green bonds') designed to channel investment into activities with demonstrably positive outcomes, such as CO_2 emission reduction, renewable energy or financial inclusion.

Boards should explicitly recognise their accountability and fiduciary responsibility for ensuring the company's responsible social performance. This is not simply a compliance exercise. It is necessary to set the right cultural and ethical tone. The tone and conviction of company leadership is critical if sustainability is to be anything beyond a top–down compliance exercise.

Accountability also calls for establishing governance structures and systems of oversight and control to allow boards to govern ESG issues in a manner that is most appropriate for the company. A small, but growing, minority of companies have established dedicated ESG/sustainability committees of the board. Stand-alone committees to lead the board's oversight of ESG risk and disclosures may be desirable where such risks are especially material and/or where establishment and monitoring of KPIs around ESG require a high degree of technical expertise.

What are the sustainability factors to focus on?

So, how do boards govern sustainability issues in practice? And how should they choose which ones to focus on? The boundaries of corporate governance and sustainability are fluid, and new issues continuously call for attention by executives and boards. There is a potentially limitless number of environmental and social factors to consider, including both 'known unknowns' (such as the impact of climate change) and 'unknown unknowns' (such as the sudden emergence of Covid-19).[19] However, the bandwidth of executives and boards is not limitless.

Building from the discussion of materiality in Chapter 4, a necessary starting point is to use the lens of materiality to identify those sustainability issues that have greatest relevance for the business and its stakeholders. But that can be easier said than done. It is first necessary for executives and boards to build sensitivity to key stakeholders and their needs. The discipline of materiality is not only to assess how ESG factors might affect the company's own financial performance directly; it is also to assess the company's broad environmental and social impact, which can include a company's exploitation of legal, but socially damaging, externalities. This is the concept of 'double materiality,' which is a core feature of the EU's NFRD. This is discussed in greater detail in Chapter 4 on ESG data and reporting.

To a large extent, the sector in which the company operates will dictate the key environmental and social risks. For example, climate change risk is fundamental to the energy and utility sectors, health and safety are fundamental to the mining sector, nutrition is fundamental to the food sector, and labour standards are fundamental to the retail sector. At the same time, not all environmental and social issues are material drivers; for example, environmental management and pollution control are typically not the main issues directly facing technology firms. While environmental and social risks will vary between sectors, one can argue that broader themes of corporate governance, sustainability management and business ethics should have strong relevance across all firms in all jurisdictions.

Robust and objective self-assessment of a company should help both executive management and the company's board to build a shared understanding of the company's specific social impacts and risks—in particular, which factors have the greatest materiality in terms of an individual company's social performance and the company's own long-term sustainability. From this shared understanding, companies can develop approaches to sustainability that best reflect the company's own needs and impacts.

INVESTORS EXPECT BOARDS TO ADDRESS THE FOLLOWING QUESTIONS RELATING TO THE GOVERNANCE OF SUSTAINABILITY

- Stakeholders—who are the company's most important stakeholders? How have they been identified? How does the company interact with them?
- Has the company undertaken a materiality analysis or stakeholder mapping exercise? How did the company come to understand and communicate its most material E&S risks? What is the process? Who is involved?
- Does the company measure, evaluate and disclose its roadmap to meeting targets and its annual progress against targets?
- Is the company committed to a net-zero business model, and, if so, does its financial and sustainability reporting disclose underlying assumptions and scenarios that align with a net-zero strategy?
- What policies surrounding ESG does the company have? Labour and human rights policies? Environmental policy? Supply chain policy?
- Does the company prepare for current and future regulatory requirements on ESG matters? How? Is the company proactive or even thinking about these issues? Is there a strategy or internal mechanism for assessing country-specific conditions and future financial risk due to environmental and social issues?
- Are there any issues with such overwhelming risk that financial models should be altered to adjust for such risk? Are sensitivity analyses needed?
- Is disclosure adequate compared with peers? How does the company measure up compared with other firms in their industry?
- How does the company fare in ESG ratings, and how could the company improve? What does a best-practice company look like within the same industry?
- To which international standards/certifications relating to sustainability does the company apply? To which should it apply?

Risk management and compliance

From a risk perspective, ESG issues can be a form of contingent liability that should be identified, managed and mitigated. Traditional risk management systems can run the risk of fighting the last war, particularly with regard to more qualitative social risks. But anticipating and avoiding future risks of this nature are the key. For example, we know that the next new ethical crisis for banks will not be Libor rate manipulation; that one has already been done. But what will be the next social controversy that surfaces about the banking sector? Is there a way for a company to 'future-proof' itself against the known or unknown future ESG risks it may face?

While risk management and compliance are activities carried out by a company's management team, the board should have clear oversight and responsibility for material sustainability issues being identified. This includes some form of accountability/communications channel to the board for those in the company who have responsibility for various sustainability issues. Many risk management systems have quantitative approaches to financial and operational risk. However, some ESG risks, particularly those relating to social and ethical issues, are more qualitative in nature, and it can be challenging for these forms of risk to be assessed with the same rigour as risks that are more readily quantifiable.

Boards can choose from four main options in assigning responsibility for oversight of ESG risk: full board, audit committee, risk committee or specialised ESG/sustainability committee. Deciding which approach is best requires consideration of a variety of industry- and company-specific factors, as well as legal/regulatory considerations in the jurisdiction in which the company is organised or listed. (For example, New York Stock Exchange listing rules require audit committee review of risk policies.)

Leaving risk oversight exclusively to the full board is increasingly disfavoured by boards themselves. The OECD *Corporate Governance Factbook* reported a sharp increase from 62% to 87% in the number of jurisdictions requiring (50%) or recommending (37%) assigning responsibility for risk to a board committee between 2015 and 2019.[20] A pattern of the audit committee taking on responsibility for risk oversight has emerged in a number of jurisdictions since the beginning of the century. Reasons for assigning this function to the audit committee include the independent composition of audit committees, a desire to ensure that oversight of financial and non-financial risk are well-co-ordinated and the historical pattern of risk management functions reporting to the CFO (who in turn reports to the audit committee).

A board typically establishes a stand-alone risk committee when operational risks (as opposed to the financial risks that are the focus of the audit committee) are particularly salient and/or the company's systems are rapidly evolving in response to such risks. A separate risk committee of the board allows directors more versed in operations than finance and accounting to take primary responsibility for overseeing the company's non-financial risk management system. In some countries (such as the US) and industries (notably banking and finance), the financial statement and account compliance burdens imposed on audit committees may leave its members with little capacity or bandwidth to play an effective role in oversight of non-financial risk.

The technical nature of a company's business may also militate for establishment of a stand-alone risk committee whose members have the requisite professional expertise and experience to understand and evaluate risks inherent in its operations. Mining, energy and financial companies typically establish stand-alone risk committees. In 2019, approximately one-third of jurisdictions required or recommended stand-alone risk committees, double the number in 2015.[21]

Investors expect boards to address the following questions regarding risk management of sustainability factors

- Environmental and social risk governance: who has responsibility for managing these risks?
- Does sustainability integration in everyday operations come from the c-suite or from the board?

- Does the board of directors or management include anyone with expertise in sustainability practices that are important for the industry in which the company operates?
- Are any compensation schemes tied to sustainability performance?
- Does the company have internal capabilities to deal with ESG risks? Does the company outsource to a public relations agency? Who would be out front if there was an ESG-related incident? Does this seem acceptable?
- Does the company have an in-house E&S/sustainability/CSR person? Where is this person in the organisation? What is this person's—or committee's—role, and to whom is the reporting line?

Linking sustainability performance with remuneration and incentive systems

To the extent that management behaviours are influenced by remuneration and financial incentives, a holistic approach to sustainability governance would suggest that material ESG factors should have links to executive pay. Incentive systems should promote positive behaviours and discourage inappropriate behaviour that brings disrepute and financial or reputational risks. These should be reflected in key performance indicators relating to ESG performance, which are likely to be sector- or firm-specific. Finding the right ESG metric or metrics that are material, measurable and assurable can be challenging, however, and well-intentioned attempts to integrate ESG into incentive structures do not always produce the intended results.[22]

To some extent, it challenges logic to award bonuses—extra pay—to an executive or employee for not violating social norms, as this should be implicit in the basic employment (if not social) contract. Arguably, there is a compelling reason to look at sustainability issues in remuneration as an 'underpinning,' or conditionality, to receiving bonus awards. In other words, inappropriate behaviour can negatively influence incentive pay that otherwise might have been earned through financial criteria alone. While loss of employment is an ultimate sanction for a behavioural breach clearly in violation of legal norms or company policy, other forms of sanction or penalty for poor CSR performance can be built into company remuneration structures.

2. NON-FINANCIAL OR NARRATIVE REPORTING

As a matter of corporate governance, executives and boards must reflect on how a company interfaces with society and stakeholders and what sustainability and ESG issues are material for report users. This also needs to be reflected in reporting, and the challenge is how best to do this. Although financial reporting is critical, we also must recognise its fundamental limitations. This begins with the observation that financial reports are axiomatically backward-looking by nature. The past can be a useful guide to understand performance and value creation, but it cannot predict the future.

Moreover, it is important to know how much (or how little) formal financial reporting actually tells us. For many companies, the book value in financial statements can often only account for a relatively small part of its valuation. In the US, 90% of the value of the S&P 500 now comes from intangible assets; in 1975, intangible assets represented only 17% of the S&P 500 market capitalisation.[23]

FIGURE 7.1 Components of S&P 500 market value

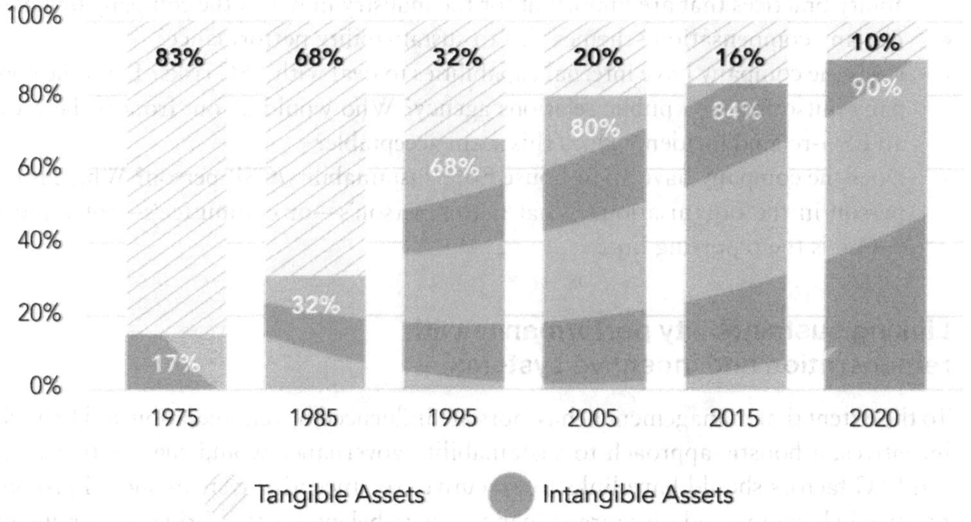

SOURCE: OCEAN TOMO, LLC INTANGIBLE ASSET MARKET VALUE STUDY, 2020

Intangible assets represent aspects of value that are not specifically accounted for on the balance sheet. This can include patents, trademarks, copyrights, brand recognition, customer data, proprietary technology and goodwill (in some markets)—as well as factors relating to ESG or sustainability issues. If this is not captured by financial accounting, then what can companies do to explain their intangible valuation—or give investors a way to look into the future rather than simply present what has passed?

At least part of the answer lies in reporting that is not constrained by financial accounting and that puts financial performance in a strategic and operational context through enhanced information that is non-financial—and often presented in a narrative context. The term 'non-financial' is widely used as a term of art. But it is a bit of a misnomer, particularly to the extent that it might lead some to question its link to a company's financial performance. But the forward-looking aspect of non-financial reporting can inform investors of risks and opportunities that can affect financial performance in the future; the term 'pre-financial' might be a better descriptor.

The journey to integrated reporting (and thinking)

The nature of non-financial reporting continues to evolve. It has come a long way, but still has a long way to go.[24] It is important to appreciate the journey and the various stops along the way. For most of the 20th century, non-financial reports did not exist or were minimal in scope.[25] Initial non-financial reports for investors and others tended to focus on 'special issues,' often relating to specific social or environmental themes in sectors such as chemicals, oil and gas, and tobacco— prompted by external stimuli such as the Union Carbide Bhopal disaster in India and the Exxon Valdez oil spill in Alaska in the 1980s.

The development of CSR reports in the 1990s began to provide a more holistic overview of social and environmental performance. The initial CSR reports were typically prepared separately from financial statements, and it was not always clear what the main audience of these reports was intended to be. It seems that investors were not the target of this early CSR reporting. CSR reports were often disregarded by investors and other financial analysts. The linkage of CSR issues to financial performance was typically not obvious, nor was it the main focus. For many investors, the discretionary nature of CSR reports, typically constructed from unaudited information of companies' choosing, gave these reports the feel of a public relations exercise, or greenwashing.

Integrated reporting is the next step on this reporting journey. It is a term of art for how corporate financial reporting and non-financial disclosure combine to provide a holistic assessment of a company's current condition and future prospects. The concept of integrated reporting is general in nature and can be applied in different ways. However, the IIRC (founded in 2010 and now part of the VRF) has developed a popular integrated reporting framework, branded <IR>, which has had been rolled out in many markets globally.[26]

Perhaps the most innovative feature of the <IR> model is that it separately considers six different forms of capital: financial, manufactured, intellectual, human, social and relationship, and natural. This presents a much broader picture of the company and corporate performance than focusing on financial capital alone. It also provides a consistent framework for assessing ESG data and other non-financial information. In spite of its progress in many jurisdictions, integrated reporting is still in an early stage of development.

While the <IR> model has had positive acceptance by many investors and companies, it is not the only way to approach integrated reporting. Some commentators find its six forms of capital approach a bit cumbersome and may find simpler models, such as the TCFD framework (discussed in Chapter 4), more intuitive. In addition, the 2020

FIGURE 7.2 IIRC framework

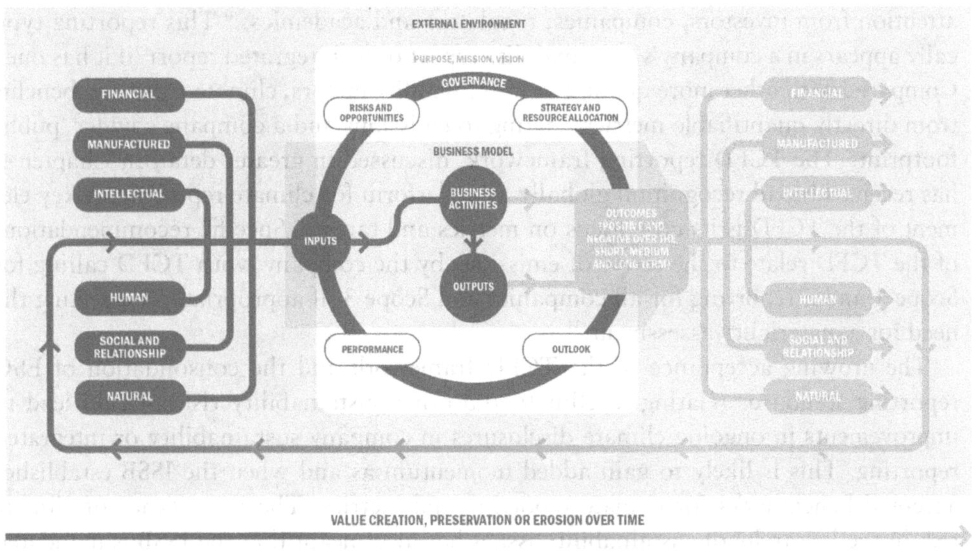

Source: Value Reporting Foundation

EU consultation on the Non-Financial Reporting Directive provides regulatory requirements for EU-based companies to focus on four distinct areas: environment, social/employee, human rights and bribery/corruption.

As an investor body, ICGN is supportive of the <IR> framework but is agnostic about endorsing <IR> or any particular integrated reporting framework over others. ICGN's governance policies focus on three primary forms of capital: financial, social and natural capital. The ICGN *Guidance on Integrated Business Reporting* states simply that 'the board should provide an integrated report that puts historical performance into context, and portrays the risks, opportunities and prospects for the company in the future, helping investors understand a company's strategic objectives and its progress towards meeting them.'[27]

The key is to augment financial reporting by integrating non-financial information into a narrative that pulls together financial, strategic, operational and sustainability performance. This amounts to 'integrated thinking' and is relevant not only for reporting but also for company management and governance.

A focus on climate reporting and accounting

Of all the ESG and systemic risks facing both companies and investors, climate change has emerged in many ways as *primus inter pares*, given its urgency and profound threats to companies (in most, if not all, sectors), financial markets, economies, societies and the natural environment. A growing number of investors include climate engagement as an important part of their ESG stewardship agenda,[28] and ICGN's GGP state that 'the board should assess the impact of climate change on the company business model and how it will be adapted to meet the needs of a net zero economy as part of a long-term strategy.' Indeed, the adoption of a net-zero strategy is becoming a key investor indicator and engagement point regarding the governance of sustainability for companies and boards.[29]

Given these dynamics, climate reporting has understandably received considerable attention from investors, companies, regulators and academics.[30] This reporting typically appears in a company's sustainability report or its integrated report (if it has one). Compared with other more qualitative sustainability factors, climate reporting benefits from directly quantifiable metrics relating to emissions and a company's wider 'public footprint.' The TCFD reporting framework, discussed in greater detail in Chapter 4, has received broad recognition globally as a platform for climate reporting. A key element of the TCFD is its core focus on metrics and targets. Specific recommendations of the TCFD relate to the scope of emissions by the company, with TCFD calling for Scope 1 and 2 reporting for all companies and Scope 3 'if appropriate,' suggesting the need for a materiality assessment.[31]

The growing acceptance of the TCFD framework and the consolidation of ESG reporting standards relating to climate and other sustainability risks should lead to improvements in ongoing climate disclosures in company sustainability or integrated reporting. This is likely to gain added momentum as and when the ISSB establishes accepted benchmarks for climate reporting and metrics. The importance of climate risk in the hierarchy of sustainability issues has also meant that the ISSB is mandated to prioritise its work on climate relative to other sustainability standards.

Although this is positive, there is a growing call by investors for climate factors to go beyond narrative reporting and link directly with a company's financial accounting and reports: how climate risks might affect the measurement of assets, liabilities, profits and cash flows. This is particularly relevant for companies that have committed publicly to net-zero targets[32] and is reflected in the 2013 Carbon Tracker report, which estimated that 60–80% of coal, oil and gas reserves of publicly listed companies is 'unburnable' if the world is to have a chance of not exceeding global warming of 2°C.[33]

This issue is not lost on the leading global accounting and auditing standards bodies; climate accounting is clearly on the agenda, as the financial materiality of climate risk can be real. In a 2019 report, the IASB published a report examining climate factors through the lens of financial materiality and concluded that climate risk has the potential to be linked into a range of accounting considerations, including:

- Asset impairment, including goodwill.
- Changes in the useful life of assets.
- Changes in the fair valuation of assets.
- Effects on impairment calculations of increased costs or reduced demand.
- Changes in provisions for onerous contracts because of increased costs or reduced demand.
- Changes in provisions and contingent liabilities arising from fines and penalties.
- Changes in expected credit losses for loans and other financial assets.[34]

Particularly for fossil fuel-based companies, asset impairment is a clear climate-related risk, as 'stranded assets' held on the balance sheet may never become economic. A visible example of this was BP's writedown of US$16 billion of stranded assets relating to its oil reserves in 2020. It begs the question of what more there is to come, not only from BP—which has committed to a net-zero strategy—but also from its energy sector peers who, to date, have not committed to net-zero strategies or made similar accounting adjustments.

On the auditing side of the equation, the International Auditing and Assurance Standards Board (IAASB) has also weighed in, noting that

> most, if not all entities, are likely to be impacted by climate change; directly or indirectly. Industries that are more likely to be directly affected by climate change include, for example, financial services (including banks and insurance groups), energy, transportation, construction, primary producers, agriculture and forestry industries.

It goes on to assert that 'climate-related events or conditions may contribute to the susceptibility to misstatement of certain amounts and disclosures in an entity's financial statements.'[35]

Although there is movement within the realm of the IASB and the IAASB, the elephant in room is arguably the US—the home of the world's largest capital market. Although the US was a signatory to the Paris Agreement in 2015, the Trump administration subsequently rescinded the US commitment, and, during that period, the US was largely absent from recent public policy dialogue on integrating climate risks into financial statements. Having said that, this is now an evolving issue that is gaining traction in the US under the Biden administration, which has reconfirmed the US's commitment to the Paris Agreement and its goals. While not singling out climate accounting, it is worth noting that the US FASB issued a staff 'educational paper' in 2021 on the intersection of ESG factors with financial accounting. It clarified:

> when applying financial accounting standards, an entity may consider the effects of certain material ESG matters, similar to how an entity considers other changes in its business and operation environment that have material direct or indirect effects on the financial statements and notes thereto.[36]

While not as explicit as elsewhere in the world, the link to climate accounting is clear.

However, climate change is explicitly on the agenda of other key US regulatory bodies relevant to investors. This includes the Office of the Comptroller of the Currency (OCC), which has established six overarching principles to support banks' efforts to focus on key aspects of climate-related governance financial risk management.[37] The US Department of Labor (DoL) has engaged with this issue through the lens of how the physical and transition risks of climate change might affect the life savings of US workers enrolled in occupational pension plans under the supervision of the Employment Retirement Income Security Act (ERISA). It launched a public consultation in early 2022 seeking input on what policies, practices and sources of information relating to climate change best protect beneficiaries' interests.[38] As already noted, the SEC has proposed rule changes that would require registrants to include climate-related disclosures in their registration statements. It has also proposed new rules requiring investment funds that market themselves as 'ESG' to provide standardised data backing up claims that the funds' investments are environmentally friendly and leaders in social and governance issues.[39]

As the US SEC continues to explore the question of climate accounting and reporting, investors generally welcome bringing the US into this debate—and bringing US companies under greater scrutiny.[40] But, as the FASB, SEC, DoL and OCC address these issues, it will be important for any standards adopted in the US to have general alignment with the IASB and the ISSB to provide the global consistency investors are looking for. Otherwise, the risk of a Towel of Babel remains vis-à-vis international standards and standards within key markets such as the EU and the US.

Notwithstanding the growing investor interest in climate accounting, the conceptual acknowledgement from the leading global accounting and auditing standard setters that climate risks can materially impact financial statements has yet to be significantly matched by action on the ground, in company audited financial statements. The 2021 *Flying Blind* report by the Carbon Tracker Initiative and the Climate Accounting Project[41] studied the 2020 financial accounts of over 100 companies, mostly on the Climate Action 100+ (CA100+) focus list of the world's leading greenhouse gas emitters. Their findings are sobering, including that over 70% of the companies did not indicate consideration of climate matters when preparing financial statements, and only 25% provided disclosure of quantitative assumptions in their financial reports.

And, even though the Big 6 accounting firms all joined the Glasgow Financial Alliance for Net Zero (GFANZ) in late 2021 to commit to a net-zero transition, 80% of auditors of 2021 statements provided no indication of whether or how they considered material climate-related matters.[42]

The reasons for this gap may be manifold. There can no doubt be technical and practical challenges that auditors face in implementing accounting for companies at the individual company level. This is not a developed area of accounting, and audit firms will need to build capacity and provide appropriate training and oversight. As this is still emerging as an issue for accounting and auditing, it is inevitable that climate accounting may be dealt with cautiously, and with some cultural resistance, by both companies and auditors, who may not see it as the role of investors to call for climate risk to be reflected in financial reports. Moreover, there is the question of self-interest. A challenge that must be recognised is that companies may have an interest in obscuring the potential accounting impacts on their business model and financial statements that might result from climate change if those impacts are deemed as disadvantageous. This may not serve the short-term interests of the company (or at least its executive management). Yet companies should not have the ability to pick and choose which accounting standards they use, nor auditors to choose the auditing standards.

Several members of the institutional investor community are seeking to prod companies and auditing firms to take more immediate action on introducing climate risks into financial reporting. The Institutional Investor Group on Climate Change (IIGCC), representing global investors managing in excess of €50 trillion, launched an advocacy campaign in 2020 to articulate investor expectations of financial statements aligned with the Paris Agreement of 2015. In 2021, the CA100+ incorporated climate accounting and auditing as part of its benchmark. This presents challenges to companies and auditors to promote the consideration of material climate risks in financial statements and to provide underlying detail on assumptions, scenarios and estimates embedded in the financial reports—particularly with regard to companies who have made some form of Paris-aligned net-zero commitment by 2050.[43]

A final observation, before we proceed to the related discussion of auditing and assurance, is that climate change is likely to be a harbinger of further linkage of sustainability factors into financial accounting. As global sustainability reporting standards consolidate, and as more consistent metrics are applied in sustainability reporting beyond climate risk, we will hopefully see an evidence trail emerge that may provide empirical grounding to establishing further links between financial reporting and sustainability risks.

3. AUDITING

The audit profession is a critical component of the financial statement ecosystem. The purpose of audits is to provide a degree of assurance that accounts provide a reliable view of capital and performance, taking into due consideration elements of both fair value accounting and prudence. The conducting of audits by audit firms is intended to provide both professional expertise and independence to fortify the accuracy and integrity of financial statements for company managers, boards, investors and other users.

Audit quality, both internal and external, is therefore fundamental to good corporate governance. But it is a complex process, involving a number of actors and a wide range of contextual factors, as suggested in the IAASB Framework for Audit Quality in Figure 7.3.[44]

The dynamics of these complexities mean that quality cannot always be assumed, and there can be an 'expectations gap' between investor needs and the reality of current audit practice. Auditor independence and professional scepticism are critical for a high-quality audit service. Exercising sufficient scepticism can be challenging in light of the business model in which the management (in practice) selects the auditors and the company itself pays for audit services. But audit firms, as commercial businesses themselves, also have their own interests at heart (including an interest to continue to serve as the company's auditor), which can create conflicts and potentially compromise independence and objectivity in their professional services. This could be influenced by the same firm providing other lucrative non-audit services or by a long-standing auditing relationship in which the auditor may be disinclined to 'rock the boat'. Notwithstanding greater attention to reducing, if not eliminating, non-audit fees and introducing mandatory auditor (partner and firm) rotation requirements seek to address these conflicts.

FIGURE 7.3 IAASB framework for audit quality

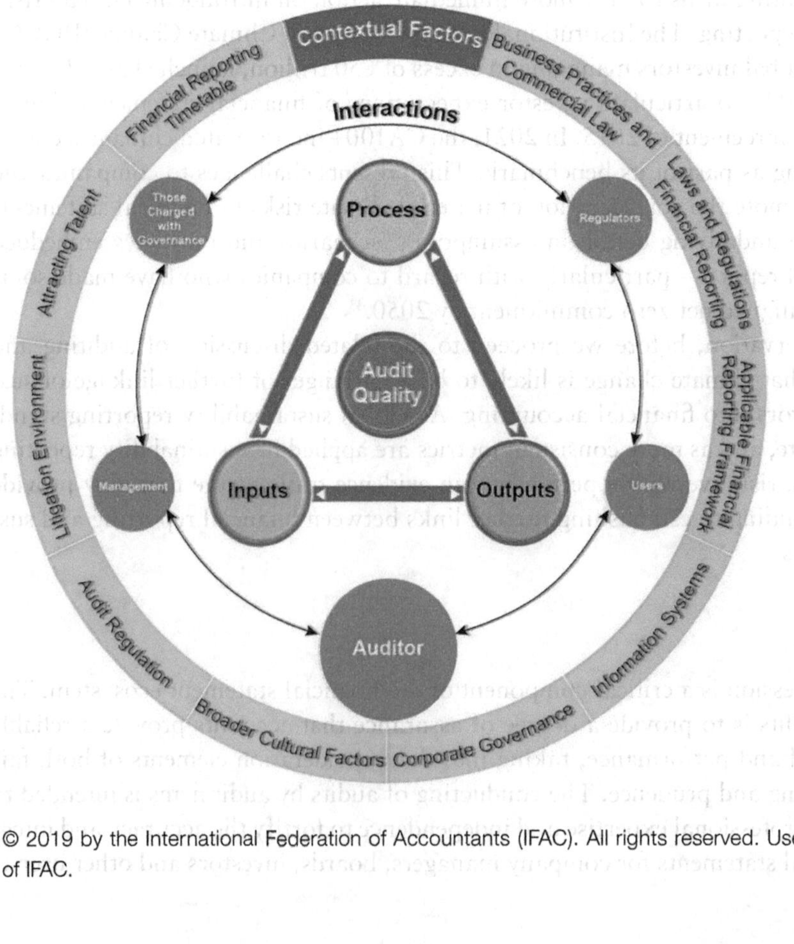

However, it remains difficult, if not impossible, for an investor or other external user of a company's financial accounts to know to what extent the auditor presented sufficient challenge to the company in the audit process, applied overly aggressive accounting principles—or may have adopted a narrow interpretation of fair value accounting to allow for mechanical application of accounting rules that run counter to the principle of prudence.

The recent high-profile failures of Carillion in the UK and Wirecard in Germany demonstrate that poor audit quality is not just a theoretical possibility. Audit independence and rigour remain a concern, particularly given the oligopolistic dominance of the Big Four firms: Deloitte, EY, KPMG and PwC. This has led to renewed scrutiny of the audit profession and whether or not it is fit for purpose.

Audit quality and governance under review

In 2019, Sir Donald Brydon conducted an extensive study of audit quality and effectiveness in the UK, stating that 'audit is not broken but it has lost its way and all the actors in the audit process bear some measure of responsibility.'[45] The scope of the study ranged from a detailed review of the audit profession itself to its regulation in the UK, the use of technology and the role of company audit committees. It also focused on the role of asset managers as shareholders, working on behalf of their beneficiaries and encouraging them to play more active roles as users of financial statements to make audit quality a more substantive component of investor scrutiny and company engagement.

The *Brydon Report* produced a wide-ranging list of recommendations for change in the audit profession and audit process. It began by redefining the purpose of audit 'to help establish and maintain deserved confidence in a company, in its directors and in the information for which they have responsibility to report, including the financial statements.' Among the many specific changes presented, one of them revisited the accounting debate stemming from potential distortions of fair value accounting and proposed that 'true and fair' be replaced in UK company law with the term 'present fairly, in all material respects.' It also suggested that the current binary reporting on audit opinions may be too narrow or simplistic, making reference to the potential use of 'confidence accounting' that reflects measurement uncertainties and provides ranges and sensitivities in additional point estimates.

Although focused on the state of audit quality and effectiveness in the UK, the depth and rigour of the *Brydon Report* has relevance for the practice of audit and the audit profession globally. It is premature to gauge the impact of the report and the extent to which all the report's recommendations will be put into practice. But the *Brydon Report* has moved the debate and is likely to stimulate ongoing reforms both in the UK and beyond.

In 2021, the UK government's Department for Business, Energy and Industrial Strategy (BEIS) launched another a wide-ranging consultation titled 'Restoring Trust in Audit and Corporate Governance.'[46] It builds from the *Bryden Report* and previous studies by UK authorities on the quality and effectiveness of audit and auditor oversight.[47] Audit quality features prominently in this consultation, and there is a broad scope under review, including proposals to clarify audit purpose and scope, audit committee oversight, audit competition and audit supervision and regulation.

Among the many issues under consideration were new obligations on both auditors and directors relating to the prevention and detection of fraud, as well as the strengthening of malus and clawback provisions in the remuneration of executive directors. In a stewardship context, the consultation also addresses the facilitation of more meaningful engagement between shareholders and companies on audit matters. The outcome of this BEIS consultation may lead to a much stricter audit regime in the UK and is likely to influence the debate on audit quality and governance globally, not just in the UK.

4. ASSURANCE OF ESG AND SUSTAINABILITY REPORTING

By all accounts, the existing frameworks for assurance of ESG and sustainability information provided by companies to investors, markets and stakeholders are incipient. Likewise, the current capacity of potential providers of assurance in these areas is limited. The diversity of reporting frameworks and standards remains perhaps the most important factor holding back the development of a generally recognised high-quality practice for third-party review of ESG reporting. Efforts towards convergence, such as those described in Chapter 4, can contribute importantly to the process of reaching market consensus on what issues are material, how they should be discussed in relation to the company's strategy and value proposition, and what scopes of audit and levels of assurance provide value.

Audit and assurance of ESG-related information collected and reported by companies potentially form a win–win proposition for management, boards, investors and other stakeholders—not to mention the audit firms themselves. From the company perspective, the process of obtaining independent assurance around ESG risks and disclosures assists boards and management teams more thoroughly to understand the ESG factors relevant to their business and the options available for measuring and monitoring attendant risks. The assurance process itself, like that around financial audits, should directly involve the board, as the board ultimately bears responsibility for the quality of the information the company provides to its shareholders and stakeholders. Regardless of how the board structures itself to oversee ESG reporting, it needs to fashion policies and procedures for its interaction with ESG assurance providers in a manner analogous to that between audit committees, internal auditors and external auditors. The process of determining the scope of the audit, planning its execution and negotiating the level of assurance provides an important framework for keeping the board, its responsible committee (if any), management and staff focused and committed.

Aspirationally, the objective should be for the scope of the audit to cover all material ESG information provided by the company and for the audit procedures to be akin to the kind of examination auditors conduct in order to provide a 'true and fair' opinion on the financial accounts. At this point in time, it is more common to see more watered-down, 'limited assurance' or 'cold comfort' opinions on ESG disclosures. These are provided after the conduct of a 'review' or merely a 'compilation' that is considerably less rigorous than the process of a full-blown examination. Even if fair representation is the ultimate quality standard investors should be seeking, investors should also support a company simply getting a start on the assurance ladder and progressing to higher assurance levels with time and experience.

Especially in the case of publicly traded companies, independent assurance provides investors and other stakeholders with a greater degree of confidence in the accuracy and completeness of the ESG-risk information provided by a company in its disclosures. As in the case of financial statements, quality auditing ensures greater clarity, consistency and comparability of reporting over time and between companies. In the exercise of their stewardship responsibilities, investors can and should let companies know their views on the quality of assurance provided on ESG disclosures. For example, the Operating Principles for Impact Management include assurance on the key principles for impact investors.[48]

While traditional audit firms bring established auditing skills and processes to the table, they also may lack sustainability subject matter expertise, as this is not a background typically required of those who provide assurance of financial accounts. This speaks to the potential need for auditors to employ multidisciplinary teams to approach assurance of non-financial disclosures. Assurance of non-financial reports also need not be limited to audit firms. ESG or industry specialists, if fortified with robust audit techniques, can provide more insight into or understanding of interpreting the accuracy, nature and materiality of non-financial information.

Growing demand for assurance is itself an importance source of impetus for the rationalisation and convergence of ESG disclosure mandates, standards, frameworks and guides. By its nature, the audit process requires a clear set of consistently applicable principles and rules against which to evaluate the veracity and comparability of company statements. Auditors can be forgiven for pushing back against providing assurance of ESG information that is presented in a *sui generis* (unique or idiosyncratic) fashion. But they also should be a force for the sort of practical convergence of reporting standards that the multi-capital framework, standard-setting institutions and the WEF have committed to work together to achieve.

The current state of sustainability assurance is still evolving and is marked by differing practices globally along several dimensions. In 2021, the International Federation of Accountants (IFAC) and the Association of International Certified Professional Accountants (AICMA and CIMA) published a comprehensive global benchmarking study of 1400 companies in 22 countries around the world.[49] While 91% of the companies studied published sustainability information of some sort, that was almost the only common feature. Only 51% had their sustainability accounts assured, and only 63% of the assurance came from auditor firms. In terms of comfort levels in the assurance opinion, close to 100% of auditor-conducted assurance was 'limited,' whereas non-auditor assurance providers provided notably higher levels of 'moderate' and 'reasonable' assurance.

The IFAC/AICMA and CIMA report also highlighted significant regional differences between where sustainability is published and by which sustainability standard. While standalone sustainability reports are the most predominant reporting format (as in the US and Canada), sustainability data are reported in annual reports in France, and other countries have a mix of sustainability, annual and integrated reporting. It is noteworthy that the incidence of not having any sustainability reporting is mainly an issue in emerging markets.

The report also lays bare the diversity of sustainability standards that are being used today. The Global Reporting Initiative (GRI) remains the most prevalent standard applied as of 2021, notably so in Latin America and Continental Europe. Yet, while the Sustainability Accounting Standards Board (SASB) still has notably less take-up globally, the SASB standards have much stronger roots in North American companies.

So, sustainability assurance, like sustainability reporting, remains on a journey. The good news is that it is more prominently on the agenda around the world. But challenges with convergence, quality and comfort levels remain.

NOTES

1. A 'B Corporation' (the B stands for 'benefit') and other impact-oriented structures have a dual corporate mission to both impact society positively and generate returns for investors.
2. OECD, *Guidelines for Multinational Enterprise*, 2011: www.oecd.org/corporate/mne/
3. European Union, *Non-Financial Reporting Directive*, 2014: https://eur-lex.europa.eu/legal-content/EN/TXT/?uri=CELEX%3A32014L0095
4. European Commission, *Proposal for a Corporate Sustainability Reporting Directive*: https://eur-lex.europa.eu/legal-content/EN/TXT/?uri=CELEX:52021PC0189
5. European Union, *Regulation of the European Parliament and of the Councils on Sustainability-Related Disclosures in the Financial Services Sector*, 27 November 2019: https://eur-lex.europa.eu/legal-content/EN/TXT/?uri=celex%3A32019R2088
6. European Commission, *Sustainable Finance and EU Taxonomy: Commission Takes Further Steps to Channel Money towards Sustainable Activities*, 21 April 2021: https://ec.europa.eu/commission/presscorner/detail/en/ip_21_1804
7. European Union Platform on Sustainable Finance, *Draft Report by Subgroup 4: Social Taxonomy*: https://ec.europa.eu/info/sites/default/files/business_economy_euro/banking_and_finance/documents/sf-draft-report-social-taxonomy-july2021_en.pdf
8. European Union, Sustainable Corporate Governance Initiative 2020–21: https://ec.europa.eu/info/law/better-regulation/have-your-say/initiatives/12548-Sustainable-corporate-governance_en
9. See the European Corporate Governance Institute webinar on Directors' Duties and Sustainable Corporate Governance (November 2020): https://ecgi.global/video/directors'-duties-and-sustainable-corporate-governance-part-1
10. Harvard Law and Business School Professors Mark Roe, Holger Spamann, Jesse Fried and Charles Wang, *The European Commission's Sustainable Corporate Governance Report: A Critique*, 17 November 2020: www.hbs.edu/ris/Publication%20Files/21-056_51410b50-5488-477a-9aa3-df8f81138e53.pdf
11. ICGN comment letter on EU Sustainable Corporate Governance consultation, February 2021: www.icgn.org/sites/default/files/2021-06/3.%20ICGN%20response%20to%20Sustainable%20Governance%20EU%20Consultation%202021.pdf
12. Directive of the European Parliament and of the Council on Corporate Sustainability Due Diligence and amending Directive (EU) 2019/1937, 23 February 2022: https://ec.europa.eu/info/sites/default/files/1_1_183885_prop_dir_susta_en.pdf
13. United Nations Human Rights Office of the High Commissioner, *UN's Guiding Principles on Business and Human Rights and OECD Guidelines for Multinational Enterprises*, 2011: www.ohchr.org/documents/publications/guidingprinciplesbusinesshr_en.pdf
14. Proposal for an EU Directive on Corporate Sustainability Due Diligence, European Commission, 23, February 2022: https://eur-lex.europa.eu/legal-content/EN/TXT/HTML/?uri=CELEX:52022PC0071&from=EN
15. European Commission, Questions and Answers: *Proposal for a Directive on Corporate Sustainability Due Diligence*, 23 February 2022: https://ec.europa.eu/commission/presscorner/detail/en/qanda_22_1146
16. www.sec.gov/news/press-release/2022-46
17. This can be referred to as 'integrated thinking,' which we will be discussing shortly.
18. Financial, manufactured, intellectual, human, social and relationship, and natural.
19. For many, Covid-19 was an unknown unknown. However, for others, with awareness of SARS, Ebola and Zika, a new pandemic was not necessarily a high-impact/low-probability 'black swan' event.
20. OECD, *Corporate Governance Factbook*, 2019, p 123: www.oecd.org/daf/ca/Corporate-Governance- Factbook.pdf
21. Ibid, p 124.

22. Alex Edmans, Why Companies Shouldn't Tie Pay to ESG Metrics, *Wall Street Journal*, 27 June 2021.
23. Ocean Tomo LLC, *Intangible Asset Market Value Study*, 2020: www.oceantomo.com/intangible-asset-market-value-study/
24. See Kathleen Hertz Rupley, Darrell Brown and Scott Marshall, Evolution of Corporate Reporting: From Stand-Alone Corporate Social Responsibility Reporting to Integrated Reporting, 25 August 2017, *Research in Accounting Regulations*, Forthcoming, Kelley School of Business Research Paper No 17-73: https://papers.ssrn.com/sol3/papers.cfm?abstract_id=3062403
25. However, reporting requirements such as the management, discussion and analysis section of corporate reporting in the US have required operational disclosures for many years.
26. See IIRC Framework: www.integratedreporting.org/resource/international-ir-framework/
27. ICGN, *Guidance on Integrated Business Reporting*, 2015: www.icgn.org/sites/default/files/2021-06/Integrated%20Business%20Reporting_0.pdf
28. A non-exhaustive list of investor and financial sector groups engaged with climate change includes the United Nations Environmental Programme Finance Initiative (UNEP FI), Climate Action 100+, the IIGCC, the UN-convened Net-Zero Asset Owner Alliance initiative, the Climate Accounting Project, the Carbon Tracker Initiative and the GFANZ.
29. We cite, for example, the Partnership for Carbon Accounting Financials (PICAF) as an initiative to promote greenhouse gas accounting and reporting standards for the financial sector: https://carbonaccountingfinancials.com
30. A good case for mandatory climate change disclosure was made by Oxford legal scholars John Armour, Luca Enriques and Thom Wetzer, 2021, Mandatory Corporate Climate Disclosures: Now, But How? *Columbia Business Law Review*, no 3: https://doi.org/10.52214/cblr.v2021i3.9106
31. Scope 1 is the company's direct emissions from its own activities. Scope 2 covers indirect company emissions coming from the amount of energy that the company purchases and consumes. Scope 3 incorporates all other indirect emissions that occur in a company's supply chain.
32. According to the not-for-profit Net Zero Tracker, 683 of the world's largest 2000 companies (as of 2022) have committed to net zero targets—but with varying degrees of scope and quality: https://zerotracker.net
33. Carbon Tracker, *Wasted Capital and Stranded Assets: 19 April 2013*: https://carbontracker.org/reports/unburnable-carbon-wasted-capital-and-stranded-assets/
34. Nick Anderson, *IFRS Standards and Climate Related Disclosures*, IFRS, November 2019: www.ifrs.org/content/dam/ifrs/news/2019/november/in-brief-climate-change-nick-anderson.pdf
35. IAASB Staff Audit Practice Alert, *The Consideration of Climate-Related Risks in an Audit of Financial Statement*, October 2020: www.iaasb.org/publications/consideration-climate-related-risks-audit-financial-statement
36. Financial Accounting Standards Board Staff Educational Paper, *Intersection of Environmental, Social, and Governance Matters with Financial Accounting Standards*, 19 March 2021: www.iaasb.org/publications/consideration-climate-related-risks-audit-financial-statement
37. Office of the Comptroller of the Currency, *Risk Management: Principles for Climate-Related Financial Risk Management for Large Banks*, OCC Bulletin 2021-62, 16 December 2021: www.occ.gov/news-issuances/bulletins/2021/bulletin-2021-62a.pdf
38. US Department of Labor, Employee Benefits Security Administration, *Request for Information on Possible Agency Actions to Protect Life Savings and Pensions from Threats of Climate-Related Financial Risk*, Federal Register, Vol 87, No 30, February 2022: www.federalregister.gov/documents/2022/02/14/2022-02798/request-for-information-on-possible-agency-actions-to-protect-life-savings-and-pensions-from-threats
39. www.sec.gov/news/press-release/2022-92
40. See ICGN Comment Letter to US SEC on climate change disclosures, 11 June 2021: www.icgn.org/sites/default/files/13.%20ICGN%20%20Letter%20to%20US%20SEC%20climate%20disclosure%2C%20June%202021.pdf
41. Sponsored by the PRI.
42. Barbara Davidson and Rob Schuwerk, *Flying Blind: The Glaring Absence of Climate Risks in Financial Reporting*, Carbon Tracker Initiative and PRI, September 2021: https://carbontracker.org/reports/flying-blind-the-glaring-absence-of-climate-risks-in-financial-reporting/

43. Natasha Landall-Mills, *Investor Expectations for Paris-Aligned Accounts*, Institutional Investor Group on Climate Change, November 2020: www.iigcc.org/download/investor-expectations-for-paris-aligned-accounts/?wpdmdl=4001&masterkey=5fabc4d15595d
44. IAASB, *Framework for Audit Quality*, February 2014: www.iaasb.org/publications/framework-audit-quality-key-elements-create-environment-audit-quality-3
45. Sir Donald Brydon, *Independent Review into the Quality and Effectiveness of Audit*, 2019: https://assets.publishing.service.gov.uk/government/uploads/system/uploads/attachment_data/file/852960/brydon-review-final-report.pdf
46. UK Department for Business, Energy and Industrial Strategy, *Restoring Trust in Audit and Corporate Governance*, March 2021: https://assets.publishing.service.gov.uk/government/uploads/system/uploads/attachment_data/file/970673/ restoring-trust-in-audit-and-corporate-governance-command-paper.pdf
47. Sir John Kingman's *Independent Review of the Financial Reporting Council* (FRC) and the Competition and Market Authority's *Statutory Audit Services Market Study*, both from 2018.
48. Operating Principles for Impact Management: www.impactprinciples.org/9-principles
49. IFAC and AICMA & CIMA, *The State of Play in Sustainability Assurance*, June 2021: www.ifac.org/knowledge-gateway/contributing-global-economy/discussion/state-play-sustainability-assurance

FURTHER READING

Robert G. Eccles and Bhakti Mirchandani, We Need Universal ESG Accounting Standards, *Harvard Business Review*, 15 February 2022: https://hbr.org/2022/02/we-need-universal-esg-accounting-standards

John Armour, Luca Enriques and Thom Wetzer, 2021, Mandatory Corporate Climate Disclosures: Now, But How? *Columbia Business Law Review*, no 3. https://doi.org/10.52214/cblr.v2021i3.9106

International Federation of Accountants (IFAC) and the Association of International Certified Professional Accountants (AICMA & CIMA), *The State of Play in Sustainability Assurance*, June 2021: www.ifac.org/knowledge-gateway/contributing-global-economy/discussion/state-play-sustainability-assurance

UK Department for Business, Energy and Industrial Strategy, *Restoring Trust in Audit and Corporate Governance*, March 2022: www.gov.uk/government/consultations/restoring-trust-in-audit-and-corporate-governance-proposals-on-reforms

Sir Donald Brydon, *Independent Review into the Quality and Effectiveness of Audit*, 2019: www.gov.uk/government/publications/the-quality-and-effectiveness-of-audit-independent-review

Oxford Union Debate, *This House Believes that Corporate Sustainability Reporting Should Be Mandated, and Standardised by FASB and IASB, for It to Be Most Useful for Investors*, 2018: www.sbs.ox.ac.uk/sites/default/files/2019-01/union_debate_transcript.pdf

Kris Douma, Principles for Responsible Investment, and George Dallas, ICGN, *Investor Agenda for Corporate ESG Reporting*, October 2018: www.icgn.org/sites/default/files/2021-06/ESG%20Reporting%20Discussion%20Paper.pdf

ICGN Accounting and Audit Practices Committee, *What Investors Want from Financial Reporting*, 2016.

ICGN, *Guidance on Integrated Business Reporting*, 2015: www.icgn.org/sites/default/files/2021-06/Integrated%20Business%20Reporting_0.pdf

OECD, *Guidelines for Multinational Enterprise*, 2011: www.oecd.org/corporate/mne/

Baruch Lev, New York University, *Intangibles: Management, Measurement and Reporting*, 2001, Bookings Institution Press: https://papers.ssrn.com/sol3/papers.cfm?abstract_ id=254345

Chapter 8

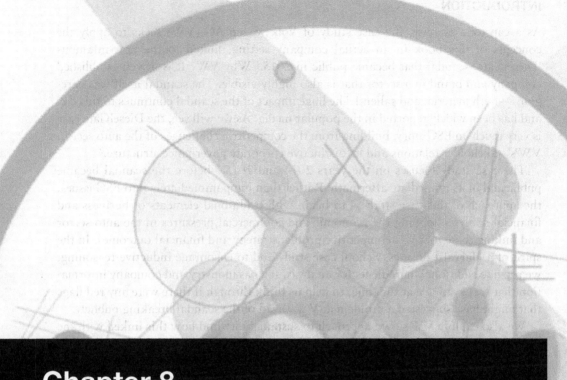

Case study: Volkswagen's DieselGate: Corporate governance and sustainability

DOI: 10.4324/9781003307082-8

INTRODUCTION

As a capstone exercise, the case study of Volkswagen AG (VW) seeks to apply the concepts of this book in an actual company setting, linked to the now-infamous 'DieselGate' scandal that became public in 2015.[1] Why VW? It is a well-established company and brand in a sector that is also highly visible. The scandal itself was egregious—both material and salient! The huge impact of the scandal continues to this day and has been widely reported in the popular media. As we will see, the DieselGate case is very much an ESG story, building from the competitive challenges of the auto sector, VW's stakeholder relations and its distinctive corporate governance structure.[2]

The case study focuses on the years 2014 and 2015—before the scandal became public and in its immediate aftermath. Rather than jump immediately into ESG issues, the approach of this case study is to begin with traditional elements of business and financial analysis: looking the economic and commercial pressures in the auto sector and linking these to VW's competitive profile, strategy and financial outcomes. In the spirit of a Harvard Business School case study and to encourage inductive reasoning, we provide additional ingredients for analysis, such as industry and company information that was available at the time, to help us think through if there were any red flags that might have suggested a problem at VW ahead of the scandal breaking publicly.

We also explore VW's own approach to sustainability and how this linked with the specific ESG issues facing the company. There are no 'right' or 'wrong' answers. But the purpose of the case is to provoke thought in terms of how ESG issues affected VW and its performance—and how investors might approach VW in terms of stewardship.

SETTING THE STAGE

Of the many companies representing German industry, VW has long been one of the most recognised, and iconic, brands of 'Deutschland AG.' As an automotive conglomerate with a long, and at times dubious, history, VW is one of the world's largest auto producers, typically running neck and neck with Japanese rival Toyota for global market dominance.

As a publicly listed company, VW is widely held by institutional investors, even though its ownership structure—and voting control—is dominated by ownership by Germany's Porsche/Piëch family, the German federal state of Lower Saxony and the Qatari sovereign wealth fund. It is included in the German 'blue chip' DAX 30 index, which ensures VW's inclusion in passive investment strategy indices based on the DAX 30, as well as other global equity indices.

In 2014, VW was the world's largest auto producer by volume—a goal articulated by then CEO Ferdinand Piëch in 2005. It produced 10.2 million vehicles, with 12 brands, and had an employment base in excess of 600,000—45% from Germany. While Germany itself represented 12% of VW sales, 26% of its production came from Germany—a high-cost production base by global standards. VW was, and remains, an important source of employment (and tax revenue) for the city of Wolfsburg and the federal state of Lower Saxony. VW's deep ties to its community are reflected in its ownership of the local football (soccer) team, VfL Wolfsburg, which competes in the world-renowned German *Bundesliga*, in a stadium named the Volkswagen Arena.

In its 2014 Annual Report, VW CEO Martin Winterkorn reported to its shareholders that, despite challenging economic headwinds, 'we successfully kept your company on a strong, stable trajectory.' Though its profitability still lagged at 2012 levels, he praised the achievement of many strategic targets, including surpassing 10 million cars per year and, by achieving record revenues in 2014, exceeding €200 billion. The letter went on to provide highlights of new model introductions across the various VW brands, as well as its geographic expansion, particularly in China and North America.

Winterkorn's 2014 letter also focused on the challenges the auto industry was facing with regard to growing pressures related to climate change and clean energy, while stressing that VW offers the widest range of electric vehicles and plug-in hybrids, as part of its 'Strategy 2018' to achieve sustainable growth. He noted that dealing with stringent CO_2 legislation 'costs us a great deal of energy, and money, too. But at VW we do not see this transition as a threat, but rather as a tremendous opportunity—one that we must and will take advantage of.' Winterkorn concludes with the optimistic tone of one leading a company that is firing positively on all cylinders: 'As you can see, VW is making itself future-proof in every area.' His handsome 2014 pay packet of €15.9 million (mostly performance-based) also suggested that the company's board shared his sense of confidence and positive achievement.

But not everyone was impressed. Apart from the positive milestones noted in Winterkorn's letter, VW was also known to be facing several financial and strategic challenges, such as chronic low profitability and difficulties in gaining traction in key markets such as the US. In April 2015, the chairman of VW's supervisory board, Ferdinand Piëch—a substantial shareholder and a former VW CEO—had just lost to Winterkorn in a power struggle.

Piëch, grandson of Wolfgang Porsche, was a prominent member of VW's founding family, known for his business acumen, his excellence as an automotive engineer, as well as his autocratic management style. Piëch had been on the VW Supervisory Board since 2002—longer than any other VW board member. His public criticism of Winterkorn, his former friend and protégé, was seen in Germany as a sensational boardroom drama, evocative of a Wagnerian opera.[3] Piëch had originally appointed Winterkorn to be the CEO of VW in 2007, as the two shared a vision of VW becoming the world's largest and most successful automotive company. But, by 2015, Piëch thought it was time to change leaders to address VW's strategic challenges. However, his attempts to win over the Supervisory Board failed, with the Supervisory Board representatives from Lower Saxony and VW's trade unions rallying to support Winterkorn. Consequently, Piëch stepped down as Supervisory Board chair in April 2015.

DIESELGATE

Yet this titillating soap opera was soon to become a sideshow. Even as Winterkorn's upbeat message was presented at VW's AGM in May 2015, storm clouds were looming on the horizon. By April 2015, VW staff had already received a report from the US International Council on Clean Transportation (ICCT) which indicated that some VW cars were emitting NOx (nitrous oxide) at 40 times the permitted levels. VW initially denied the existence of a 'defeat device' that allowed these higher emissions to pass undetected in normal testing. But, on 18 September 2015, the US Environmental Protection

Agency (EPA) published a Notice of Violation outlining its complaints against the company, and, by 23 September 2015, Winterkorn had stepped down as VW CEO.

This DieselGate saga set in motion a series of events that have severely impacted both the company's value and reputation. Immediately following the announcement in 2015, VW's market value dropped almost 50%, from €84 billion to €46 billion. Since then, over €30 billion has been set aside to cover legal liabilities relating to class action suits, mainly from the US.[4] Although VW senior management initially claimed to be unaware of these defeat devices, the US Department of Justice indicted Winterkorn and other VW executives in 2018 for conspiring to rig emission test results. In April 2019, German prosecutors filed aggravated criminal fraud charges against Winterkorn.

VW's minority investors—for the most part asset managers investing on behalf of asset owners, including pension funds—had a right to feel unhappy, as well as disenfranchised. Important questions are raised:

- Should they have seen this coming? If so, how?
- Is there any relationship between VW's governance structure and its emission scandals?
- What expectations should investors now put to the VW management and supervisory boards in their engagement?

OWNERSHIP

Starting from its origins in the 1930s as a creation of German industrial policy by the Nazi government, VW has had a unique ownership structure, reflecting a mixed strategic agenda as an agent of German industrial policy and as a publicly listed private-sector company. As of the time of the case study, in 2014, Lower Saxony maintained a 20% stake in VW, with the blocking rights of a 25% shareholder; it also had two delegated representatives on VW's 20-member Supervisory Board. The Qatari sovereign wealth fund held a significant 17% stake and also had two members on the VW Supervisory Board.

Importantly, the majority of VW ownership has been held in the hands of the Porsche and Piëch families, whose roots date back to VW's founding father Walter Porsche. Collectively, the families as of 2014 controlled 52% of the company's equity (through their sole voting shareholding in Porsche Automobil Holding AG), though this holding is dispersed through various Piëch and Porsche family members.

In spite of VW's status as a German 'blue chip' company in the DAX 30 index, institutional shareholders and other minorities represented only 11% of the company's ownership in 2014.

VW STRATEGY AND COMPETITIVE POSITION

Strategy

- 'Our goal is world leadership'—Ferdinand Piëch, 2005. This vision was shared by Piëch's protégé, Martin Winterkorn, who in 2007 became VW CEO and, over time, a rival to Piëch.

- Multibrands: 12 automotive brands, multiple customer segments.
- Geographic diversity: critical mass in key markets.
- Focus on technology, innovation and customer satisfaction.
- Strategy 2018: 'most sustainable automotive company in the world.'
- 'Preserve German jobs' (CEO Matthias Müller, 2017). An implicit, if not explicit, component of this strategy is to rely on German employees and production. Of VW's 600,000 employees, 45% are from Germany. Note that, in a global context, Germany is a relatively high-cost labour market.

Competitive position

- *Market share/stable customer base*: VW benefits from a strong European customer base, particularly in Germany. However, its market presence is less strong outside Europe, where VW faces considerable competition. China and the US are important markets for VW if it is to establish its global leadership goals, but its market positions are less established in these markets, and VW has had historical difficulties gaining traction in the US.
- *Scale and diversity of product lines: brands and geographies*: VW is well diversified geographically, although its market positions are generally stronger in Europe and still developing in other global markets. Given the size of the North American market, VW only generated around 10% of its sales in the US and Canada—a relative weakness. Its upscale models, such as Audi and Porsche, are lower volume, but much more profitable than VW branded models.

  Although VW's disclosures break down its profitability by its automotive, commercial vehicle and financial services units, it did not break down the contribution of the individual VW brands to overall profit. But an article in *The Economist* in 2016 indicated that the VW-branded models themselves accounted for over 40% of revenues, but only around 20% of operating profits.[5] Perhaps more importantly, VW does not provide a geographical report on its sources of earnings. Investors are not made aware of VW's commercial success and profitability (or lack thereof) in key growth markets such as the US and China.
- *Reputation for technical quality, innovation and customer satisfaction*: this has been a traditional strength of VW and other German automakers and has enabled VW to place a pricing premium on its top brands and compete successfully in other mass markets outside Germany.

FIGURE 8.1 VW sales by geography 2014

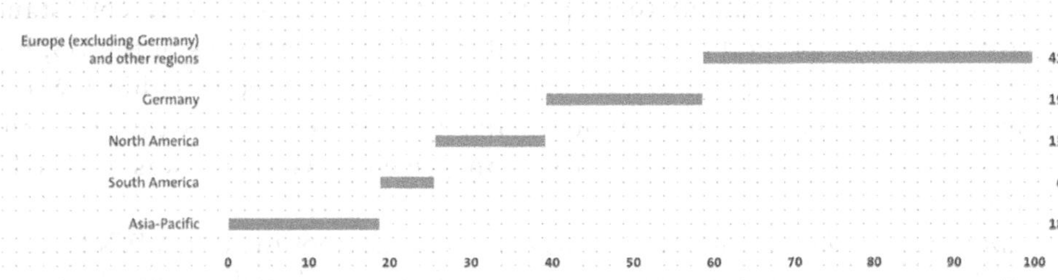

Source: VW Annual Report 2014

- *Operating efficiency/cost base*: this is one of VW's key strategic challenges, given its strong presence in high-cost Germany. While Germany accounted for around 12% of its sales in 2014, 26% of its production was in Germany, and 45% of its entire labour force was German. Although this may have real or perceived benefits in terms of product quality (*Standort Deutschland*), it also puts VW at a competitive cost disadvantage vis-à-vis its competitors—particularly in the mass-market segment.

  There was also a stark contrast in efficiency between VW and Toyota—its arch-rival in terms of production volume. According to a 2014 brokerage report by Sanford C. Bernstein (now Bernstein Research), Toyota's car production per employee was more than twice the level of VW's.

FIGURE 8.2 VW car production per employee 2015

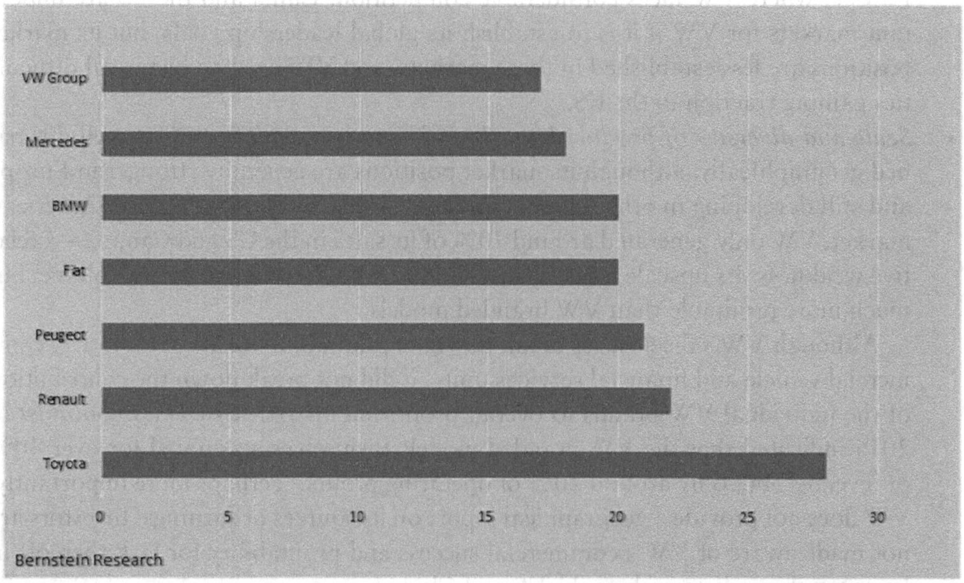

- *Ability to adapt business model to accommodate industry 'disruptions,' such as eco-friendlier vehicles*: the 'Strategy 2018' that was guiding VW in 2014 clearly established its ambition to be the most sustainable automotive company in the world, and, at least until the DieselGate scandal became public, VW was regarded positively compared with peers in the Robeco/SAM benchmarking of its environmental and social performance. But, in many ways, the scandal was catalysed by VW's inability to adapt its auto production to US emissions standards in a more profitable way. So it had to either suffer losses in the US, give up trying to build share in the US market—or cheat. Someone within VW ultimately chose to cheat, although it remains unclear exactly how this was sanctioned and to what extent senior VW management in Germany was involved in this decision.
- *Financial stability to withstand cyclical downturns*: prior to 2014, VW's financial performance and financial strength was satisfactory, although not highly profitable. Its credit ratings by Moody's (A-2 long-term, P-1 short-term) reflected a strong

financial position and ready access to global capital markets. Of note is that rival Toyota maintained the highest possible AAA long-term rating—a rarity in industrial company ratings, particularly for such a risky sector as the automotive industry. This reflects Toyota's strong market share, particularly in Japan, its operating efficiency and a very conservative balance sheet, with limited debt.

- *Stakeholder relations: employees, customers, communities*: the employee voice is strongly represented in VW, reflecting in part that 50% of its Supervisory Board is elected by its employees, including two members of VW's four-person audit committee. It is worth noting that all these employee-elected Supervisory Board members are German, which is understandable for reasons including logistics and language. However, given the fact that 60% of VW's workforce is based outside Germany, some critics of the co-determination system express the concern that the labour representation on the VW board may be advocating more on behalf of the German workforce (eg not exporting too many jobs) than on behalf of the workforce generally.

With a 20% stake in VW, the federal state of Lower Saxony brings a broader public policy perspective to VW as a hugely important employer and source of tax revenues. This relates not only to the operations of VW as a legal entity, but also to the broader supply chain network supporting VW, which provides a wider base of economic activity that benefits Lower Saxony directly and Germany more generally. VW's ownership of the *Bundesliga* football team Vfl Wolfsburg clearly reinforces its links with its local community, but it also raises questions of capital allocation and strategic fit.

As VW recognised the importance of customer satisfaction and brand loyalty, it was positioning itself in late 2014 as customer-friendly, particularly in the new era of eco-friendly cars. Its promotion of diesel engines as an environmentally better solution increased customer sales. But this environmental positioning was severely discredited as a result of the emissions scandal, with the effect of VW customers suffering the consequences of making an important consumer spend on false pretences. The long-term implications of this for VW's brand and customer loyalty are challenging to assess or measure.

FIGURE 8.3 VW sustainability performance 2014

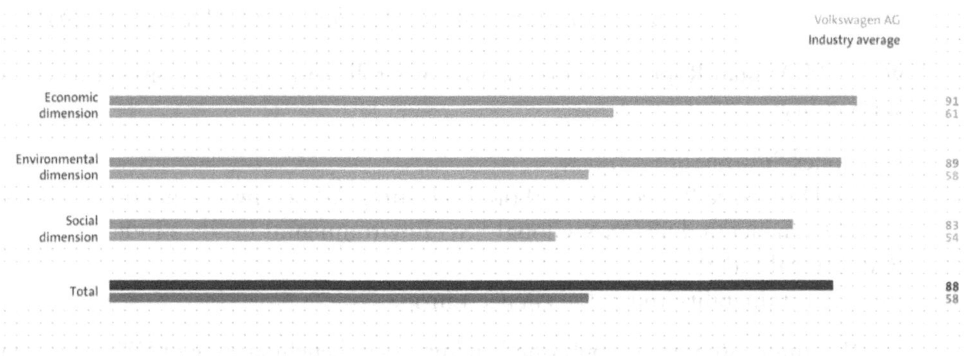

Source: VW Annual Report 2014

VW SUSTAINABILITY PERFORMANCE

In 2014, VW presented itself very credibly to its shareholders and stakeholders with regard to its strategy for industry leadership as a producer of environmentally friendly vehicles.

FIGURE 8.4 VW approach to sustainability 2014

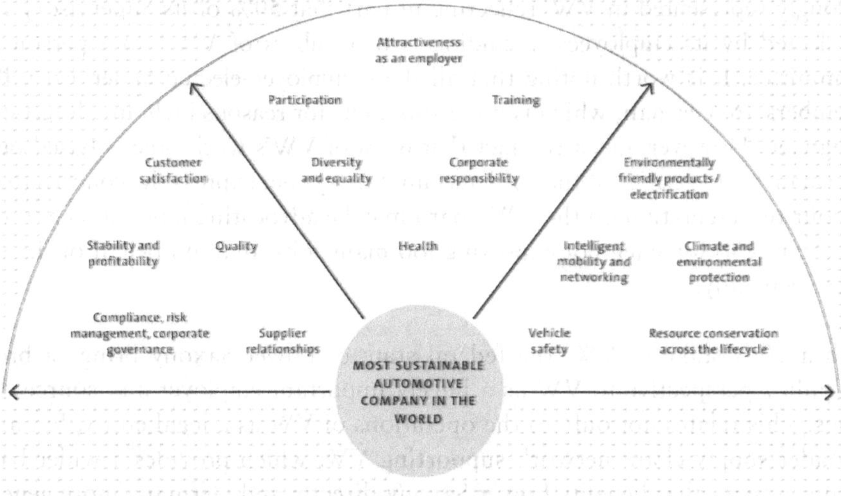

Source: VW Annual Report 2014

From VW's 2014 Annual Report

> Our pursuit of innovation and perfection and our responsible approach will help to make us the world's leading automaker by 2018—both economically and ecologically.
>
> The automotive industry is currently experiencing fundamental change. Look no further than the increasingly stringent CO_2 legislation. This costs us a great deal of energy and money, too. But at Volkswagen, we do not see this transition as a threat, but rather as a tremendous opportunity—one that we must and will take advantage of.
>
> As you can see, Volkswagen is making itself future-proof in every area.
>
> *Source: Professor Dr Martin Winterkorn, Chairman of the Board of Management of Volkswagen Aktiengesellschaft*

VW's 2014 Annual Report cited the company's following recognitions with regard to sustainability:

- Dow Jones Sustainability Index.
- Carbon Disclosure Project: 99/100 on disclosure, 'A-' on environmental activities.
- Global Compact and STOXX Global ESG Environmental Leaders Index.
- ECPI Ethical Index.
- Ethibel Sustainability Index Excellence Europe.

The 2014 Annual Report also published an impressive benchmarking of VW's sustainability performance vis-à-vis its peers, conducted by the independent data firm RobecoSAM.

This analysis showed VW clearly ahead of the industry average across the three dimensions of RobecoSAM's sustainability model: economic, environmental and social. Similarly, the 2014 ESG ratings of the analytics firm Sustainalytics ranked VW in third place out of 47 automotive competitors. It was regarded as an 'industry leader' in terms of environmental performance and an 'outperformer' in its social performance. However, its governance performance was only rated as 'average.'[6]

Corporate governance at VW in 2014

VW's Supervisory Board (*Aufsichtsrat*) and the Management Board (*Vorstand*) as of December 2014 are presented in Appendix V below. Typical of a large German company, the Supervisory Board had 20 members, half investor-elected, half employee-elected. Three of the ten employee representatives, including VW's deputy chairman, were representatives of employee councils or unions. VW's Management Board comprised ten executive directors and was chaired by the CEO, Martin Winterkorn, in 2014. As typical of a Management Board structure, all the Management Board members are subordinate to Winterkorn.

The distribution of investor-elected directors on the Supervisory Board reflects VW's ownership blocks. As of December 2014, members of the Porsche/Piëch family held five of the ten investor board seats and controlled the Nomination Committee with two of the three seats. Being a member of the Porsche/Piëch bloc did not ensure that family members were consistently in accord with one another on every issue facing VW, but one unifying feature between family measures is the preservation of Porsche/Piëch family control.

Two of the ten investor seats were taken by Qatari representatives, given the state's 17% holding in VW. Reflecting VW's ownership stake of 20% by the federal state of Lower Saxony, two positions on VW's board were taken by the prime minister and the minister of economics of Lower Saxony.

The two-tier board structure in Germany results in different interpretations of independence. In an Anglo-Saxon unitary board structure, any employees on the board would be regarded as non-independent. Similarly, family members with controlling ownership stakes would also not be regarded as independent. However, VW considers all its Supervisory Board members independent, including five members of the Porsche/Piëch family, two representatives of Lower Saxony, and the two representatives from Qatar.

In contrast, the 2014 *Proxy Alert* by the proxy advisor ISS stated that only one of the 20 members on VW's board (Anna Falkengren, CEO of SE Banken) was to be regarded as independent. While the board representatives linked to either the workforce or investors with control blocks are clearly non-independent, given that SE Banken at the time was one of VW's 'house banks,' the independence of its CEO, Falkengren, could also be called into question.

A Porsche family member (Ferdinand Oliver Porsche) was also chairman of the four-person audit committee—a committee that calls for 100% independence in many leading corporate governance codes. Two of the seats were held by employee representatives, whose main experience was in works councils and not the accounting and audit of financial statements.

Ferdinand Piëch—former VW CEO—was chairman of VW's board in December 2014 and also sat on seven other corporate boards, some of which were within the overall VW group.

QUESTIONS: VW'S GOVERNANCE ECOSYSTEM

1. *Sector dynamics*: what are the competitive characteristics of the automotive sector? What are the keys to success in the sector, and where are the key risks?
2. *Competitive position*: how would you characterise VW's competitive position? What are its key strengths and weaknesses?
3. *Governance influencers*:
   - *Controlling ownership*: are there private benefits of control applying to Piëch and the Porsche family?
   - *Family dominance*: what are the implications of ex-CEO and controlling owner Piëch chairing VW's supervisory board?
   - *State ownership*: does VW's 20% ownership by Lower Saxony, with board representation, commit the company to a social agenda in Lower Saxony, and Germany more generally, that might conflict with the company's long-term commercial development and sustainable value creation?
   - *Employees*: given the 50% representation of employee-elected directors on VW's Supervisory Board, how will this influence the company's strategy, particularly vis-à-vis its high-cost German workforce? How are the interests of VW's employee representatives linked to the interests of the federal state of Lower Saxony? Are VW's stakeholder relations with its employees a source of strength or weakness?
   - *Minority shareholders*: where did minority shareholders/institutional investors sit in this pecking order?
4. *Strategy*:
   - How was VW's strategy in 2014 influenced by its governance structure?
   - How does VW's strategy relate to its competitive position?
   - Do you perceive any disconnects?
   - How might competitive pressures for VW to establish itself profitably in the US have catalysed the emissions scandal?
5. *VW sustainability performance*:
   - What are the key ESG issues facing VW?
   - How strong is VW's sustainability performance in the following areas:
     - Environmental?
     - Social?
     - Governance?
   - How did ESG factors influence the DieselGate scandal?
6. *Corporate governance and board effectiveness*:
   - Is DieselGate a failure of board oversight?
   - What does it say about the company's culture and values?
   - What does it say about the company's internal controls?
   - What might have prevented the scandal from occurring in the first place?
   - Are there changes to VW's governance system that minority investors might recommend to ensure their interests are protected?

APPENDIX I

Auto sector

The automotive sector includes both passenger cars and commercial vehicles. Demand is typically correlated with economic growth. In 2014, the global economy was gradually showing recovery from the financial crisis of 2008–9. Linking this to the auto sector, the Economist Intelligence Unit's 2014 forecast was for medium-term global growth of 4–5%. Emerging markets, China in particular, grew as sources of demand.[7]

Against this seemingly benign macroeconomic background, the auto industry itself is an intensely competitive sector, with a large number of manufacturers, including a number of 'national champions.' According to rating agency Standard & Poor's, the auto sector is regarded as a moderately high-risk industry, with key macro risk factors of economic growth and cyclicality, which in turn reflects consumer confidence and budgets. This sensitivity can be significant. For example, in the period 2007–9, auto companies' aggregate revenues dropped by over 30%.[8]

Auto manufacturing is capital-intensive, which results in high barriers to entry and generally low profit margins, particularly for the mass market. More upscale models benefit from brand appeal, with established upmarket brands (Mercedes, BMW, Volvo, Audi) providing much stronger profit margins, albeit at lower production volumes; mass market cars, such as VW, Seat and Skoda, are produced in greater volume and generally are much less profitable per unit. Although these national brands often benefit from local home loyalties, competition between brands for market share is intense—and can be price-based.

The risk of product substitution has not affected the auto market historically, as both personal and commercial demands for mobility have continued to grow. But the risks associated with climate change affect many sectors, including the automotive sector. In particular, the shift from fossil fuels to hybrids and electrically powered vehicles is leading the industry to important changes, which could affect the competitive dynamics of its competitors. These climate dynamics have more generally led to a greater awareness of sustainability issues in the auto sector, particularly to the extent that sustainability factors might lead to product differentiation and competitive advantage within the sector.

As of 2017, Toyota and VW were still neck and neck in world leadership, according to the OICA World Ranking of Auto Manufacturers, with Toyota producing 10.5 million vehicles and VW producing 10.4 million.[9] However, the field was very crowded, with 12 other auto firms producing in excess of 2 million vehicles that year, suggesting a very competitive market.

But this world leadership by volume production contrasts significantly with the market values of the leading producers. Even though VW's and Toyota's production volumes were virtually the same, Toyota's market capitalisation in 2017 was more than twice that of VW, reflecting its relative efficiency and profitability.

Competitive advantage: keys to success in the sector

- Market share/stable customer base.
- Scale and diversity of product lines: brands and geographic markets (customers and manufacturing facilities).

- Strong design, engineering, technology, innovation and customer service.
- Operating efficiency/low-cost base.
- Financial stability to withstand cyclical downturns.
- Ability to adapt business model to accommodate industry *'disruptions,'* such as eco-friendlier vehicles.
- Stakeholder relations: employees, customers, communities.

APPENDIX II

Statement of strategy from VW's 2015 Annual Report

> The Volkswagen Group sent a strong signal with the launch of its Strategy 2018 in 2008. The clear and ambitious goals triggered significant momentum within the Company, laying the foundation for the Group's significant success in recent years. In this context, and in light of the fundamental changes both in the automotive industry and within the Company itself, now is the time to realign the Volkswagen Group, both technologically and strategically. The basis for this realignment is our Strategy 2018, in which we defined four goals that are intended to make Volkswagen the most successful, fascinating and sustainable automaker in the world:
>
> 1. Volkswagen intends to deploy intelligent innovations and technologies to become a world leader in customer satisfaction and quality. We see high

FIGURE 8.5 VW statement of strategy 2015

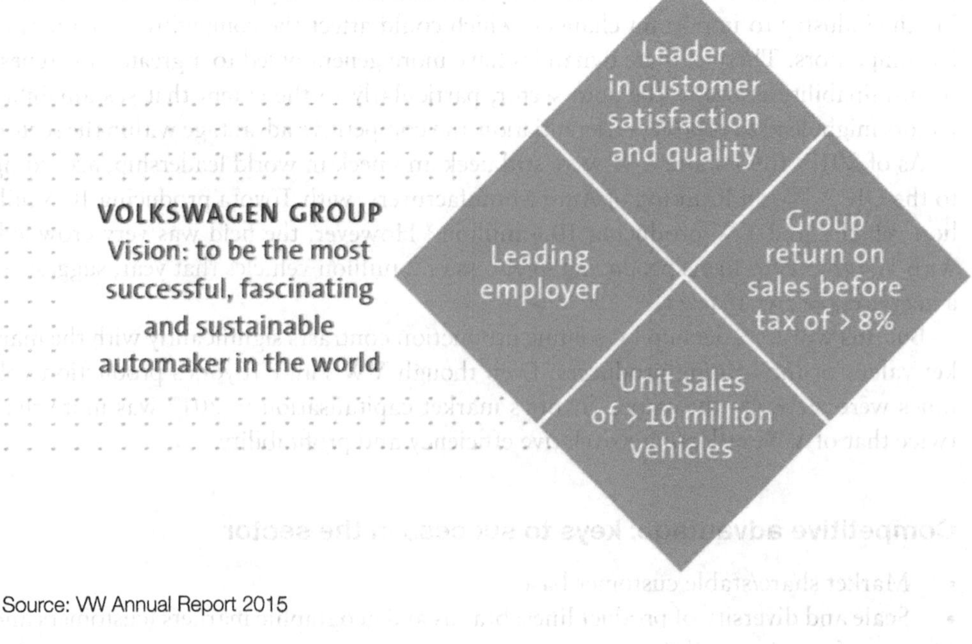

Source: VW Annual Report 2015

customer satisfaction as one of the key requirements for the Company's long-term success.
2. The goal is to generate unit sales of more than 10 million vehicles a year; in particular, Volkswagen intends to capture an above-average share of growth in the major growth markets.
3. Volkswagen's aim is a long-term return on sales before tax of at least 8% so as to ensure that the Group's solid financial position is guaranteed and that it retains the ability to act even in difficult market periods.
4. Volkswagen aims to be the most attractive employer in the automotive industry. The aim is to have the best team in the sector: highly qualified, fit and above all motivated.

(VW Annual Report 2015)

APPENDIX III

VW share price performance 2014–20

Figure 8.6 illustrates VW's comparative share performance vis-à-vis the S&P 500, Toyota and the DAX 30. Note the sharp fall in VW's share price in late 2015 after news of the emissions scandal became public. Although its share price has recovered somewhat from its low point in 2016, its performance still lags the S&P 500 and DAX 30 indices—as well as Toyota—VW's arch-rival.

FIGURE 8.6 VW share price performance 2014–20

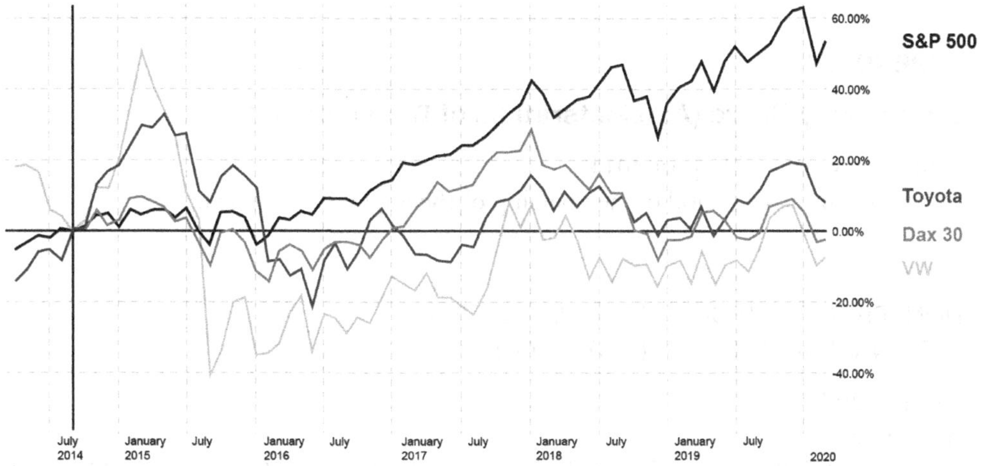

Source: *Financial Times*, 2020

APPENDIX IV

GERMAN CORPORATE GOVERNANCE

German corporate governance is noted for two distinctive features:

1. *Two-tier boards*: the Supervisory Board (*Aufsichtsrat*) consists entirely of external (non-executive) directors. The Supervisory Board of a typical large German company is large, usually 20 people. The company's Management Board (*Vorstand*) is typically much smaller and comprised of the company's senior executive team.
2. *Co-determination (Mitbestimmung)*: a key feature of a German Supervisory Board is that 50% of its members are elected by shareholders, and the other 50% are elected by the labour force; trade union representatives are also elected to represent employees. This gives German governance a much stronger orientation to employees. This can be rewarded by positive employee/stakeholder relations, but can also result in higher labour costs, particularly for the German workforce.

While the ownership of large German companies traditionally involved cross-shareholdings with other corporates—and significant ownership stakes by the leading German banks—this has largely disappeared, and many of Germany's largest corporates are widely held.

Germany's Corporate Governance Code (Kodex) was introduced in 2002 by a government-appointed commission. It was last updated in 2017. Its statement of company purpose is not shareholder-focused: 'it is the obligation of the Management Board and Supervisory Board to ensure the continued existence of the enterprise and its sustainable creation of value in conformity with the principles of the social market economy.'

APPENDIX V

Supervisory Board (Aufsichtsrat) as of December 2014

Source: VW Annual Report 2014

* = beginning or period of membership of the Supervisory Board.

HON.-PROF. DR. TECHN. H.C. DIPL.-ING. ETH
FERDINAND K. PIËCH (77) (CHAIRMAN)

16 April 2002*

Appointments:

Germany: AUDI AG, Ingolstadt, Dr. Ing. h.c. F. Porsche AG, Stuttgart, MAN SE, Munich (Chairman), Porsche Automobil Holding SE, Stuttgart

Global: Ducati Motor Holding S.p.A., Bologna, Porsche Holding Gesellschaft m.b.H., Salzburg, Scania AB, Södertälje, Scania CV AB, Södertälje

BERTHOLD HUBER (64) (DEPUTY CHAIRMAN) IG METALL

25 May 2010*
Appointments:
Germany: AUDI AG, Ingolstadt (Deputy Chairman), Porsche Automobil Holding SE, Stuttgart, Siemens AG, Munich (Deputy Chairman)

DR. JUR. KLAUS LIESEN (83)

2 July 1987–3 May 2006*
Honorary Chairman of the Supervisory Board of Volkswagen AG (since May 3, 2006)

DR. HUSSAIN ALI AL-ABDULLA (57)

Board Member of Qatar Investment Authority and Board Member of Qatar Holding LLC

22 April 2010*
Appointments:
Global: Gulf Investment Corporation, Safat/Kuwait, Masraf Al Rayan, Doha (Chairman), Qatar Investment Authority, Doha, Qatar Holding LLC, Doha

AHMAD AL-SAYED (38)

Minister of State, Qatar

28 June 2013*
Appointments:
Global: Qatar Exchange, Doha; Qatar National Bank, Doha

JÜRGEN DORN (48)

Chairman of the Works Council at the MAN Truck & Bus AG Munich plant, Chairman of the General Works Council of MAN Truck & Bus AG and Chairman of the Group Works Council and the SE Works Council of MAN SE

1 January 2013*
Appointments:
Germany: MAN SE, Munich; AN Truck & Bus AG; Munich (Deputy Chairman)

ANNIKA FALKENGREN (52)

President and Group Chief Executive of Skandinaviska Enskilda Banken AB

3 May 2011*
Appointments:
Global: Securitas AB, Stockholm

DR. JUR. HANS-PETER FISCHER (55)

Chairman of the Board of Management of Volkswagen Management Association

1 January 2013*
Appointments:
Germany: Volkswagen Pension Trust e.V., Wolfsburg

UWE FRITSCH (58)

Chairman of the Works Council at the Volkswagen AG Braunschweig plant

19 April 2012*
Appointments:
Germany: Eintracht Braunschweig GmbH & Co KGaA, Braunschweig; Phantoms Basketball Braunschweig GmbH, Braunschweig

BABETTE FRÖHLICH (49)

IG Metall, Department head for co-ordination of Executive Board duties and planning

25 October 2007*
Appointments:
Germany: MTU Aero Engines AG, Munich

OLAF LIES (47)

Minister of Economic Affairs, Labor and Transport for the Federal State of Lower Saxony

19 February 2013*
Appointments:
Germany: Deutsche Messe AG, Hanover; Demografieagentur für die niedersächsische Wirtschaft GmbH, Hanover (Chairman); Container Terminal Wilhelmshaven JadeWeserPort-Marketing GmbH & Co. KG, Wilhelmshaven; JadeWeserPort Realisierungs-Beteiligungs GmbH, Wilhelmshaven (Chairman)

HARTMUT MEINE (62)

Director of the Lower Saxony and Saxony-Anhalt Regional Office of IG Metall

30 December 2008*
Appointments:
Germany: Continental AG, Hanover; KME Germany GmbH, Osnabrück

PETER MOSCH (42)

Chairman of the General Works Council of AUDI AG

18 January 2006*
Appointments:
Germany: AUDI AG, Ingolstadt; Porsche Automobil Holding SE, Stuttgart; Audi Pensionskasse – Altersversorgung der AUTO UNION GmbH, VVaG, Ingolstadt

BERND OSTERLOH (58)

Chairman of the General and Group Works Councils of Volkswagen AG

1 January 2005*
Appointments:
Germany: Autostadt GmbH, Wolfsburg; Porsche Automobil Holding SE, Stuttgart; Wolfsburg AG, Wolfsburg; Allianz für die Region GmbH, Braunschweig; VfL Wolfsburg-Fußball GmbH, Wolfsburg; Volkswagen Immobilien GmbH, Wolfsburg
Global: Porsche Holding Gesellschaft m.b.H., Salzburg

DR. JUR. HANS MICHEL PIËCH (72)

Lawyer in private practice

7 August 2009*
Appointments:
Germany: AUDI AG, Ingolstadt; Dr. Ing. h.c. F. Porsche AG, Stuttgart; Porsche Automobil Holding SE, Stuttgart; Schmittenhöhebahn AG, Zell am See
Global: Porsche Cars Great Britain Ltd., Reading; Porsche Cars North America Inc., Wilmington; Porsche Holding Gesellschaft m.b.H., Salzburg; Porsche Ibérica S.A., Madrid; Porsche Italia S.p.A., Padua; Volksoper Wien GmbH, Vienna

URSULA PIËCH (58)

Supervisory Board member of AUDI AG

19 April 2012*
Appointments:
Germany: AUDI AG, Ingolstadt

DR. JUR. FERDINAND OLIVER PORSCHE (53)

Member of the Board of Management of Familie Porsche AG Beteiligungsgesellschaft

7 August 2009*
Appointments:
Germany AUDI AG, Ingolstadt; Dr. Ing. h.c. F. Porsche AG, Stuttgart; Porsche Automobil Holding SE, Stuttgart; Porsche Lizenz- und Handelsgesellschaft mbH & Co KG, Ludwigsburg
Global: PGA S.A., Paris; Porsche Holding Gesellschaft m.b.H., Salzburg

DR. RER. COMM. WOLFGANG PORSCHE (71)

Chairman of the Supervisory Board of Porsche Automobil Holding SE; Chairman of the Supervisory Board of Dr. Ing. h.c. F. Porsche AG

24 April 2008*
Appointments:
Germany: AUDI AG, Ingolstadt; Dr. Ing. h.c. F. Porsche AG, Stuttgart (Chairman); Porsche Automobil Holding SE, Stuttgart (Chairman).

Global: Familie Porsche AG Beteiligungsgesellschaft, Salzburg (Chairman); Porsche Cars Great Britain Ltd., Reading; Porsche Cars North America Inc., Wilmington; Porsche Holding Gesellschaft m.b.H., Salzburg; Porsche Ibérica S.A., Madrid; Porsche Italia S.p.A., Padua; Schmittenhöhebahn AG, Zell am See

STEPHAN WEIL (56)

Minister-President of the Federal State of Lower Saxony

19 February 2013*

STEPHAN WOLF (48)

Deputy Chairman of the General and Group Works Councils of Volkswagen AG

1 January 2013*
Appointments:
Germany: Wolfsburg AG, Wolfsburg; Sitech Sitztechnik GmbH, Wolfsburg; Volkswagen Pension Trust e.V., Wolfsburg

THOMAS ZWIEBLER (49)

Chairman of the Works Council of Volkswagen Commercial Vehicles

15 May 2010*

Members of the Audit Committee

Dr. Ferdinand Oliver Porsche (Chairman)
Peter Mosch (Deputy Chairman)
Annika Falkengren
Babette Fröhlich

Members of the Nomination Committee

Hon.-Prof. Dr. techn. h.c. Dipl.-Ing. ETH Ferdinand K. Piëch (Chairman)
Dr. Wolfgang Porsche
Stephan Weil

VW Management Board (Vorstand) as of December 2014

Source: VW Annual Report 2014

PROF. DR. DR. H.C. MULT. MARTIN WINTERKORN (67)

Chairman (since January 1, 2007), Research and Development

1 July 2000*
Chairman of the Executive Board of Porsche Automobil Holding SE
25 November 2009*
Appointments:
Germany: FC Bayern München AG, Munich

DR. RER. POL. H.C. FRANCISCO JAVIER GARCIA SANZ (57)

Procurement

1 July 2001*
Appointments:
Germany: Hochtief AG, Essen
Global: Criteria Caixa Holding S.A., Barcelona

PROF. DR. RER. POL. DR.-ING. E.H. JOCHEM HEIZMANN (62)

China

11 January 2007*
Appointments:
Germany: Lufthansa Technik AG, Hamburg; OBO Bettermann GmbH & Co. KG, Menden

CHRISTIAN KLINGLER (46)

Sales and Marketing

1 January 2010*
Appointments:
Germany: Messe Frankfurt GmbH, Frankfurt am Main

DR.-ING. E.H. MICHAEL MACHT (54)

Production

1 October 2010–31 July 2014*

PROF. H.C. DR. RER. POL. HORST NEUMANN (65)

Human Resources and Organization

1 December 2005*

DR. H.C. LEIF ÖSTLING (69)

Commercial Vehicles

1 September 2012*
Appointments:
Global: SKF AB, Gothenburg; EQT Holdings AB, Stockholm

HANS DIETER PÖTSCH (63)

Finance and Controlling

1 January 2003*
Chief Financial Officer of Porsche Automobil Holding SE
25 November 2009*
Appointments:
Germany: Bertelsmann Management SE, Gütersloh; Bertelsmann SE & Co. KGaA, Gütersloh

ANDREAS RENSCHLER (56)

Commercial Vehicles

1 February 2015*
Appointments (as of 1 February 2015):
Germany: Deutsche Messe AG, Hanover

PROF. RUPERT STADLER (51)

Chairman of the Board of Management of AUDI AG

1 January 2010*
Appointments:
Germany: FC Bayern München AG, Munich

NOTES

1. It was also suggested in the Preface that one might wish to begin the book by reviewing this case study, to sensitise the reader to how the VW case relates to issues that will be discussed throughout the book.
2. The authors are grateful to Professor Christian Strenger, Academic Director of the Corporate Governance Institute at the Frankfurt School of Finance, for his detailed notes on this case.
3. Kate Connolly, VW Boss Martin Winterkorn Defeats Chairman Ferdinand Piëch, 17 April 2015, *The Guardian*.
4. The class action suits were product liability actions brought on behalf of purchasers of VW cars and securities law class actions on behalf of the holders of the company's American Depository Receipts.
5. *The Economist*, Emission Impossible, 5 March 2016.
6. Sustainalytics, *ESG Report*, 2014.
7. *The Economist* Intelligence Unit, 31 July 2014.
8. Standard & Poor's, *The Auto and Commercial Vehicle Manufacturing Industry*, 19 November 2013.
9. OICA World Motor Vehicle Production 2017.

Index

Page numbers in italics refer to figures. Page numbers in bold refer to tables. Page numbers followed by 'n' refer to notes.

9781032308784